Chris
MORTON

UNTIL THE CAN RAN OUT

Chris
MORTON

UNTIL THE CAN RAN OUT

CHRIS MORTON MBE & BRIAN BURFORD

First published 2005
Paperback edition first published 2007

STADIA is an imprint of
Tempus Publishing Limited
The Mill, Brimscombe Port,
Stroud, Gloucestershire, GL5 2QG
www.tempus-publishing.com

British Library Cataloguing in Publication Data.
A catalogue record for this book is available from the British Library.

ISBN 978 07524 4337 9

Typesetting and origination by Tempus Publishing Limited
Printed in Great Britain

CONTENTS

ACKNOWLEDGEMENTS

Chris Morton: This book has been a long time in the making. At one stage it seemed that it wouldn't have seen the light of day. Initially, Richard Clark began working with me on it, but too much of his time was taken up by his position at *Speedway Star*. But then Brian came on board and I soon realised what was expected of me to produce a book! Without Brian to coax me and teach me in my writing, this book would still be on my 'to do' list. His experience and knowledge of the process was invaluable. Our mutual passion for speedway helped drive us on and I feel we worked well as a team. Brian worked tirelessly on the research and the factual detail, gathering information from all available sources, allowing me to concentrate on my memories and experiences. I have a great deal to thank Brian for, but most of all for agreeing to work with me on this book and finally getting it to print.

A special thanks to Ged for writing the foreword and for many, many years of support as my mechanic and good friend in the pits, and to Steve Cooney for his input and interest and, of course, for his expertise as a mechanic during my racing days. Thanks also to Gary Miller, my first mechanic. We learned together and had some good times in my early days. Martin Bean and Sue deserve recognition for their support throughout my long-track campaign. I would also like to express my appreciation to all the riders, managers and friends for contributing their stories for the final chapter of this book. I'm pleased that we are still in touch after so many years of travelling and racing together. I have had a great deal of sponsors over the years; without their assistance I would not have been able to have the equipment needed to compete at the top level. I would like to thank them all for their help and assistance. My family has been there from the very beginning, through all the good times and bad, triumphs and disappointments, and it seems inadequate just to express my gratitude, but I hope they all realise how much I have appreciated their support. I would like to dedicate this book to Jackie, who has been my rock, my Mum and Dad and the rest of my family.

Including the above I have also been inspired, influenced or impressed by the following: Soren Sjosten, Chris Pusey, Ivan Mauger, Peter Collins, Eric Boocock, Ian Thomas, Dave Morton, my Dad as 'George the Welder' (he could make anything), Bob Sexton, Steve Casey, Dent Oliver, Ted Howell, Bob Dylan, Richard Clark, Loudon Wainwright III, The Beatles, Carl Glover, Wishbone Ash and their album *Argus*, Derek and Clive, Tony Rickardsson, Led Zeppelin, AC/DC, Fats Waller, Billie Holiday, Frank Sinatra, Mark Winterbottom, Russ Hodgson, Doug Wyer, Deep Purple, Reg Wilson, Joe Cocker, Sam Ermolenko, Keith Rushton (you make your own luck), Hans Nielsen, Jim Rowlinson, Peter Green's Fleetwood Mac, Leith Mitchell, Bruce Penhall, Jason Crump, Erik Gundersen, Greg Hancock and Billy Hamill. This is not an exhaustive list.

A special thank-you to all my sponsors. Here are some of them: Shepley Equipment, Jim Rowlinson, Trackstar Equipment, Weslake, Dunlop, Groundwork, TNT, Coldshield Windows, Filtrate, Dem Plant, Jawa, Sandy Martins, Godden, Pipercross, Barum, SEXTONS, (Bob & Janice) Arai Helmets, Regina Chains, Iveco, Kestrel, Gatefield Van Hire.

Brian Burford: I would like to thank the following people for their help and assistance in the research and writing of this book: Mark Sawbridge for all the photocopying of the relevant articles and reports from various publications of the time, Richard 'Clarkie' Clark for his inspired input, Mike Patrick for his patience, Ken Carpenter for always responding to my 'It's that time of year...' request, Gordon Day, a mine of information, Ged Blake and Steve Cooney for their entertaining anecdotes and all the ex-riders and managers for their memories of Chris. A special thanks to Chris and his family for all their generous hospitality. It has been a very enjoyable experience and such an honour to work with a man whose abilities I had admired on the track. As always, thank you to all the staff at Tempus Publishing for their continued support for speedway racing. A big note of thanks to Phil Handel for his advice – even though it's not always heeded – and support, and John Chaplin for his guidance and help over the years; thanks amigo! Not forgetting my own Mum – 'I'm a farmer's daughter' – who always supports me. It's often said that speedway racing is like a family; therefore, having made many friends in the sport over the last few years, I would like to dedicate this book to my speedway family – you know who you all are.

FOREWORD

by Ged Blake

You are watching the news, then they hand over to the sports desk, where the presenter then goes on to cover all the breaking headlines for the day. He gives a general round-up of any other relevant sporting action before saying the immortal words about the match being shown later: 'Look away now if you don't want to know the score.'

This is a sporting story of a man who is speedway through and through. If, like the majority of fans across the planet, you pay your entrance money to see some action, you know that when this man was in town that was exactly what you were going to get. Not blessed as the best gater in the world, most of his races were won the hard way – from the back. Not a pleasant thought for the rider in front, who half the time never knew which way to look as he came steaming past. Here was a man on the track who would not give an inch to an opponent, but be on his side and you would feel secure enough to know that help was around if you needed it.

A measure of the man, and one of the reasons we stayed as a partnership for so many years, happened in the first full year I worked for him. It was over in Denmark. I'm not sure whether it was an open meeting or a round of the World Championships. I seem to remember it being the first of many long weekends away from home. We had ridden midweek in the UK, then gone over on the ferry to do the meeting. It's strange, that first trip, one of excitement and a bit of apprehension. Here I am, married with a family, and leaving them for the first time to go away for several nights. Everything happens at such a pace until you adjust to it. We arrived at Esbjerg and then had a moderate drive to the track at Vojens. One thing I do remember was that it was dry that day – a thing that over the next twelve or so years was a rarity at Vojens! We did the practise okay, then it was time to load up and get off to get showered and find something to eat. The hotel used by the speedway fraternity is the Slukefter Kro Hotel, which was only a short drive away. We pulled into the car park and made our way to reception. By this time it was fairly busy as the rest of the boys had a head start on us. Everybody was checking in and getting sorted. The one thing I did notice was that all the riders were sticking together and leaving all the mechanics to sort out their own arrangements. This was an area in which I was short on experience and for a moment I didn't know what to expect. Mort had gone off to reception and I was standing there in a crowded hotel, yet still feeling alone. Looking round, I was trying to decide what to do next just as I saw Mort walking back to me with keys in his hand. He just quietly said: 'Come on, we're in room three,' and off we went together. I can't put into words what that gesture represented, but it made me feel part of something that has lasted from that day to this.

Off the track Chris Morton was one of the most approachable riders you would ever meet. He would always have time to sign autographs for the kids and chat to the fans – yes, even if things had not gone well on the night.

This book charts the career of a man of whom, if you go and see him race, you expect the unexpected. You watch that never-say-die attitude, always expect to be on the edge of your seat and never know what will happen next. I could go on and on but most of all, when he's up at the tapes and the green light goes on, for God's sake, DON'T look away now.

INTRODUCTION

Unfortunately, not everyone can become World Individual Speedway Champion because, as it says in the *Highlander* movies, 'There can be only one' – in this case, one a year. When you consider how many riders sit on a speedway bike and take their first tentative ride, it's only a very small number that even get the opportunity to race at the top level, never mind compete in the World Championship. The various track bars, clubs, magazines and periodicals often trot out the eternal question: who was the best rider never to win the World Championship? The answer is always one that sparks a great debate and names like Jack Parker, Vic Duggan, Eric Langton, Dennis Sigalos, Billy Sanders, the Moran Brothers, Dave Jessup, Kenny Carter and Phil Crump are all commonly mentioned.

The question is: just how do you measure a rider's ability? Quite often it is not the most naturally talented of individuals or the most exciting of racers that wins the big prize. Instead it is the most dedicated and determined – or ruthless! But being a World Champion doesn't necessarily mean that you are adored for your success – especially in Britain where the press in particular are keen to knock you down – it is usually the hard-working, all-action racers that earn their points from the back that have the crowd on their feet.

Enter one Chris Morton, a world-class performer who would have been a World Individual Champion more than once if only natural ability was a factor in lifting the title. But Morton's Achilles heel was his lack of prowess from the start. His dashes from the back made him one of the most popular riders of his generation, but how his many adoring fans must have wished that he was equally adept at starting as he was at passing his rivals from the back. But it takes more, much more to be a top racer. The sport's politics plays a big part, even when, seemingly, it's not directed at you. Preparation, equipment and the necessary funds for reinvestment all have a major role in a racer's speedway career. And then, of course, there is that stingy mistress Lady Luck, whose whimsical glance and sleight of hand can be the difference between success and failure.

Chris Morton, or 'Mort,' was one half of the duo – with his boyhood buddy Peter Collins – that put the Ace back into Belle Vue Speedway throughout the 1970s and 1980s. For many, they were Belle Vue Speedway and an Aces team without them was not, well, the Aces. Personally, I have never seen two such exciting British riders in the same team such as Mort and PC. Of course, Collins did win the World Championship, while Chris won almost everything else but the big one. It is a pity but Mort's World Final record isn't a true reflection of his ability or his success that he enjoyed during an eighteen-year career that included a brief comeback. I believe that it was Morton and Collins that restored the British heart in Belle Vue following the tragic death of Peter Craven in 1963. Ivan Mauger may have brought success back to the club, but Mort and PC were the heart and soul of Belle Vue for over ten years. Following the closure at the end of the 1987 season of the old Hyde Road track at 'The Zoo,' the club moved to the greyhound stadium at Kirkmanshulme Lane. But it was Chris Morton who brought the Hyde Road tradition with him. It was no coincidence that the Aces' fortunes began to take a step back following Morton's retirement at the end of the 1990 season, because the last link of that magnificent era of Hyde Road heroes had been broken forever. It's interesting to note how popular and successful speedway racing was during the years that Morton graced the magnificent track at Hyde Road in Manchester. Speedway was stunned when the doors at Wembley had been closed, but the demolition of 'The Zoo' left deep wounds from which the sport has yet to make a full recovery.

All this tradition is part of Chris's speedway career. He graced the tracks during a golden era for speedway when big crowds and big stars were everywhere and also when falling crowds and dubious decisions signalled its depressing decline. He experienced celebration and disappointment, clashed elbows against some of the greatest riders of all time and witnessed first hand some of the arguments and politics that shaped the sport. But, above all, he performed with distinction and commitment wherever he chose to throw a leg over a 500cc speedway machine – whether that was before 100,000 spectators or 1,000.

While looking back through the old records and books during the course of our research for this book, Chris Morton was often described as 'a quiet man.' And yet on the track he was anything but quiet. If Chris was in the race you knew full well that four laps of dazzling action was about to take place. Speeding around the outside of his rivals, spectacularly broad-sliding his machine as he wrestled a bike that was ready to spit him off at any moment in protest, Chris Morton was a double dose of 'e's – entertainment and excitement. And that, ladies and gentleman, is what Chris Morton and speedway racing was all about.

Brian Burford
January 2005

PROLOGUE

Although it was a strangely uncomfortable feeling, it was a very familiar sign; the gnawing in my gut was one of those indicators that my body was preparing itself because it knew something extra special was about to be demanded of it. The rush of adrenalin that was pumping in my veins was a welcome feeling, and the next few minutes were going to be the most significant in my life since I drew my first breath.

At only nineteen years old, the last three years had been a steep learning curve, but I had responded by progressing beyond my childhood dreams. But I was no longer a child, I was an adult and my dreams had grown as my self-belief took flight. It was down to me now, as I was about to have my mettle tested. A siren sound cut the tense atmosphere. That not only meant that I had two minutes to be lined up and fully prepared to race, it was also a countdown for me to summon my resolve for the mighty task ahead. I was cool. I pulled on my helmet, put my gloves on and checked my goggles were perfectly clean before carefully pulling them over my helmet. I could feel the light pressure of the foam inside the facemask that would protect me from the flying shale press against my face. I was ready for this moment; the only thing that stood between me and my greatest achievement to date was the battle of desire and determination between four men. As I prepared myself, my breathing was steady and I felt that I was in complete control. I was totally focused with not a shred of doubt about my ability to achieve my desire.

As I walked out towards my machine I was thriving on the occasion; the emotion and the anticipation of the crowd was part of the fuel that powered my determination to achieve my greatest moment. Ten years earlier I had sat up there in the stands of this monumental arena as a child, watching people do what I was doing now. I sat astride my machine. I checked my fuel was turned on – already done – touched my plug cap – a small ritual – and then I felt a couple of encouraging pats on my back. This was it: I was pushed off; my machine was keen to do battle as it immediately fired up. I felt the excitement of the gigantic crowd increase, as I could hear them over the noise of my engine. Subconsciously I switched off the noise from the crowd as I built my concentration and I closed myself off from any outside distractions. Now I could only hear the noise of my engine, providing the soundtrack for my self-motivation – making sure I left nothing to chance.

As I lined up at the starting tapes I felt the confidence grow within me, which was justified because I had been a sensation tonight by maintaining the form that had got me this far. This was it, my last race in the last round to qualify for the biggest night of my career. All I needed to do was to score 2 points. Each of the four riders in this race could also qualify and we all needed points. I expected no favours – it had been incredibly tight in the 1976 Intercontinental Final. I was up against the best Australian and the best American. The three of us had 8 points each. The fourth rider was a very experienced Swede who was in need of a race win. I was on gate two with the Australian on my left in gate one, the Swede was next to me on gate three with the American off gate four. The fidgeting and settling-down ritual was over. As I waited for the green light to come on that would put us under starter's orders, I knew that I required 10 points to be sure of a place in my first World Championship Final. This was it; there was no turning back, there was no time for any more adjustments or last minute advice – it was down to me now. At nineteen years old I was at the start of a journey that had already taken me around the world. It was going to take me a lot further than that, not just by travelling but also in many other ways.

ONE

THE PARTINGTON GANG

Bruce Wayne, as his alter-ego Batman, had successfully 'kerrracked and krrushed' The Riddler with the help of his doting other half of the dynamic duo, Robin, so Gotham City was safe for at least another week. Holy smoke Batman! It's time to go to speedway – to the Batmobile! Okay, the Ford Pop.

This was the Saturday-night ritual; it was midsummer during the mid-1960s. On a Saturday night from late March through to late October, we would watch *Batman* on television, and then at six o'clock the Morton family, George and Hilary – 'Mum and Dad' – Dave, Chris and Gina – 'the kids' – would jump in the old Ford Pop car (30mph just cruising, 40mph pushing it a bit, 50mph flat out!) and drive the ten miles or so to Belle Vue Speedway. We had to be in our seats in M Stand for the start of the meeting at seven o'clock. Speedway had been our chosen sport to support.

My first visit to Belle Vue Speedway that I can remember was one Saturday night after my elder brother Dave suggested how great it would be if we could go to watch speedway tonight like our friend Peter Collins. 'Yes' said I, not really knowing what it was, but my spark of interest won me the job of asking our parents if they would take us to watch speedway – I was seven years old. In the year of 1964 the Morton family went to watch speedway at Belle Vue on about ten occasions. By the end of that year we were all hooked!

I didn't know much about speedway at this time or what a thrilling history the club had. What little I did know I learnt from my father. But as time went on I learned more about the history of the club and the standing it held within speedway racing.

Belle Vue, Manchester, was one of the most successful and glamorous clubs in Britain. Known as the Aces, they were one of the pre-war giants of speedway racing. Riders like Eric Langton, Frank Varey, Max Grosskreutz and Bill Kitchen were among the stars that made the sport and Belle Vue a household name. Incredibly, they won four successive league championships before the outbreak of the Second World War, which brought an end to their success. As hostilities began to gather pace speedway racing, in line with all other sports, was forced to close.

Unbeknown to me, speedway racing in the 1960s was going through something of a crisis. The boom period that followed directly after the war was well and truly behind it and the crowds were falling. The death in 1963 of England's popular double-World Champion, Peter Craven, was a disaster for the sport in Britain, which was by then desperately trying to reinvent itself. Craven's passing was especially felt at Belle Vue as he had been an Ace for most of his speedway career, and it took the arrival of Sweden's Ove Fundin to lift some of the gloom that surrounded 'The Zoo' at that time. The handicap system that had been introduced in 1962 to spice things up was still in operation when I first went to speedway.

My parents tell me that I saw Craven race, but I don't have any recollection of it, as I would have been only three or four years old. But at least I know that I was in the presence of such a legend. In 1964 Belle Vue were recovering from the shock of the loss of one of their greatest ever riders and, despite all the action and excitement that a sport like speedway can generate, Craven's death cast a shadow over the entire season.

Belle Vue were the reigning National League Champions, but the sport's top league had shrunk in number to just seven clubs. The Aces finished in a mid-table position and experienced a mediocre season – it was a difficult period for the club following Craven's death. One of the highlights of that year was the Great Britain v. USSR Test Series, which caught the imagination of the public and the media, even though the Soviets lost all three Test Matches.

It was New Zealand's Barry Briggs who won the World Championship that year on a rain-soaked track in Gothenburg. Briggs was one of the riders who were still handicapped at the start in Britain. This began in the early 1960s with Briggs, the late Craven, Ove Fundin, Ronnie Moore and Bjorn Knutson – known as 'the Top 5' – were all handicapped twenty yards at the start to spice up the action. This controversial rule was just one of the problems that faced the speedway bosses during the winter months. Another was that the top league wanted one of the Provincial League tracks (the lower division) to move up to swell the numbers in the top flight. They refused, as they were happy in the PL and deep divisions existed between the two groups. Threats and counter-threats followed, that eventually led to the RAC ordering an inquiry, which was headed by Lord Shawcross. Finally a compromise was agreed and a new British League was formed in time for the 1965 season. It was one big league and provided the supporters with much more variety and supplied a much-needed shot in the arm for the sport.

But all these politics went unnoticed in a eight-year-old like me. I was just thrilled by the speed, the atmosphere and the sheer excitement of a Saturday night at Belle Vue Speedway. Later, of course, the politics of the sport in its various forms would have a bearing on my career. Not that I was worried about that now, as all I wanted to be was a speedway rider.

In 1965 we went regularly to watch the Belle Vue Aces, but my awareness of the significance of that season was about zero – yet in about eight years' time I would be competing in it thanks to an injured rider whose skills we were yet to admire.

I can clearly remember Dick Fisher was the captain and rode at number one – even the child who had already decided he was going to be a speedway rider when he grew up would never dream that he also, one day, would become the captain. Other members of the team were Norman Nevitt ('Rev-it Nevitt'), Gordon Macgregor, Cyril Maidment, Bill Powell, Sandor Levi and Jim Yacoby. Vic White made a number of appearances, with the Aces getting a little help from Taffy Owen with his immaculate chrome bikes. I also remember a lad called Dave Scofield. Was that also the year Dent Oliver made a comeback? My Mum and Dad would give Dave and I 1s 6d to get in through the turnstile on the Redgate Lane entrance. We would then have a good look in the Wright Wood Photo Kiosk at some of the great photos of our favourite riders.

When the time got to about 6.45 p.m. we would make our way up to M Stand to meet up with our parents to sit in our regular spot. I can still hear The Rolling Stones' *(This Could Be) The Last Time* blasting out of the tannoy system as we walked up the wooden steps to our seats. Usually we sat down just in time for the parade. You just knew you were in for a good night of thrilling racing when you heard *Tokyo Melody* (whoever thought of using this piece was a genius). As *Tokyo Melody* faded away, the scene was now set for the St John Ambulance people and the pushers to march out to *Colonel Bogey*.

At the back of the stand on the first corner, about thirty fairgoers started their ride to the top of the 'Scenic Railway' and got a brief glimpse of speedway racing as the riders drop the clutch for the start of heat one. This match could have been against our local rivals from just over the hill, the Halifax Dukes – affectionately named by my brother Dave as 'Halifax Flukes'. I must admit, whoever we were riding against was never that important to me; the main attraction was to soak up speedway in all its glory.

During the mid to late 1960s a group of families from a village about ten miles away called Partington used to take their children to Belle Vue every Saturday night. Some of these kids were to become speedway riders with varying degrees of success. You may remember some of these names, as they have now become part of speedway's memory: Dave Trownson (Trout), Peter Collins (Wee Collie Extra), Wayne Hughes, Andy Reid, Steve McDermott, Dave Morton (Big Mort), and myself Chris Morton (Little Mort). If you remember seeing stupid kids running onto the track to pick up goggles discarded by the riders, it was probably one of our little group.

My brother was the master of this game; at one point he had amassed six sets of gas goggles, which he had retrieved from the track, and usually not without fierce competition! My brother announced to me one day, as he polished and caressed his prized possession of six sets of gas goggles, that not only were they once owned by Cyril Maidment (affectionately named by him as 'Ci Maido'), his favourite rider, but they would also be the first goggles he would use when he started riding. He was aged about twelve at the time. Dave Morton's finest moment of skill and stupidity – although it earned him raging glory from any budding goggle-grabber – was when a yellow/black helmet colour came off during a race. My brother lacked the will, or common sense, to overcome the strong desire to possess a helmet cover, even if it meant running onto the racetrack during the race, as he knew by the end of the race it would be picked up by one of the pushers.

On lap two the helmet colour came off, all the riders passed by and then old Mort, without any hesitation, jumped over the fence and ran across the track during the race. He grabbed the helmet colour, ran back and climbed over the fence and then ran straight round the back of the stands, knowing that the officials would be after him. He stayed in hiding for a few races while the heat died down. This was one prize that was priceless to a future speedway rider.

My future source of major inspiration was in the Belle Vue team of the previous year, 1964, but a policy of no foreign riders in British League was to rob others – and me – of the excitement of watching Soren Sjosten in 1965 for two seasons. This may in some way have helped me observe all the riding, because kids tend to have an infinite belief in their favourite. But without Soren I just admired individual skills. Dick Fisher was Mr Reliable as a trapper (maybe I should have taken more notice!). Sandor Levi never stopped trying. Cyril Maidment would have been an obvious replacement for Soren as my favourite, but he was Dave's – not allowed – therefore I could only admire my older brother's choice of idol. Week after week I would watch Cyril perform his passing trick – I had this skill firmly fixed in my mind, stored up in my own bag of tricks, long before I was ever to use it. Cyril would tease his opponent, and thrill the crowds in the process. He always performed it on the pit corner, usually on the last lap. He would come in wide – we all knew what was coming – then he would have his victim wondering where he came from as Ci Maido flashed past on the inside to take the chequered flag, thanks to a masterfully timed and performed 'hook back'.

One thing that made a speedway night complete would be a chance to meet the riders and get a few signatures in the old autograph book. One night springs to mind when I was in the Baveria Suite, which was part of the whole Belle Vue Complex, and it was where the fans could meet their favourite riders after the meeting. You would eagerly await the entrance of your idol, just to see them in the flesh and to get an autograph. In the Baveria Suite there was a stairway up to an upper balcony where we could get a first glimpse of the riders as they came in. Adult supporters and speedway staff would chat and drink with the riders, while kids were passing messages around as to which riders had come in and where they were.

Just like any busy bar, drinks were put on any available table or ledge. There was one such ledge near the bottom of the stairway, which was full of drinks. A few riders had already come in. Norman Nevitt and Dick Fisher were both looking immaculate in suit and tie. Then in came someone whose appearances were not as frequent as others, and not looking quite as immaculate as his aforementioned colleagues in his donkey jacket, but he was in! He was immediately spotted by one of our lookouts who, true to his cause, rushed down the stairs to let us all know that Cyril Maidment had just come in. Maybe some of you out there remember this crazy kid running down the stairs and sending all of the drinks that were sat on the ledge at the bottom of the stairs flying. His name was Peter Collins and, although anonymous at the time, this was his first bit of the limelight at Belle Vue as drinks and glasses were scattered all over the floor.

My autograph book, I am sure like many others at the time, had Taffy Owen's autograph at least every sixth page. It was not that Taffy was a big hero of our gang, but he was a speedway rider, he was at all the after-meeting clubs and he had an autograph that was a bit fancy and flamboyant – it fascinated us kids. Taffy's bikes were a credit to him, all chrome, sparkling and immaculate-looking, but Taffy was one of those who learned his trade the hard way. He wroteoff a few bikes before he made a name for himself, which would not be until 1968 with the Belle Vue Colts, when the Second Division was formed.

This Division was introduced to help develop new young talent. From 1965-68 the British League had been one big league, but the two-tier system was formulated and it proved to be extremely popular. Belle Vue entered a second team called the Belle Vue 'Colts' and, despite the complaints from the then-Canterbury promoter Johnnie Hoskins that the club were using ex-First Division riders, the Colts won the league with an invincible performance around Hyde Road. Taffy Owen was the star of the Colts side, but other riders like Ken Eyre and Eric Broadbelt would go on to serve the Aces side in the senior league – and I would rub shoulders with them during my climb up the ladder.

Speedway had become a major influence on a lot of the kids' lives in Partington, including me. It wasn't just about going along on a Saturday night; we lived it so much we would ride our pushbikes as speedway riders. We quickly developed the skill of 'broad-sliding', which is the basic 'speedway trick' (as described by Michael Lee) of flicking your bike into a broad slide without the use of brakes – it's easy when you know how!

Our apprenticeship probably started on Peter Collins' father's farm. Bill Collins allowed Peter's mates to play there. One of our favourite pastimes was doing massive broad-slides in the yard. We would howl into the farmyard as fast as it was possible on a push bike and then drop the bike into a slide. We would do it in different styles with onlookers having to guess whose style we were imitating. We were just having fun, but we were developing skills that would be invaluable in just a few years' time. It wasn't long before we were looking to get motorbikes to ride with Peter on his farm and the track nearby. Peter Collins had been riding his motorbike, a 98cc James, since he was about six or seven years old.

One day my brother and I found an old Lambretta Scooter 197cc that had been dumped and it looked like it had been in a crash. We dragged it back to our house for my Dad to have a look at it and assess its suitability as a track bike. My Dad took this bike to his garage where he did car repairs, and within a few short weeks he had transformed this wrecked scooter into a superb bike. After taking all the pressed steel panelling off it was stripped back to the bare chassis and fitted with a cross bar like a motorbike. Footrests were added and he made a fuel tank like a speedway bike. Apart from the small scooter wheels it was now a motorbike, not a scooter, or as referred to by the motorcycling fraternity a 'Pansy Wagon'. 'George the welder' had worked his magic and we now had a bike to ride on the farm, or the nearby track. I was about eight years old.

My first ride on a motorbike was a rude awakening. It was while the Lambretta was being transformed from a piece of junk to an impressive motorbike with little wheels. My Dad at the time had a Capri 80cc Scooter to go to work on – he worked as a welder at Manchester Airport. One day he decided it was time to test my ability to ride a motorised thing. I suppose a father would be thinking: 'In a few weeks time he will be riding a bike on the track, he's eight years old so let's just teach him some basics.' Dave had already had a go on this 80cc scooter; he was ten years old and was quite competent.

Now it was time for his young brother to have a go. I had watched Dave ride this scooter around the small yard where my Dad did his car repairs for a few weeks now, so I knew – or so I thought – how to do it. It was easy… well, it looked easy anyway. 'Do you want a go Chris?' my Dad said. Of course I did, anything my big brother did I wanted to do. I obviously couldn't touch the floor (I probably still wouldn't), so I was perched on the seat with my Dad holding the bike up giving me the basics. He was getting a novice going; nay, getting an absolutely raw, wet-behind-the-ears beginner going. As all first timers do, I listened intently as my Dad said: 'Set the revs steady and very slowly let the clutch out. Don't just let it go all the way out when it starts to move. Keep letting it go slowly and keep the revs low and steady.' Easy; anyway I had seen our Dave do it loads of times.

I then did what all first-timers do, which was the exact opposite of what my Dad said. What first timers do is this: as soon as the clutch bites you panic, let it go all the way out instantly and become a passenger in charge of the throttle, which you unknowingly twist to increase the revs. It was quite a culture shock as an eight-year-old, going from pedal power to 80cc 10-horsepower in one jump. Any natural talent for riding a motorbike that was apparent to onlookers at my first grass-track meeting seven years later was having a day off on this day. I took off, or the bike took off, with me on it at a fair old rate. We travelled about ten yards in a dead-straight line; not a glimmer or sign of control and I crashed head-on into the side of a garage wall and wrecked my Dad's scooter. There was more to this motorbike-riding thing than meets the eye!

My first ride and first crash didn't deter me in any way though. I think my decision to ride motorbikes and to be a speedway rider had been born before

I had my first ride/crash on my Dad's scooter, so I just needed to acquire a few basic skills. It wasn't long before my Dad finished the repairs to the Lambretta that had been dumped, and we thought it was fantastic. We had a great track on some waste ground near to the Collins' farm. We could get to it from one side near to our house and from the farm Peter could see, or hear, when we were there and he would come down to the track from the other side of the field. We would then spend the day riding round, racing and trying different things. Learning to slide was the main skill we developed, as well as a desire to win.

It wasn't long before we found another scooter, and that got the same treatment as the first, so my brother and I had a bike each. So that was the start of it all for me. While all the other kids were playing football or getting into trouble – there was plenty of that in Partington – we were riding track bikes on a field and having a great time.

However, we had a pathetic situation with the local police. My brother and I had a 300- or 400-yard walk along a main road to the waste ground to where the track was. My Dad was very strict about the rules: absolutely no riding on the road. We adhered to this to the letter; even Dave – who had his moments of fighting authority – never broke this rule. If the police came across us pushing the bikes along the road it would be: 'Where are you going with that son?' 'Whose is it?' 'Is it taxed?' You can see it from their side: a little kid with a motorbike and they think you've nicked it. Anyway, the bottom line was that it was illegal to push a motorbike without having a licence or it being taxed, and both of those were not going to happen.

My Dad entered into a running battle with the local fuzz over this. We weren't causing anybody any harm, we were keeping out of trouble and having a bit of fun. It was an obvious complaint from my Dad's side. 'Go and catch some proper criminals instead of pestering young kids,' he would say. At one stage the police were threatening to prosecute. In the end he told them to piss off, and said 'I am not going to stop them pushing the bikes on the road, so do your worst!' Nothing ever happened.

While Dave and I were out riding our bikes, my sister Gina, who is four years younger than me, had developed an interest in horse riding. This is something she has been involved with ever since – she began when she was about nine years old. Gina's interest was something that has got my daughters riding horses and it was great fun, but no safer than riding motorbikes. And just like speedway bikes, they have no brakes!

Partington County Primary School was my first taste of formal education, following in the footsteps of my brother. I was okay at school. I was aware of the importance of school but none of it came easily so it was an effort being average. I was looking for something to inspire me, but school never managed to deliver. Weekends were the highlight of the week. We were riding our bikes all weekend – if we had enough money for some petrol – and then on Saturday night we went to Belle Vue. We could want for no more.

Other than speedway, the Belle Vue complex had many other attractions. It was a great concept in entertainment, ranging from the reality of the speedway racing to the fantasy of the fairground. I can remember the 'All-in Wrestling' at the Kings Hall, with names like Billy Two Rivers and Big Chief. There were a number of function halls, including the previously mentioned Baveria Suite, while the other Suites were the Cumberland, the Kensington and the Kendal. These were mainly dancehalls, with Caesar's Palace being a popular place for a drink.

Occasionally, usually during the interval while Alan Morrey was announcing 'Good evening folks, once again it's lottery time,' we would go for a wander around the fairground. There was a tunnel behind the stand at the end of the home straight and it was kind of magical walking through the tunnel into the fairground. I would look in awe at the magnificence of the 'Bobs' – said to be the biggest switchback in Europe – and commit myself to one day being brave enough to go on it. But I was unable to fulfil that commitment, as the Bobs did not survive beyond my childhood. It was said that they had been sold to America, but I fear the truth was that they had become too old and decayed and they had to be scrapped. Therefore I would have to prove my bravado some other way. We would take a quick ride on the Scenic Railway and maybe catch sight of the first race of the second half. A real favourite was a go on 'Shoot the Rapids', or go and watch the 'Water Chute', and get wet. But, none of this was ever going to compete with the draw and attraction of the speedway. One thing that was a major attraction was the zoo, until the cost became too great and it closed before many of the other facets were lost. In Manchester, Belle Vue was probably most famous for its zoo and this was to become the affectionate nickname for the speedway: 'Are you going to The Zoo on Saturday?' There was something for everybody at Belle Vue.

On race nights we always went in at the pop side, (popular side) because we were not rich enough for the posh side, which was the start and finish straight. But after the interval the stewards allowed spectators from the pop side to come through. We would often take advantage of this because we could go around to the pits and get a good view of the pits action. It was a hive of activity, usually a lot of novices warming-up bikes or trying to get them going, and occasionally there would be a team member signing autographs at the fence.

Watching the racing was great, but the next best thing and occasionally even better was just soaking up the mish-mash of action in the pits: watching mechanics changing sprockets – why did they do that? – taking out engines and cutting tyres. There were so many things going on. A mechanic would rush in for a spanner, somebody would shout for a spare bike, (probably Alan Morrey) then out would go a bike for a rider with twenty seconds left of his two minutes' time allowance. Sometimes this was where the action was, it was like being backstage at the theatre, witnessing the off-stage drama and chaos, while the audience enjoyed a good performance up front, unaware there was a backstage performance as well.

One other very important factor that was a little more powerful in the pits was the smell. That very distinctive aroma comes from a combination of alcohol fuel (methanol), and castor-based vegetable oil, which is used for lubricating the engine. When the engine is run the unmistakable, and dare I say addictive, smell is produced. Your first smell at the start of a new season was, ironically, like a breath of fresh air. One trick that us lads would do with our track bikes was to put a small amount of castor oil in our petrol to simulate the smell at speedway. It plays a big part in the attraction of the sport.

Local grass-track racing was something that had become appealing to the Partington Gang. It had similarities to what we were doing with our own track bikes and, more to the point, we had noticed some of the better grass-track lads getting a chance at speedway. We were all keen followers of the local grass-track scene. It was obvious that this was going to be the stepping stone into the world of speedway.

In the late 1960s my Mum and Dad would take us all to the local grass-track meetings, where we would watch local talent like Johnny Cox, Grahame Drury, Dave and Chris Baybutt – these had all had a go at speedway – but the real hero was Chris Pusey. If Chris Pusey was at a local grass-track meeting he would usually clean up. Following his rapid success in grass-track racing, Belle Vue Speedway had snapped him up around 1968. As he quickly developed his speedway skills he uniquely adapted them to his grass-track style – he was sensational.

His performances on the grass were formidable. We watched him develop a unique style on the grass that we all found to be an inspiration. Instead of riding into the corners with the power off and with the wheels in line, the traditional grass-track method, he was coming into the corners flat out, broad-sliding in speedway style – he was a revelation to us. What he was doing so successfully was basically what we were doing on our little tracks on the farm, riding speedway on grass. We found him so entertaining as his style was all or nothing – usually 'all' – and he was very colourful with his polka dot leathers, which got more and more elaborate as his confidence grew. Chris had what can only be described as a raw talent. There was no calculation in Chris Pusey's riding; he rode on instinct, with a strong desire to win. I have since described him as a contradiction in terms in as much as he was 'controlled chaos.' The way he rode a speedway bike was sometimes amazing, often defying the laws of physics.

I can recall an incident that sums Chris up a treat. Tapes go up, Chris Pusey's in front and an easy race win is on the cards. But no, he has forgotten to turn on the fuel! First lap, on the back straight the bike packs up and three riders fly past. Chris, quick to realise the error, turns on the fuel, but by the time the engine starts up again the other three are half a lap in front. You can sense from the crowd that they fancy him to maybe catch up and, just maybe, get a point. But I suspect old Pusey wants his first place back. What ensued was entertainment just as raw as his talent, you could see him metaphorically roll up his sleeves and for the next three laps it was pure Pusey. He certainly caught them up, and with half a lap to go scrapped and nudged his way to the front and took the chequered flag to a standing ovation.

Chris Pusey represented hope for us lads wanting to be speedway riders. He was young and the story of how he learned to ride was very similar to what we were doing. He was a teenage hero and a massive inspiration. I consider myself to have been lucky to have got to know him, and enjoyed some good times in Australia with him back in the 1970s – more about that later.

Apart from having to deal with the rigours of formal education, the real valuable learning that was going to be the foundation for my future was moulded outside of school. Maintaining these old track bikes was a skill on its own, the budget for funding this passion coming from minimal pocket money, a paper round, and occasional spud bashing.

From seven years old, along with my mates, I did a self-styled eight-year speedway apprenticeship because during the summer months this group of lads from Partington could religiously be seen at Belle Vue Speedway every race night throughout the season. We would have been riding our bikes during the afternoon, playing at speedway, then go and watch how it was really done by the professionals. Just as kids do, we were going to be speedway riders when we got older, but we never had any way of knowing if what we were doing was going to make us good enough. We did not have any way of measuring our skills against anything but ourselves – a kind of blind faith. School holidays couldn't come quickly enough for the chance to ride our bikes every day, or when we could afford the petrol. I can clearly remember hot summer days when I could fill my gallon can up with petrol, take it down to the track with my bike to meet the rest of the lads, where I would ride until the can ran out.

TWO

I COULD HAVE BEEN
A DREAMER

There was a cold snap in the air but I could feel sweat slowly trickling down between my shoulder blades. The start marshal barked fog out with his orders as we tried to settle at the tapes. Every speedway season ended like this. Floodlights squinting through October gloom, that fireworks smell arriving at least a month earlier than expected, the shivers that were as much down to excitement as they were temperature.

As I got my front wheel in line I glanced across at the bright red leathers and caught his eyes watching me. Soren Sjosten, that bundle of Swedish dynamite, knew I stood, or rather crouched, at the tapes between him and first prize. Pride was at stake; I understood that. I wasn't just any opponent astride a Jap, I was the future, and I threatened Soren's great past. His job was to teach people like me a lesson; my job was to learn.

The staring was over. Tapes, green light, throttle and clutch became the world for that split second that always seemed like an age. Nerves and engine reached fever pitch before that moment of release, arms straining to wrench from the sockets as the tyres bite and the waiting is over. I was on the white line and the fence flashing by on my right, but there was no sign of Soren. I could hear his engine over my shoulder but it mingled with a faint roar from the packed Hyde Road terraces. 'MOR-TON, MOR-TON, MOR-TON,' accompanied my slide into the pits turn. 'MOR-TON, MOR-TON, MOR-TON,' rang out as I bent low over the handlebars to build up speed over the start line, a lap behind me already. 'MOR-TON!!!!' A ruler snapped across my desk as Hyde Road vanished from view and Blessed Thomas Holford School in Altrincham sprang into its place. It wasn't Soren Sjosten, international speedway rider, glaring at me – it was my teacher! It wasn't an engine I could hear ringing in my ears, but laughter.

'MORTON! PAY ATTENTION BOY.'

The class sniggered as I returned from where I'd been, a bright shade of crimson and in deep trouble again. Not because I'd failed to hold Soren Sjosten at bay for four laps. No, I was still years away from making that dream come true. Dreaming, that was the problem. Looking back, I would say it was their problem and not mine.

I was a speedway rider years before I even sat on a speedway bike. I won the war without realising what wars were about. I helped John Wayne tame the American West. I sank battleships, drove steam engines, flew jet planes and beat Soren Sjosten, my first speedway hero, fair and square over four laps. But at school I wasn't known as the greatest general, the navy commander, sensational Belle Vue schoolboy signing and next World Speedway Champion. I was the dreamer. They used to taunt me with rousing choruses of the old Everley Brothers hit *Dream* and I used to go away and sulk... or dream.

I was never anything special at school. I always felt they were missing something. I knew there was something inside me that they weren't catering for. That's probably where the dreaming came in, as nobody could understand that I wanted to be a speedway rider. And I wasn't interested in anything else I thought they wanted me to be. I had ambitions of my own and made the classic mistake of not concentrating hard enough on anything but my dreams, because I thought I knew better. Riding speedway wasn't all that mattered to me; I understood I had to do reasonably well at school, but I wasn't prepared to give it my best. I was content to do just enough to keep the teachers off my back. Now I'd give anything to go back and educate myself. But dreaming? I recommend it. Sometimes, they even come true! For some the dreams became reality a lot quicker than they did for others.

One of these dreams was in front of me and it seemed like a vision. I know that sounds a little dramatic, but to see a real grass-track bike in the yard at Bill Collins's farm was stunning. It was 1970, I was thirteen years old and while looking at this bike with Bill he was telling me all about it, his pride and enthusiasm was palpable – this was his son's first 500cc grass bike. Peter Collins had worked at a local market garden for a few years and this was the fruit of his labours. It was a 500cc Stacey Jap; a long-stroke 500cc Jap engine in a Harold Stacy frame to be exact. Although we were used to seeing these types of machines at the grass-track races we attended on a regular basis – as we were able to walk around the pits and look at the bikes – to see one in isolation in Bill's yard was so impressive.

At the time I had a 197cc Villiers, which I thought was the business, especially when compared to the 175cc Bantams that most of the other lads were using – including PC. But Peter Collins had now set a new precedent and a total shift into the real world; from that day forward nothing would ever be the same – playtime was over! I still had a couple of years to wait, but the path to follow would soon be taken.

For me, the next two years were agony. It would even be a further twelve months before my brother Dave would be able to afford to buy a grass-track bike for the 1971 season when he was seventeen years old. I was now fourteen, turning fifteen in the July of 1971. Dave was proving a major success on the local grass-track scene and he found himself getting a trial for Crewe Kings. I was involved with this proper racing as a helper, just soaking up the atmosphere and gaining experience. I was still riding my track bikes more or less on my own, although sometimes I would ride with Andy Reid who was a friend – he went on to ride for Glasgow.

I had a really old 350cc BSA Goldstar. It must have been a 1940s or early 1950s model as it had a rigid rear frame, usually with a sprung seat, but I had given it the 'track bike' treatment. I don't remember where I acquired this bike, but I do know the attraction was the rigid frame – it would be just like a speedway bike. I stripped off all the junk, including the sprung seat, which I substituted with a homemade affair. I replaced the heavy front forks with a set of 175 BSA Bantam forks and there you have it, as near to a speedway bike as I would get for a couple of years. It wasn't the easiest thing to ride on our waste-ground track, but what it did teach me was how to slide a bike with a bit of four-stroke power.

I don't know exactly how I came to be in the pits, but I was feeling quite privileged standing in the riders' enclosure at Belle Vue in 1971. Not only that, I was standing next to double World Champion Ronnie Moore. There had been an incident involving Alan Wilkinson and Alan Cowland and a bit of a scuffle broke out on the track. There was tremendous tension in the air and before anyone had a chance to calm it all down, the track on the pits bend was full of riders, mechanics and supporters all scrapping. It was a little sad for speedway, as it was a very rare occurrence – but it was great excitement for a fourteen-year-old.

As 1972 was looming towards us, the Morton family had a difficult decision to make. Dave had finished his first season in 1971 in competitive racing and had been a success. Meanwhile, Peter Collins had taken British Speedway by storm with a sensational first season with National League Rochdale. Bill Collins had taken me to see some of the meetings and PC was being heralded as Britain's great white hope – the new Peter Craven. He finished with an average of over 9 points a meeting for the Hornets and also doubled-up with Belle Vue, who won the league championship that year. I recall that such was the excitement surrounding his debut season that PC was quoted as saying that everyone was getting carried away and that he didn't believe all the hype that was being spouted about him. All this was great for us Partington kids, but I was champing at the bit to be racing as well. I had been left behind to carry on riding my bike while PC and Dave were doing it for real. I desperately wanted to make that step too, but all I could do, for the time being at least, was dream about it.

My parents recognised this and they had decided they could help me to buy my first bike. I would be finishing school in the spring – around April – and then I would start work when I was sixteen at Shell Chemicals, so I would be earning a regular wage. The timing, however, of this very significant event in my life wasn't quite right. It would need a bit of rule-bending for me to be able to make the most of this opportunity.

As I would be sixteen in July, I would miss more than half of the grass-track season because you can only have a competitor's ACU National Licence at the age when you reach sixteen years old. 'It wasn't my idea, Your Honour, it was my Dad's, and he made me do it,' I applied for a licence giving my date of birth in March instead of July so I could start the season. Not the crime of the century, but I was only fifteen when I first rode in senior grass-track meetings.

It's not generally known but there was no junior grass-track racing for us at that time. When we all began racing bikes, all we knew was what we had learnt by riding against each other in the fields around our homes. There were no training schools for under-16s in speedway or grass track. Within a couple of years of my entry into grass track, a fairly good junior grass-track scene was established, but there was very little about at that time for me. During the mid to late 1970s, it was an accepted route that an aspiring speedway rider would begin his career in junior grass track and, as the two disciplines are similar, they have complimented each other.

Indeed, England's first World Champion Tommy Price extolled the benefits of grass-track racing in his book *Tommy Price's Speedway Mixture*: 'You can learn much from grass-tracking; I regard it as the most instructive step to the cinders. Most important of all is a sound mechanical knowledge and the ability to prepare your own motors.' So even in the immediate post-war years, grass-track racing was a training ground for any would-be speedway rider. Although I didn't know it at the time, I was following a well-worn path of progress.

We purchased my first bike from Graham Drury, a 250 BSA C15, in a Ray Drury frame. Ray tuned it; and for a little 250 it went like a rocket, compared to anything else I had ever ridden up to then. My first meeting was in April 1972, about seven miles from home in Woolston, Warrington. It was a local grass-track meeting – probably organised by a local club. Both Dave and I were there, Dave on his 500cc Hagon Jap and me on my 250. We cleaned up and won about six little trophies each. This was the very first time I had competed in anything really and it was a revelation to me – I was ready for more. At the end of the meeting one of the riders came up complaining to my Dad that we should not have been there, it was not for professionals, you shouldn't be allowed to come in here and take all the trophies and prize money. Dad tried to explain that I had never done it before and it was my first meeting, but he wouldn't believe it. I knew it would not all be as easy as that, but it was a very satisfying and surprisingly easy first meeting. I could certainly handle a lot more of this winning lark.

I did about twenty to twenty-five grass-track meetings in 1972. My Mum and Dad had a Mini car at the time, and my Dad had worked a bit of the 'George the welder' magic on an old mini sub-frame and made a trailer so it could carry three bikes. So the little Mini with its 'George the Welder'-inspired trailer was an essential part of our equipment. That little set up saw us through the first couple of years.

Both Mum and Dad would be my chauffeurs for some time yet. Whenever my Dad had to work at the weekends it was my Mum's job to act as driver. My Mum had to train herself on driving with a trailer, which was a skill that she never completely mastered. It was a very familiar site on the roads around Cheshire; this little Mini pulling a trailer loaded up with grass-track bikes at the weekends.

Dave was now a regular in the Crewe Kings side and I was his mechanic, along with my Dad. Only months earlier the nearest I had been to speedway pits was at the back of Belle Vue by the big steel-mesh gates where you could only see a few of the second-half riders. The team riders pitted around the corner from these steel gates behind a tall concrete fence so you could not see them, or what was going on in the big boys' pit area. Here I now was around all this action. It was a smorgasbord of essential information for an eager young racer – I loved it. But I would have to wait for my chance, which would come sooner than I expected.

THREE

NO MORE PIPE DREAMS

I was sat in the back of the Morris Minor van that was my brother's trusty speedway vehicle. It was September 1972, my leathers bag and helmet were also in the van, along with Dave's speedway bike and all his gear. I was a little apprehensive; I was going to have a ride on Dave's speedway bike in a novice race in the second half of the meeting at Crewe – but I was cool! So there I was, sixteen and a speedway bike virgin. Sure, I had a few months experience of grass-track racing on my 250 grasser, I had sat on my brother's speedway bike lots of times – you know, dreaming what it might be like to race on it – and I had even warmed it up for him in the pits, but I had never ridden a 500cc speedway bike in my life before.

My first ever experience of moving along on a speedway bike under its own power was riding round to the tapes for a race. Now, for all you people out there who have never ridden a speedway bike but can ride a motorbike, I can tell you from experience that it is ten times harder and nowhere near as easy as we make it look. I was now sat on a bike twice as powerful as my grass-track bike. Twelve months previously I was riding on a field on a Villiers 197, now here I was going up to the start in a real speedway race.

As I was told, I did a practice start as I made my way around to the starting tapes. My God! It felt like a rocket ship! I did a start like I would on my grass-track bike and I have got to say it scared me. There was such raw power that was in my control – or not as the case may be – that I just gave it a handful of throttle and dropped the clutch. It was probably one of the best starts I was going to make for a long time, but it was only a practice. By the time I had got to the tapes I had now completed my first few hundred yards on a speedway bike and track, and had done about three practice starts. As I rolled up to the tapes I was bricking myself – reality is so different to the dream. It all happened so quickly: green light on, (don't give it too much throttle, remember it's so damned powerful) tapes up, drop the clutch.

I wasn't kidding about it being a rocket. As the other three riders went forward I went straight up, my front wheel pawed the air, I did a complete loop and the bike landed on top of me – first race over! I had only travelled about three yards! Riding a speedway bike is a fine skill, get it wrong and it will let you know. That was a harsh lesson for me and a very important one. Not because I got hurt, but I found out it was not as easy as I thought it was. That little incident may have contributed to my not being one of the best gaters in the world.

Of course, I mastered the skill of using the power of a speedway bike fairly quickly and, as the 1972 season came to a close, I had a few second-half rides at Crewe. I managed to get a ride at Belle Vue in the last meeting of the season in their second half – thanks to the loan of my brother's bike.

And then that was it; at the end of October 1972 there was no more speedway until March 1973, but we had the end-of-season dance in the Cumberland Suite to finish off the season. For the last few weeks I had noticed a particular girl in the suites at Belle Vue during the end-of-meeting drinks. We had had a few brief chats, nothing substantial, but I was very aware that I was always looking to see if she was in.

The end-of-season dance was no exception to my hoping for her presence. In fact, more than just looking to see if she was there I was going to make a move. I was sixteen, I didn't have a girlfriend and this girl seemed very special to me. When I walked into the Cumberland Suite there she was, sat with her two friends at a table – just the three of them. I went up to the bar and got myself a pint of lager because it looked manly and grown-up, boldly went over to the three girls and plonked my pint on the table and said 'do you mind if I sit with you?' A great chat up line! It was all done very clumsily, but I was no master at this stuff. The night went okay, the usual bit of chat, bit of dancing, and then she suddenly announced that she had to go – her mates were already out the door. I asked if I could walk her home and she agreed that I could walk her to Redgate Lane, which was a few hundred yards away. That was where it happened, the first time I kissed Jackie Evans. My encounter, or at least the significant part of my encounter, had been brief but indelible.

Unfortunately, as it was the end of the season, I wouldn't have the chance to see Jackie at the speedway, but as I had her phone number I would arrange to go and see her in Manchester or something – that was my plan anyway. Jackie lived about half a mile from Belle Vue whereas I lived twelve miles away. I had obviously not left the same impression on Jackie as she had on me, because when I phoned her religiously every week to arrange to see her at the weekend, I would get the baby-sitting or washing-my-hair routine every time. I was persistent, but after a few months I was slowly becoming resigned to the fact that love at first sight for me was going to take a few more viewings for Jackie Evans.

For a young man itching to make his mark as a speedway rider, the winter months were long. But there was much to talk about for speedway fans when Aces' number one and reigning World Champion Ivan Mauger was forced to move from Belle Vue by the controversial Rider Control board. Belle Vue won the league title for the third successive season in 1972 – the first team to win the title three years in a row since the British League was formed in 1965 – and Mauger had been a big influence on the success of the club and also on the young up-and-coming riders. When the news came through that Mauger would not be permitted to ride for the Aces, there was much speculation as to where he would eventually ride in 1973. Despite all the different clubs that were linked with him, it was the seemingly unfashionable West Country team Exeter that sensationally secured the signature of the multi-World Champion. A new era had begun for the Falcons and also for the Aces too.

My experiences with Mauger would be mainly as a rival on the track instead of a teammate. But in 1969 it seemed that the Belle Vue management had decided that it would be a good idea to give its famous name some credibility. Since the new British League was launched in 1965, Belle Vue's highest league position had been an embarrassing tenth place and they mostly finished in the lower half. This was particularly uncomfortable when you realised what a glorious and successful history the club had. My knowledge at the time of the team's poor performance was almost non-existent – I just loved watching the racing at Belle Vue. Perhaps if they were top of the league and winning trophies, then their performances would have been more obvious. But I was just happy to be supplied with good racing.

Dent Oliver's youth policy was just starting to bear fruit in 1969, but if Belle Vue were going to win the league it would take something extra special. That something special came neatly packaged in the form of reigning World Speedway Champion Ivan Mauger – later to be fondly known as the 'The Big I' as his status became prolific.

I didn't realise the meaning at the time, but Ivan Mauger had an important influence on me when I was eleven years old. In 1967 I can bring to mind the 'Peter Craven Memorial Trophy' meeting, and my speedway world at that point was limited to Belle Vue, a trip to Sheffield once, Halifax (Flukes), once, and one World Final that year. So when this rider from Newcastle called Ivan Mauger won the Peter Craven Memorial Trophy it meant very little to me; and he more than likely made it look boring by making every start and winning with very little excitement. He must have been a bit special because I can remember my Mum saying how pleased she was that he had won the meeting, and how he deserved some success. Well that was just the start for the 'The Big I' and the Belle Vue link. After winning the meeting, Ivan Mauger was paraded around the track and I was right up by the fence to get a good look at this deserving winner. I have a very vivid picture in my mind of a young Ivan Mauger with a beaming smile holding this magnificent trophy with about twenty gold shields around its base just waiting for the winner's name to be engraved each year. That was the first year of this meeting, so the first shield read '1967 Ivan Mauger' – would this eleven-year-old dare to believe that the shield for 1974 would read '1974 Chris Morton'?

In 1969 Belle Vue became the home track for Ivan Mauger, who was soon to be identified as 'Mr Professional' by his peers. This professional approach was to bring some serious success during the four-year stint that 'The Big I' did as a Belle Vue Ace. Although Soren Sjosten was always going to be my favourite rider, watching Ivan around the Hyde Road circuit was an absolute pleasure, and it was only a matter of time before he would beat the long-standing track record set by Peter Craven back in 1958.

After the 1972 season had finished Peter Collins had been chosen to ride for the British Lions in Australia. Amazing things were happening, especially when you consider that just two years earlier he was at school. My brother had finished a successful first season with Crewe, but unfortunately he suffered a serious compound fracture of his left arm.

It was a bizarre accident that occurred in a second-half race. At the end of the race Dave just over-slid after the finish line going into the corner. As he was getting up, a novice rider who was about half a lap behind and did not have a clue how to lay down a bike (a perfect advert for the American system, no licence until you can lay a bike down) ran straight into Dave, who instinctively held up his arm to protect himself. There you go, one seriously broken arm and an incredible amount of pain. This was the first of a series of broken bones that would plague my brother throughout his career.

For me, the winter months of 1972/73 consisted of riding at the Belle Vue Training School on a Saturday, and then during the week I'd work at Shell Chemical at Carrington in Cheshire – affectionately known locally as 'Joe Shell'. In the early 1970s Joe Shell was to employ a few speedway riders – myself, my brother, Peter Collins and the Ellesmere Port rider Wayne Hughes.

During that winter the training school was run by Dent Oliver. Although conditions were often very poor due to the weather, a great effort was always made to ensure that the training schools were able to run. There was an incredible resilience towards the bitter British winter by everybody concerned. This was a great foundation for me. As the 1973 season started to approach, I had made some serious progress since my first experience on a speedway bike at Crewe – the three-yard disaster at the end of the previous season!

My days at the training schools in 1972/73 are a little vague as I was only looking ahead. I wasn't very interested in who I was practicing with because I just wanted to win, but a number of lads started out at about the same time. I remember Geoff Lyons – who was sponsored at the time by Jim Sephton, who became the promoter at Ellesmere Port – and I occasionally had a ride on Geoff's bike. He had two brand-new Jawas and was the envy of us aspiring novices. I remember Barry Booth, who was a good friend of Paul Tyrer who had come through the training school regime and was an established member of the Belle Vue team. Barry, on the other hand, was a good novice but never held down a regular team place, although he was always one for the up-and-comers to beat.

One lad who is a very good friend of mine to this day is Steve Casey. He started at the same time as I did and we spent that winter learning our trade. As my career took flight, Steve steadily made progress and went on to ride for Ellesmere Port and later Newport. He tells me he beat me once at the training school, but sadly for him I cannot remember that ever happening. But if he wants to believe that he once beat Chris Morton, I can live with that.

Throughout the winter I had watched the top novice lads and raced and beaten a few, and I thought some of them looked quick. Then one day in February Eric Broadbelt, who had just returned from Australia, came along to try his new bikes. It was a revelation to watch from the inside of the track as to how you really do it. I had spent the whole winter watching novices like myself, but seeing the difference in speed and technique between novices and a rider of Eric's level at that time gave me a serious message that said 'there's still work to do.' What I saw him do was ride the engine to its limit and squeeze out every ounce of power. I had seen this done many times, in many races, by many riders, but the difference was that I had now had a winter's experience on a speedway bike and could now relate to what I was seeing him do. At that moment I recognised the major difference between riding a speedway bike and *racing* a speedway bike.

I started the 1973 season as a Belle Vue novice by riding in the second-half races at Belle Vue and Ellesmere Port. The Port was looked upon as a 'feeder track' for the Aces as they had taken over the licence from Rochdale, who closed at the end of the 1971 season following poor attendances. Things were looking good, apart from one thing.

During the winter I had telephoned Jackie Evans several times – more like every week – for a date. I didn't realise at the time but she was only fourteen, so she wasn't ready for a pushy pubescent sixteen-year-old just yet. But I just knew from our encounter at the end of the previous season that there was a spark to be kindled.

One day it happened. It was during a Bank Holiday and we had a meeting at Belle Vue against Wolverhampton in the afternoon followed by the return in the evening at Wolves. At the time a friend called Jack Bassett did a lot of driving, spannering and generally helping out for Dave and myself. He was aware of my interest in Jackie and he decided to play Cupid.

He invited her to come along with some friends in his car to watch the meeting at Wolverhampton, where we had already arranged he would mechanic for me as I was riding in the second half of the meeting. I knew nothing of his plans. Jackie had convinced her parents to let her go, and Jack Bassett had promised them he would get her back for an agreed time. So off they went to Wolverhampton in his Dad's Hillman Hunter full of people. My Mum, Dad and I had trundled down to Wolverhampton in the Mini with its Mini sub-frame trailer and my bike. I rode in the second-half novice races; I had won a race and felt good. Jack then told me he had got Jackie with him and did I want to come home with him? My Mum and Dad didn't seem to mind so that was it. With four of us in the back of the Hillman Hunter it was a tight squeeze but I made sure I sat next to Jackie. We hit it off straight away. She was only fourteen and studying for her CSEs (equivalent of today's GCSE) at the time. I don't think I was a great influence on her studying as we moved into the 1973 season and my career began to take shape.

Speedway for me was developing fast. On loan from Belle Vue as a raw rookie, in April I became an Ellesmere Port team rider. The team was known as 'the Gunners' and by mid-May I had broken into their side in a match against Canterbury. We lost 47-31 and I failed to score. But a week later I scored 6 points as we defeated Berwick and then I had my best meeting of my debut season at Crewe when I scored 12 points. That was significant because it was at Crewe, where I had had my first ignominious public appearance on a speedway bike, and it was also where my brother had begun to make a name for himself – all in all, not bad for a sixteen-year-old.

Among my teammates were Graham Drury – the number one and skipper – Robbie Gardner and Gerald Smitherman. Gerald went on to found GTS Products, which has become a familiar name in the sport for the quality of his racing accessories such as leathers, covers and so on. Most of the riders were part-timers and they had day jobs. But Paul O'Neil had come over from New Zealand to be a speedway rider and he took me under his wing. He was very good to me, had a lot of experience and was very helpful. All of them offered me help and I think they could see that I was a young lad coming through. Jim Sephton was the promoter of the Gunners and he was a massive help and influence to all us young lads at Ellesmere. As I mentioned earlier, he got involved in speedway through sponsoring Barry Booth, and as Barry and I were competing at the training schools at both Ellesmere and Belle Vue, he took an interest in me. He oversaw everything and was a bit of a gentleman.

Ellesmere Port's meetings were on a Tuesday. We would leave home in Partington at about 5 p.m. for a 7.30 p.m. start. As our relationship was developing, Jackie was always invited to my meetings at the Port and when she could get away with it she would wag off school in the afternoon. She would take a change of clothes to school with her for speedway, get a bus from school into Manchester City Centre and then catch another bus from Manchester to Partington – the whole affair would take about three hours. Although very young, we were both absolutely serious about each other and were sure our future would be together.

To my way of thinking, Ellesmere was always a gater's track. There weren't too many places where you could pass, but I found one or two ways of doing it – but it wasn't easy. I wasn't a gater, I was a racer, so that made it more difficult and, of course, the riders there were more experienced than I was. Just as grass track was the route to speedway, so too was Ellesmere a route to Belle Vue.

My weeks now required some planning and skiving from work at 'Joe Shell' as an apprentice 'Hairy-Arsed Pipe Fitter' – as the saying goes. This may sound a bit crude, but they were and no doubt still are always referred to by this title. Other trade options at Joe Shell, to name just a few, were fabrication fitter (my brother's choice), electrician and plant operator. As I am sure you can imagine, a chemical plant site has an enormous amount of pipe work, and it was a pipe fitter's job to maintain these systems. This would also include servicing chemical pumps, valve systems, manufacturing simple parts and generally whatever else was needed to keep the plant going. For example, we would work in workshops repairing valve seats, then have the repaired valve pressure tested in a sealed test bay up to incredible pressures before they would then be put back onto the site in situ. At times it could be highly technical work, at other times you could be up to your neck in crap trying to handle a big valve out of its position in the system because it was leaking and in desperate need of repair. A chemical plant is a fascinating complexity of pipe work and machinery, but also a dirty filthy place out on site. Once familiar with it the fascination soon wanes – familiarity breeds contempt.

During my time at Joe Shell – which went from September 1972 to October 1974, representing two speedway seasons – on many occasions I had a need to leave work early to get to a speedway meeting somewhere in the country. As meetings during the week usually started at 7.30 p.m. or later, some of the tracks I could get to after I finished work – these were Belle Vue, Sheffield, Ellesmere Port and Halifax, with Wolverhampton, Birmingham and Cradley Heath being locations we could 'just about' reach in time for the racing. However, the rest of the tracks required at least the afternoon off. Throughout my two years as an apprentice we also did a day release at Stretford Technical College of Further Education. If I needed to leave early I would just sweet talk the lecturer into letting me go early – my rising fame in Manchester had its benefits! When I was back on site at Joe Shell I would use my holidays when I had to, but there was one trainer who had seen PC go through a couple of years then go off to Aussie, so he had an understanding of the great opportunity that was ahead of me and would always give me the time off whenever I was under his instruction. All in all I enjoyed my time at Shell; I learned some basic engineering skills, and some good basic grounding. Shell had strict safety rules because of the risky business they are in and this gave me a good sense of danger and risk awareness.

I was managing quite well to integrate the two careers, although my sights were set high for my speedway career, I was pretty carefree about my career at Shell. My grounding and general approach was guided by an inbuilt thought or consideration. This was a rather grown-up and boringly sensible approach I had heard from my elders and went along the lines of 'although you are looking like making a success of this speedway thing, it is very important to get a career or trade behind you old boy'. It was a sensible approach that lasted until I had the opportunity to go to Australia. Then I never looked back.

With the away meetings I needed help as I was still only sixteen, so I couldn't drive and my Dad could only get a limited amount of time off work. Jack Bassett was a rock driving me all over the place in the – inherited from Dave – grey Morris Minor van, with the legacy from my childhood travels in the Ford Pop, 30mph cruising, 40mph pushing it a bit, 50mph flat out, with the benefit of 60mph downhill! I was also managing to fit in a busy grass-track schedule. Jim Rowlinson sponsored me on the grass. He had been helping Peter Collins, but during 1973 PC's speedway career had really taken off, so Jim offered me the grass bikes.

In June Chris Pusey broke his arm racing in Poland for the Great Britain under-23 team, which eventually gave me a chance to go into the Belle Vue side – the dream was developing before my very eyes. My first meeting for Belle Vue was away at Cradley Heath, and I scored a credible 6 points; proving I was ready for the British League's higher level of racing.

While I was doubling up for Belle Vue and Ellesmere Port, Dent Oliver was the team manager at Belle Vue. I think his health was deteriorating at this time. This was brought home to me with a jolt when one Saturday night at Belle Vue I was walking back from my van towards the pits when I saw Joe Shaw supporting Dent, who had collapsed onto a car bonnet. Joe called me over with obvious concern and urgency in his voice and asked me to get help. It wasn't long after this incident that Dent sadly died. I had only just started to get to know Dent through his training schools and the Aces, but in the short time that I had known him and his wife Laura they had made me feel really welcome at Belle Vue. I attended his funeral at Stockport near Manchester and contemplated a relationship that might have been. Dent had a great reputation and his work with the youngsters was a credit to him.

In a matter of months I had gone from being a raw novice to a competent and valuable member of a club I had supported from the age of seven. I cannot deny I had dreamed about becoming a Belle Vue Ace. I don't think I could ever be considered as arrogant, but even at the age of sixteen, nearly seventeen, it felt like my destiny. I just took it in my stride; it felt like my place to be in this team. It had certainly come about sooner than I thought it would, but that was not going to stop me from staking my claim. I didn't feel any euphoric elation at this realisation of a dream come true. It really was a matter of course – the first step along a road I had planned years before.

I had spent my years at school believing that life beyond school would hold something special and something worthwhile through speedway. I could quite easily have been wrong. I had nothing to base my faith on, apart from Chris Pusey and, much later, my own friend Peter Collins. But what Peter did was to prove that what we had been doing as kids was going to work. I think what Chris Pusey was showing us in the late sixties was that if this rough-arsed Scouser could do it, then so could us rough-arsed Partingtonians. Pusey was our role model, our hero. So when the opportunity was presented to me to join the Belle Vue team I greeted it with enormous pride – a pride that never left me – and got on with the challenge. Be careful what you dream about, it just may come true.

Of course reality is never that simple, and although I managed a 6-point average in my part season for Belle Vue in 1973, the end of the season taught me a lesson I would have to endure at many levels: 'You must first learn how to lose before you know how to win'. It was the 1973 Knock-Out Cup final, Belle Vue *v.* Reading. It was a memorable final with the climax being the famous run-off between Anders Michanek and Peter Collins after both teams had finished on equal points after the second leg at Hyde Road.

Peter was carrying a damaged left hand and had moved his clutch lever over from the left to the right-hand side of his handlebars, and amazingly he operated both the clutch and throttle with the one hand! Furthermore, his left hand was taped to the bars as he had no gripping power due to the injury. The home and away legs resulted in a draw and left the cup to be decided in a run-off, with each team nominating one rider. Whoever won the race, his team would win the cup.

I stood and watched a most amazing race develop between Peter Collins for the Aces and Anders Michanek for Reading – regarded by some as the greatest race ever staged at Hyde Road. Michanek made a predictable fast start and, as expected, PC made a smart move on him to take an early lead. Michanek instantly came back with a counter-move on the next corner to regain the lead. Clearly both riders were not giving up without a fight as one rider out-manoeuvred the other on one corner and then he would find his move had been countered at the next. Both riders were obviously pushing the limits and leaving themselves no opportunity to consolidate the race. It was, predictably, decided by the last dash to the chequered flag with PC taking the win by half a wheel on the line. It was an absolute pleasure to watch two world-class riders battle to the last inch. Belle Vue had won the 1973 Knockout Cup final. The record shows I scored 0 points.

As I received my winners' medal I felt like a complete fraud; winning surely is about winning. I had not done any winning. I never considered myself part of that win and quite rightly so. As far as I was concerned I had lost, and that cold miserable feeling you get when you lose is what stokes that strong desire to win. I really believe losing is an important part of winning. It was an experience that I did not want to repeat. That meeting had taught me a valuable lesson: I did not like being a loser – especially on a winning side!

That victory also silenced some of the critics who said that Belle Vue wouldn't win anything without Mauger. There were some who thought that the Kiwi's departure to the West Country would spark a downward trend in fortunes. After completing the league and cup double in 1972 it was always going to be hard to repeat that – especially when Pusey got injured. But they hadn't reckoned on the desire that young riders like PC, Wilkie and Paul Tyrer had, and I considered myself to be in that group even if I didn't feel much like a winner.

After the Belle Vue Knock-Out Cup win and my private, but probably self-induced, feelings of humiliation at having no part in the matter, I had the winter months to plan my 1974 season. My brother had gone off to New Zealand to ride, and generally to have a good time. PC was riding for Great Britain on the Australian tour, while I had a winter of weekend training schools at Belle Vue. The winter months of late 1973 and early 1974 were a bit mundane after the swift rise in my speedway career through the previous season. I had passed my driving test in October 1973, which gave me some freedom and as I now had some money from racing I was able to trade in the old Morris Minor van – okay, scrap it – for an Austin Maxi. Pure luxury!

Despite the distraction caused by me, Jackie had finished school and achieved some reasonable results in her exams. She obtained a job working for an insurance broker. We spent as much time together as we could, but this was mainly at the weekend due to the fact that we were both working. Having started my apprenticeship in the September of 1972, my apprenticeship with Joe Shell was now in its second year. Life was great for this seventeen-year-old, but I couldn't wait for March to come around so I could get on with the new speedway season as a full-time Belle Vue Ace.

Jim Rowlinson gave me the very welcome news that he would be fully sponsoring me on the grass track and speedway for the 1974 season. I considered myself to be extremely fortunate to be under Jim Rowlinson's wing, because I was following in the footsteps of Chris Pusey and Peter Collins. For the new season I was kitted out with two speedway bikes with the new short-stroke Jap engine. In a bid to compete with the now-tremendously successful

Czechoslovakian Jawa engine, the Jap agent, George Greenwood, had developed the short stroke. On the grass tracks I would ride in the 350cc and 500cc events. It was a fantastic arrangement, because all I had to do to was turn up at the grass-track meetings and ride. Jim's mechanics, the famous Horris and Harry would do the rest, and this allowed me to continue grass-track racing and concentrate on my speedway.

I still had an enormous amount to learn and 1974 provided some very positive learning. It was clear I had the ability to win races, but how would I cope with individual meetings and the specific races when the pressure was on? As the early months of the season progressed I found the short-stroke Jap engine was very competitive but a bit unreliable. Far too often the con rod – which attaches the piston to the flywheels – would break to devastating effect, completely smashing an engine to bits – both internally and externally. I was, in effect, the test pilot for these engines. I was grateful at this stage of my career, but their lack of reliability would be their downfall. But when these engines held together I had some fantastic results.

Through my teammate, Paul Tyrer, I had a pits helper called Gary Miller. He was enthusiastic and he was nicknamed by PC 'Terry Tinsel' because of his flashy overalls that he had made that had 'Mighty Mort' emblazoned on the back. Gary had been helping speedway riders and began by cleaning Ole Olsen's leathers when he was racing at Newcastle as a fresh-faced Danish rider. Gary and I got along really well. We shared similar tastes in music and also had the same sense of humour. Consequently we had many a laugh together.

During a mid-season spree I won the Peter Craven Memorial Trophy at Belle Vue and the British Junior Championship at Canterbury. Winning the Peter Craven Memorial Trophy meeting filled me with great pride. I had watched some of the legends win this meeting in the past as a child, not least the 'Big I' himself, Ivan Mauger. For me to win this against a strong field was a great boost for my confidence, and I was still only seventeen. My deciding race was against my hero Soren Sjosten in heat seventeen and we both had unbeaten scores. My daydream was becoming a reality as I was leading Sjosten. But Soren's challenge ended on the second lap when he retired with a broken chain, which meant I had clinched a very prestigious trophy.

The following week I was the favourite to win the British Junior Championship, although it wasn't a great shout to be 'the favourite' on a track I had never seen before and did not have any practice on. The first time on the track would be my first race. This meeting really was a test of my mettle. But I held my nerve and went through this meeting unbeaten and was crowned British Junior Champion.

In the process I pushed the up-and-coming Steve Bastable into second place and Neil Middleditch took third. Middlo, as Neil would be called, went on to become the current Great Britain team manager, but he enjoyed a successful career on the track before sampling more triumphs as the team manager of the Poole Pirates Speedway team. We all met in what would turn out to be a decisive heat fifteen. Bastable and I both had unbeaten scores, while Middlo had already dropped a point to Eric Dugard. On paper this really was a pressure race, the type of which I had been wondering about during the winter. You can imagine my pride when I passed the chequered flag in first place.

The *Speedway Star* report of the time described the surface at Canterbury as a track prepared for 'a gater's night,' but this didn't prevent me from weaving my way past Keith White and Martin Yeates in heat eleven after I had missed the start – this would be a familiar occurrence as my career progressed. It was one of the few thrilling moments in the meeting – not that I knew much about that because I was concentrating on my own performance.

Just how committed I was to winning the meeting can be illustrated by my opening-race win. I didn't know this at the time because it was reported later, but apparently I had knocked four-fifths of a second off the three-lap track record, that was held by Trevor Jones, to lower it to 55.2 seconds. I think I must have backed off a little bit on the last lap because although I recorded the fastest time of the night, I didn't grab the track record. But I had no idea that there was a three-lap track record!

By winning this title that was previously held by PC, I had kept the British Junior Championship at Belle Vue for another year. This went some way to making up for my lack of input during the Knock-Out Cup final against Reading. It was my first 'major individual' trophy in speedway, but at this time it didn't hold quite the same amount of prestige and significance as it would later on. Later it would form part of the World U21 Championship qualifying process – formerly known as the European U21 Championship. It's interesting to note that despite the presence of some very good riders in the meeting that would go on to forge successful careers for their club and, in some cases, country, I was the only one in that line-up that would qualify for a World Championship Final.

In late September my season came to a grinding halt when I did something really stupid. It was at a grass-track meeting, and I was riding in both the 350cc and the 500cc races. It was a very full programme with heats, semis and finals, so it could be nine races if the meeting included an unlimited event. Being a fairly small guy I would get tired in the later races of these meetings, especially during the six-lap finals. As this meeting progressed my arms were feeling the strain. A common problem is forearm fatigue, as the muscles in your forearm start to pump up and go into spasm and fail; this becomes acute during six-lap finals at the end of the meetings. When this occurs you have to slow down to reduce the strain. I was in a six-lap final at the end of a busy meeting.

Gerald Short was in front of me and I was in second place. I wanted to beat him and having raced hard for five laps I caught him up, but during this time my arms had become fatigued over the last two laps. I had rested them as much as I could, riding with one arm down the straights while trying to shake out the fatigue from the free arm. On the last lap my arms really had gone completely, and I made a stupid decision. As I lined myself up to go around Gerald on the last corner, I decided I would ride through the fatigue! Now I don't know what I thought riding through this warning sign that my body was giving me meant but, surprise, surprise, halfway around the corner my arms turned into jelly. This sort of abuse, pushing your body to the limit, is okay in the gym, but at 70 mph on a grass-track circuit it becomes what is termed as 'a right shitter'. I completely lost control, crashed heavily and broke my collarbone – that'll teach me!

Belle Vue were in a tight battle at the top with Exeter, but my injury, and also the ones sustained by Alan Wilkinson and Paul Tyrer, put a big question mark over the Aces' ability to regain the league championship. Nonetheless, it was building up to an exciting climax, just as we were thrashed at Ipswich 54-24, Exeter were getting a drubbing at Sheffield. With matches in hand we felt that we could just top Exeter. We had a trip to Wolverhampton and they were without Ole Olsen, who was on the injured list with a broken ankle.

But, just to add spice to the occasion, Wolves were threatening to use Mauger as a guest replacement for Olsen. But we were still confident of getting a result there. Then we were due at Sheffield followed by a home fixture against Halifax. All three meetings were matches that we felt that we could get the required 5 points from to pip the Falcons and clinch the league championship. But in the end the league championship wasn't decided on the track, but in the headquarters of the Speedway Control Board (SCB). Before we could turn a wheel in those three vital matches the title had been handed to the Falcons. Exeter lodged a protest during their 40-38 defeat at Wolverhampton about Wolves' use of Australian Ricky Day as a guest. The SCB upheld their protest and ruled that they should not have used Day as a guest from Second Division Birmingham. And that was it, game over – Exeter had won their first league championship in the top flight. Chris Pusey in particular went on record to say that the team was gutted to lose the championship like that. It's hard to take when you lose a championship on the track even though you may have given your all for the team, but it's even worse when it's taken out of your hands by suits in a bland office somewhere.

As it was now near the end of the season – only October left – that was it, the end of my riding for 1974 – or so I thought. In early October I got a call from the British Speedway promoter's office. John Louis had dropped out and did I want to go to Australia as a member of the British Lions Touring Team? This was a bolt out of the blue. I would have to give up my apprenticeship at Joe Shell! That thought lasted for about a nanosecond. Although it was a surprise, I had put another point on my average and the two individual meetings that I won hadn't gone unnoticed by the selectors. I always felt that if you want to compete in any sport at the highest level it requires your full attention and commitment. If you don't pledge your undivided concentration to the job in hand you may never find out what your best is. There comes a time when a decision has to be made, October 1974 was that time for me.

I remember talking to my trainer at Shell Chemicals about the opportunity to go to Australia. He had also trained PC for two years before he upped and left for a tour in Australia. He said: 'What are you waiting for? Don't give this place a second thought.' This was an absolutely unbelievable opportunity for me as an eighteen-year-old. I was no longer a 'hairy arsed pipe fitter,' I was now a full-time professional speedway rider and I was off to Australia!

FOUR

THE BIG TIME – ALMOST

Going off to Australia was a massive adventure. It was also a big test for any relationship, being separated for four months. It was tough for Jackie, being left behind while I went furthering my skills Down Under. We both knew our love was easily strong enough and my going to Australia was never in question. Saying your goodbyes to loved ones for a four-month trip is not an easy undertaking, and it was the most difficult goodbye I had ever done. But, as I walked through into the departure lounge with the other seven people – who I did not know very well, if at all – I had this sharp sense that something special was happening to me. This trip would be a big step up the ladder in my development, both professionally and personally.

In the 1974/75 British Lions Tour of Australia we had seven riders and a manager. As well as myself there was Nigel Boocock (captain), Doug Wyer, Reg Wilson, Jimmy McMillan, Eric Broadbelt and Kevin Holden, with Wally Mawdsley as our team manager – who later became known as 'Uncle Waz.' For me it was a little bit like the first day at secondary school: you know you are big enough to deal with the situation, but a little apprehensive not knowing anybody that well and not knowing what to expect. Of course, I knew the guys but only really to race against. For the next four months we would be living together.

This was my first trip on a jumbo jet. They really are enormous and I was stunned by their sheer size. I never doubted the ability of this monster to fly but it really is a revelation the first time. After the initial overwhelming impression that the Boeing 747 had on me and, aware it would be my bit of space for the next twenty-four hours or so, I settled down to enjoy the trip. All the guys were really friendly and I knew I was in for a whole new experience. They seemed excited for me. Jimmy Mac told me how all the tracks were big and racy. 'You will love it,' he said. 'Sydney Showground is a bit scary though!' and then, aware of its breathtaking reputation and my apprehension, he added: 'But you'll be alright.' My lifelong appreciation of Bob Dylan was born on that flight to Aussie thanks to the in-flight entertainment. It was an out-take from the double album *Before the Flood*, a live recording of Bob Dylan and The Band performing *Like a Rolling Stone*. My young receptive ears were impressed; Bob Dylan was going to be a companion for a long time.

Nigel Boocock had spent a lot of time in Australia and had a lot of friends with whom he could stay, so he didn't always stay in the hotels with us. This meant that with most hotel rooms being twins we paired up: Reg and Doug together, Jimmy Mac and Broady, leaving Kevin Holden and me to pal up. We were both rookies, although Kevin was a little older than me – about twenty-three at the time. Both Kevin and I hit it off right from the start, even though we were competing for a team place. It was a six-man team with the seventh man at reserve patiently – more like impatiently – waiting for a poor performance to give him a chance, but we were still able to develop a strong friendship. Reg Wilson nicknamed us 'Irish Parliament' (everybody talking, nobody listening) and this was because of something to do with our naivety and inexperience – Reg was full of little witticisms. His favourite recital, which we would get at least once a day, was as follows:

Well you can oil 'em boil 'em
Fry 'em try 'em
Shoot 'em boot 'em
Guaranteed not to
Wear tear rust or bust
And if you haven't got one
We'll get you one.

My first two meetings were actually individuals, the Winfield International at Newcastle and the Frank Arthur Memorial Trophy at Sydney. I scored 3 and 5 points. I was picked at reserve for the First Test, and this was expected because I was returning from a collarbone injury. I had anticipated riding against a State side for the opening matches, but the important thing was that I was getting some racing in to get race fit.

Traditionally Australia is said to be the country where the sport of speedway racing originated. Well, the legendary Johnnie Hoskins always said that. This was merely one facet of the Aussies' desire to put one over us Poms in the Test Series. The rivalry between England, or Great Britain – the old country – and Australia in any sport has always been intense. England's Rugby Union World Cup victory in 2003 was all the sweeter because we took the title in the Aussies' own back yard. And speedway racing was no different. This was speedway's equivalent of the world-famous Ashes Tests that are a feature of cricket.

After a few years in the doldrums following the back-to-back championship success of Jack Young in the 1950s, Australia had some talented young riders emerging, such as Phil Crump, Billy Sanders, Phil Herne, John Titman and the experienced but volatile John Langfield. These were all riders that I would be banging handlebars with on a regular basis as my career developed. Some of them I had already had the pleasure of trading elbows with, but doing so in their own back yard would be a different experience to the one in the British League.

The First Test was at Brisbane and we lost it 62-45. Dougie Wyer was in sensational form, scoring 17 points, dropping his only point to John Titman. But we were having problems with their starting procedures, which if employed in the British League would be looked upon as cheating. Basically, it was green light on, go! There was plenty of rolling at the start and the tapes were almost ignored. We couldn't get to grips with it at all, but, significantly, when we did get ahead on the first turn we usually provided the race winner. Our team manager, Wally Mawdsley, asked for a meeting with the Australian Speedway Control Board to clear up the problems before the Second Test at Brisbane.

I was brought in to replace Kevin Holden after he had two point-less rides, and I passed John Langfield to score my first international point. He wasn't very happy and had a go at me in the pits after the race. This turned out to be our first disagreement – round one – because almost twelve months later Langfield and I had an almighty dust up. However, there was no indication that he had taken a particular dislike to me because he apologised after the meeting. Not that I was bothered, far from it. It was just a racing incident as far as I was concerned.

The unusual thing about racing in Australia at that time was that the races were three laps instead of the traditional four because the tracks were so big. It was flat-out racing too; you needed a fast motor for many of the circuits. In Australia these tracks were often used for car racing such as midget cars and sedans and that was why they were so much bigger.

We won the Second Test 58-50 and once again Dougie 'Nugget' Wyer was in great form. His Sheffield teammate Reg Wilson was also riding well – as he did in the First Test. The difference this time was that Eric Broadbelt scored 9 points and put behind him the rough time he had experienced in the First Test. I scored 4 and it was nice to level the series. But as Christmas approached we lost the next two Tests at both Newcastle and Sydney. We got very close at the Fourth Test, losing by the narrow scoreline of 55-53. I scored 5 at Newcastle and 4 at Sydney, but couldn't prevent us from going into the festive period losing the series 3-1 with three Tests remaining.

I would phone Jackie after every meeting to let her know how I got on and when I could I would write home to my parents. It was a strange Christmas for my Mum and Dad because while I was away in Oz, Dave was racing in New Zealand. Christmas in Australia under the warm sun is different but I would highly recommend it!

The Fourth Test was scheduled for Boxing Day at Liverpool and the Aussies clinched the series, winning 57-51. Liverpool was a bit like Ipswich, so it was more like a conventional speedway track. I replaced Kevin Holden in heat seven, but while I rounded my teammate, Doug Wyer, I found that Billy Sanders had fallen in front of me and I had no chance of avoiding him. I ran over his back wheel and I remember that I rolled over and over and my bike was airborne. Luckily a headache was my only injury, but my bike was wrecked – it was a write-off.

It was disappointing to lose the Ashes, but if it wasn't for some mechanical problems I felt sure that we would have won that Test. At the time I think that we had underestimated the strength of the Australians and they used a horses-for-courses policy to great effect. But the starting procedures were a shambles throughout the series and the lads were often lodging protests – including me! Before we left for Australia, critics wrote us off as 'no hopers' and it was a pity that we couldn't make them eat their words.

During the Sixth Test at Adelaide I was involved in a 'photo finish' with the in-form Phil Crump, and we provided some great racing. At one stage the crowd were on their feet and the locals told me that that was the first time that had occurred for many years. As a team against the Australians we were up against it. As the record shows, we only managed to win two Tests – including the final one at Perth – to lose the series 5-2. I loved Perth; at over 500 metres in length it was more like a long-track circuit. We rode at Perth at the end of the series and by this time I was starting to show real signs of progress from my few months of living the dream. I top-scored in the final Test Match with 14 points, and won a Pairs meeting with Nigel Boocock at the last meeting in Perth before flying back to the UK.

I had formed a strong friendship with Kevin Holden, which I was looking forward to developing over time, but sadly he died a young man on 27 April 1977 – leaving a wife and two children. His death was a shock to everyone and a sad, sad loss of a good man with a big heart, and I lost a good friend. Holden was riding for Poole at the time and had showed considerable form, when he died in heat five of a Knock-Out Cup clash against Reading. He was chasing the Australian Bob Humphreys along the straight at Wimborne Road when he appeared to crash for no apparent reason. It later transpired that he was dead before he hit the deck because of a torn aorta – which is one of the main veins that feeds the heart. The meeting was immediately abandoned and he was only twenty-seven.

I came back from Australia in late January 1975; the Australian experience had lived up to all my expectations. I went over there as a young eighteen-year-old lad, still wet behind the ears, and it turned out to be an incredibly valuable three months of learning about racing, preparing machines and life. When you are part of a touring team you see how other people set up their equipment and you learn new ideas. After all, at eighteen you really know bugger all in the great scheme of things. That type of tour, or any experience that makes you look closely at yourself over a few months, does help you to grow up. Any self-respecting eighteen-year-old thinks he knows it all; the Aussie trip checked that pretence! I knew I had learned a bit more about many things, but most importantly I knew I had a lot more to learn. Therefore, I was keen to get on with the new UK season.

My equipment for the new season had not yet been finalised. I had completed all my 1974 racing on the short-stroke Jap's. Although they had given me some credible success, their reliability was in question. I was getting advised by a number of people to move over to Jawas. I had competed in Australia on a Jawa and I was starting to think this way myself, but Jim Rowlinson still had great enthusiasm for the Jap. I was willing to start the season with them and see if their reliability had been improved. However a rather heart-rending set of occurrences decided the way I should go. While I had been away in Australia, Jim had a technical idea he wanted to try out. He acquired a blank cylinder head casting for a short-stroke Jap in order to create a special cylinder head with the valve angle in a more upright position. The engineering work on this head also had innovative ideas applied to it: most engines are production models that only allow you to modify what has already been done, but this was a blank canvas and Jim was able to form this cylinder head into something special. While I was increasing my knowledge Down Under, Jim was spending all his available time building this prototype engine that he had high hopes for.

On my return to the UK I went along to see Jim and tell him of my experiences over the past few months. During my visit he unveiled his pride and joy: a brand spanking new short-stroke Jap with his special priceless cylinder head. It was arranged that I was to give it a run out at the Belle Vue Training School.

I was excited about testing this brand-new engine with this unique cylinder head and special angled valves. It also had an improved con rod to overcome the devastation caused by them breaking – weak con rods were the Jap's achilles heel. It felt good as I warmed the machine up in the pits, and I was told to take it easy for a few laps. I managed to avoid the temptation of seeing what it could do during its first run and did what I was told: 'Take it easy, just run the engine in.' It felt great – definitely something special. Next time out I would put it through its paces; and that was what I did. I was part way through the second four-lap test when it happened. For anyone with an ear for a sweet-sounding engine, the noise that an engine makes when the con rod breaks is like a kick in the head, it sounds and feels really painful. It's like a sound effect from a science fiction movie, metal against metal, steel on steel. It's an engineer's and mechanic's nightmare.

When a con rod breaks the flywheels are doing about 8,000 revs per minute, generating about 45-plus brake horsepower. The con rod connects the piston to the flywheels while they are happily joined together, the flywheels go round and the piston goes up and down in the barrel and the valves on the cylinder head all work how they should… then BANG! The con rod breaks, usually near the top where the piston joins it – the weakest point – and in an absolute split-second the piston, with nothing to stop it, goes straight up the barrel and smashes into the top of the cylinder head while the con rod, now without the piston to guide it and 45-plus BHP of energy to show off, wants to get out – and it usually does!

I was horrified when it blew; it was brand new. I could not believe it. I had a sickening feeling in my belly that was about to get worse. I knew straight away it was the con rod failing again – so much for the new improved type. As I surveyed the damage the devastation was predictable. The con rod had smashed through the front of the barrel, smashed the front crank cases and then carried on round, smashing the back of the crank cases and burying itself in the magneto at the back of the engine. Fairly standard sort of damage, but on further inspection I could see a crack in the cylinder head – the special unique cylinder head. The force of the piston had split the cylinder head right through the inlet and exhaust port. It had taken Jim months to engineer this special head and in a split second all his hard work was in ruins. When I took the engine back, Jim was his usual philosophical self, a kind of 'Oh! Another one gone,' until I pointed out the damage to the cylinder head, then the blood drained from his face. His disappointment was clearly evident and I had never seen him so deflated. That was really the end of the short-stroke Jap; that con rod breaking caused far more damage than wrecking one engine. Not long after that, the Jap was out of production and I rode a Jawa during the 1975 British season.

As I embarked on a new season I felt that my experience gained in Australia had boosted my progress in becoming a more complete international speedway rider. My target as a club rider was to achieve an average of over 9 points per meeting, which was likely to put me in the top ten to fifteen British League riders in the country, which at that time really put you in the top twenty riders in the world. Qualifying for the World Speedway final at Wembley was also a target, but to be fair I realised I had a bit more to learn for it to be something I could genuinely influence.

Everything that I learned from my first full season and my trip Down Under I put into practice during 1975. Belle Vue had a great team that year, but our local hero Chris Pusey left the Aces and joined the Halifax Dukes. His brother, Geoff, who had doubled-up with the Aces from Stoke, joined us and Russ Hodgson also became a full-time Ace after impressing at Middlesbrough. The departure of Chris 'Polka Dot' Pusey left a bit of a hole in the team and it was clear to most people that the Belle Vue management expected Wilkie, Paul Tyrer and myself to step up to the mark and support PC and Soren. It was time for us young guns to come of age.

Racing for Belle Vue was really going well, with the Peter Collins and Chris Morton partnership really starting to develop into something formidable. Team riding on the Hyde Road speedway track provided both Peter and myself with some of the most enjoyable and creative racing throughout both of our careers. It was great fun to do and at the risk of sounding conceited, if it looked half as good as it felt, it must have been a great spectacle to watch.

I got off to a good start, scoring double figures on a regular basis and in a league match at home to Coventry on 7 June, I scored my first full maximum with a 12-pointer as we defeated the Bees 49-29. I had already scored some paid maximums in 1974, but to go through the card unbeaten really meant that I had, in my eyes, come of age. As it turned out, our next fixture was at Swindon who eventually finished bottom of the table, but we lost 40-38 and I scored 6 points. In the final analysis this surprise defeat probably cost us the championship.

Another ambition started to bloom in 1975 when I became a regular in the England side, riding with stars that I used to watch at Belle Vue when I was a kid. Riders like Martin Ashby, Ray Wilson, Terry Betts, Malcolm Simmons and now friend but childhood hero Chris Pusey were my teammates. A Test Series was arranged with Sweden with five matches in the UK and five matches in Sweden. My brother Dave was also a regular for England, riding at the time for Hackney, and at one point in 1975 topping the British League averages with an average of over 10 points per meeting. At this point in our careers, Dave had the edge on me, helped by his prolific gating. Or was it his cheating ability? Probably both! An England team with three rough-arsed lads from Partington still seemed like a dream to us, but it was happening.

This series proved to be a bridge too far for the weakening Swedish speedway nation who did not have the strength in depth that the England side now possessed. England won the series on English tracks 5-0, and also won 5-0 in Sweden. That aside, the experience for me was invaluable. I scored 11 points for England at Belle Vue, and going over to Sweden to ride in three of the matches over there I scored 3 at Kumla, 6 at Stockholm and with my best score, 7, at Eskilstuna. Dave also rode in three meetings in Sweden and was second-top-scorer to Martin Ashby at Vetlanda. Ashby was by this time an old campaigner, and an obvious choice of captain being the steady, straight-laced chap to keep us young whippersnappers in line.

Young enthusiastic sportsmen can be a bit boisterous at times; and an element of practical joking had developed between Peter Collins and Chris Pusey. One of Chris Pusey's favourite tricks when you were in the shower was to take a handful of toothpaste or Radium B, the muscle liniment, and slap it on your balls! The effect is quite devastating, and it really is 'great balls of fire!' Of course, this behaviour was strictly between the younger members of the team and was looked on with some disdain by Martin Ashby.

On one occasion after one of the Test Matches in Sweden we were all arriving back in the changing rooms in dribs and drabs. At one time there was Peter Collins, Malcolm Simmons, Dave Morton and myself, while PC was on a mission to get back at Chris Pusey for his Radium B antics. While my brother kept a lookout watching for Chris Pusey's return, PC laced Chris Pusey's underpants with Radium B. Job done, stage set, he went in the shower as the rest of the lads came in. PC finished his shower and was getting dressed. Out of the shower came Chris Pusey and Martin Ashby, whose clothes were next to each other. To PC's horror, Martin Ashby took the Radium B-laced underpants off the hook and put them on! Pusey is nearly dressed by now and there is not a whimper of discomfort from him.

Martin got as far as starting to put his trousers on when he realised he had a problem. YES! His balls were on fire! He quickly ripped off his undies, but it was too late as the Radium B had done its deed. Now Martin was very aware of what had been going on between PC and Pusey, and so put two and two together and came up with what he knew was the right answer. He turned to PC and roared 'HAVE YOU DONE THIS?'

By this time PC was quivering; he is not a fighter and I don't think he wanted to start here. His answer to this question would determine whether he got a smack in the mouth or not. Martin had steam coming out of his ears, not to mention the warm glow from down below. PC answered, with a note of fear in his voice: 'No, it wasn't me'. Martin turned to Pusey and asked him the same question. But Pusey was far more convincing and, obviously stifling his amusement and fully aware he was the target, said 'don't look at me'. Without any evidence PC had survived the smack in the mouth, but only just!

I continued my progress in 1975 and I had established myself as second only to Peter Collins in the Belle Vue team, finishing with a 9.26 average. And just to show that it was no fluke, I retained the Peter Craven Memorial Trophy. It is essential for a racer to be at his best and to be in a competitive team; and that is what Belle Vue was, both within the team and against our rivals. By the end of the 1975 season we had finished second to Ipswich in the league title race by just 1 point.

John Berry, the Ipswich boss, had put together a cracking team that was extremely tough to beat and our battles with them were always the ultimate test at league level. Throughout July and August we went an incredible fourteen league matches without a defeat – eventually losing to Exeter 41-37. However, in the middle of that run, we defeated Ipswich on aggregate to progress to the next round of the Knock-Out Cup. We lost at Foxhall Heath by 6 points, but it was enough to see us through to meet Oxford, who we defeated both at home and at their track.

We then saw off Cradley as well in the semi-finals to set up a final against Leicester. After feeling like a loser when we won the cup in 1973, there was no way that I was going to experience that kind of deflation again. Throughout the cup matches I scored well. It was a similar story in the Inter-League Knock-Out Cup – a competition that included the National League (Second Division) clubs – when we easily fought through to the final where we met our Northern rivals, Halifax, who now included Chris Pusey. It was the competition's first year in operation and we won the first leg at Halifax 40-38, with Pusey top-scoring for the Dukes with 11. At Hyde Road we took them apart with a 50-27 win and we won our second cup to become the cup kings of the British League.

My World Championship campaign really started in earnest in 1975 as I made it through a British Semi-Final to get through to the British Final for the first time. Although I only finished with 5 points in a meeting that saw John Louis lift the British title, I was very aware that this meeting had given me some essential experience.

Something that I was starting to notice was some riders' indifference to the Individual World Championship trail. Riders who you would consider a threat and a challenge at club level would crumble under the mental difficulty of the World Championship – where every race mattered and demanded your total commitment and concentration. I recognised that this was my own failing during the 1975 British Final and I realised that if I was going to even get to a World Final, let alone win one, it required a totally different approach than the one for club racing.

It became clear to me, as I saw some top quality club riders fail miserably at World Championship semi-final level, that it wasn't about being good at riding a speedway bike. We could all do that and some that failed could do it better than some that were successful. I realised it was about 'making it happen', and that was a phrase that would, in time, become my mantra. Racing at club level can become routine; yes, you have to lift your game for certain teams and certain opponents, but fail to win a race at club level and it is unlikely to have a devastating affect. But at World Championship level that all goes out of the window because every single race is special. It's not just going out and winning; it does not happen like that because it could be a matter of life or death to the other riders in the race. Race wins at club level happen because you can do it. Race wins at World Championship level happen because you make them happen; and that is the difference – one is physical the other is psychological. My mantra 'make it happen' was born from this observation. Without this I would never get past a British Final, never mind become World Champion.

The grass-track scene was still a vibrant proposition at this time and Dave and I paired up for a unique meeting. We took part in Britain's first major grass-track

Best Pairs Championship at South Shropshire's small track at Lydham. We took part in five qualifying heats and made the final where we met the Baybutt brothers, Chris and Dave, and the grass specialist Julian Wigg – older brother of Simon – and Mike Garrad. Dave got a good start and led the way, but I thought that my bike was going to seize in the final and I was in third place. I didn't push that hard and just did enough to maintain third. It proved to be enough and we won the meeting with 26 points.

I don't think we realised the significance of what we had done – winning a pairs event as brothers, and on grass – and as Dave's speedway career developed, his injuries prevented him from maintaining his great form that he had displayed at Hackney during 1975. But winning this pairs meeting was something different and a unique achievement.

As the cold blast of October marked the end of another British season, I looked back on the campaign with some satisfaction. My main aim now was to qualify for the World Final and I knew that the only way to make it happen was to gain as much experience as I could. My relationship with Jackie had already withstood one winter trip Down Under and all the indications were that it was going to be tested again with another Aussie adventure in the pipeline. There wasn't a great deal anybody could do about it. I packed my bags and prepared myself for another tour.

FIVE

THE LONG, HOT SUMMER OF 1976

AC/DC blasted out their inspirational electric bagpipes solo on *It's A Long Way To The Top (If You Wanna Rock 'n' Roll)*. Chris Pusey turned up the volume of the hire-car radio. This was our chosen anthem, and we all mimicked playing bagpipes along with AC/DC as we drove down to the beach in Perth, Australia. Their vocalist, the late and much-missed Bon Scott, may have been singing about their climb up the rock and roll ladder, but this song became the metaphor for our climb up the speedway ladder. It was my second consecutive year representing the British Lions Down Under and this year we had a strong team. We were ready to rock and roll, and give those Aussies a pasting!

This tour was managed by John Berry and fielded a strong team: Peter Collins ('PC'), Chris Pusey ('Bushfire'), Doug 'Flyer' Wyer ('Nugget'), John Davis ('Mavis'), Dave Morton ('Big Mort'), Gordon Kennett ('Gordon Bennett') and myself ('Little Mort') against an Aussie side with some class acts. But they did not have the strength in depth in their side beyond their top three of Phil Crump, Billy Sanders and Phil Herne. As we travelled between states the Aussie side was strengthened by local track specialists. One of these was the old campaigner John Langfield. An example of the edge that this tour had was augmented during a 'friendly' at Newcastle near Sydney. Australians are extremely hospitable and always made us feel very welcome off the track, but when national pride was at stake it's a serious matter for both the Aussies and the Brits.

I have seen a few fights in my time between speedway riders and this was the nearest I ever came to fighting as I watched, with Phil Crump, a real Ashes scrap that I had started – or was at the start of. Confused? I was. We were easily winning the series at this point, 3- or 4-0 of a seven-Test Series. About eighty miles from Sydney is Rockhampton, which was to host a pre-Sydney Test 'friendly' meeting, and being warmed up and taken out of mothballs for this Test was John Langfield.

John was clearly on a mission to show the young whippersnapper (me) that speedway was a serious business and he did not take kindly to any messing about; and if I did mess with him, it would mean trouble. In my first race I was partnered with Doug Wyer. John Langfield was on gate two, I was on gate one, with 'Flyer' Wyer on gate three and Phil Herne on gate four. John Langfield had a reputation for being a troublemaker. I had raced against him the previous year but had hardly noticed his presence – apart from that moan at Brisbane, but that is quite a common occurrence during a tough international meeting. Prior to that, I may have seen him at Belle Vue with some team when I was about eight or nine years old. But his presence was about to become indelible on my memory.

As we started to come up to the tapes I performed a practice start. Remember I am just nineteen years old and still learning my trade. I did notice that the rider on gate two was at a strange angle, pointing towards gate one, but in my naivety I thought little of it and suspected he didn't know what he was doing. However, I was about to be subjected to a bit of bullying and lesson-teaching by the old cock.

Green light on, set the throttle to the right revs, relaxed my breathing, lean forward slightly, focus intently on the tape-release mechanism, tape release activates, tapes go up, drop the clutch, Go! Go! Go! Not a bad start, level with the bloke next to me on gate two, I thought. But what was Langfield doing? He was aiming for the centre green and he's going to bring us both off! He ran into me, causing me to hit the kerb, and I was very nearly on the grass and out of the race – I just managed to stay on.

By the time I had dealt with this sabotage attempt I was thirty yards behind at the back. I soon caught the nutter up and I was very much in a mood to race! Now it was my turn to teach a few lessons, but my lesson was about racing. I proceeded to do what I do and did for the next eighteen years: race. He did everything he could to stop me getting past; all the no-no's, like chopping across the front wheel and stuffing me up against the fence. Once I realised what his game was, I did the old trick (which was a new trick to me then). I kidded him into thinking I was coming around him, but when he came across to stuff me I nipped inside him, a beautiful clean pass – 'beat him'. I was very pleased with myself; I paraded around to the pit entrance at the end of the race with a well-earned third place and a 4-2 against the Aussies.

John Langfield's lesson had not gone according to plan so he must have decided to use Plan B, the 'beat the shit out of him' method! As I rode towards my pit area, I was suddenly dragged off my moving bike and manhandled to the floor, as he tried to lay a few punches on me. Now I'm not much of a scrapper, but I'm not getting beat up for doing nowt. So, I am just ready to fight back when John was dragged off by Gordon Kennett and John Davis, who then proceeded to give him a good seeing-to. This inspires the Aussie Bob Valentine – who was ready for the next race with his helmet on – to come to John Langfield's rescue. So he gets stuck in and, of course, Chris Pusey is well in among this somewhere. I feel a gentle grip on my arm from behind pulling me back. It's Australian captain Phil Crump, who says: 'You don't want to get involved with all that' and we both stand back watching my fight with John Langfield develop into a brawl. There were now about fifteen people involved, riders, mechanics and staff, some fighting, some doing the old 'that's enough now break it up' bit. I saw my brother Dave with Bob Valentine's helmeted head in a headlock bashing it against the pit fence! It was, at the time, a bit overwhelming for me because I didn't understand the subtleties of what John Langfield was trying to do. Probably just as well, or he might very well have intimidated me. As it was, it did not affect my racing one bit. I found it rather odd that someone who was so angry with me could be the perfect host off the track by taking us water-skiing – as did a lot of the Aussie riders – and he generally looked after us well.

That was my first lesson in Aussie-style psychology. Well John, it didn't work, but it did teach me something: the place to fight and win battles is on the track. As Soren Sjosten would say to a rider who did him an injustice, in his strong Swedish accent: 'You in my bloody book mate!'

We thrashed the Aussies in the first five matches. Only Phil Crump provided any real resistance. Occasionally Billy Sanders or Phil Herne would back him with some useful scores, but by and large the Aussies were a disappointment. I scored double figures at Perth and Newcastle and it wasn't until Sydney when some 'doctoring' of the track allowed the Australians to stop us and prevent an embarrassing Test-series whitewash.

We were 5-0 up, with the Sixth Test at Sydney in the famous, exciting and sometimes intimidating Sydney Showground. It was quite a large circuit at 509 metres (557 yards or one-third of a mile) and fairly narrow for a large track, but it had good banking, which lends itself to fast racing, being just inches off the concrete safety fence. This was sometimes described by Peter Collins as 'The Danger Fence' – he always said this deliberate twist of the term safety fence as an ironic jest, and many tracks could own that tag. Danger aside it was a good, entertaining circuit, but you had to be brave. It had a reputation for being dangerous and that was not without foundation. It had seen many bad accidents, including a number of fatalities.

As we walked around the track before the meeting it was obvious to us that a job had been done on the track to try to unbalance the touring side. A 7-0 defeat would be a major embarrassment for the Aussies, so the track was prepared as it had never been before. It had lots of dirt and was rough and quite dangerous; you could ride the track but it was not safe to race on. Rain shortly before the meeting made the surface even more treacherous. As a team we felt the meeting should not be run as the track was too dangerous. The referee insisted that we ride, so we did. I don't know how the Australian riders felt about the conditions, but as we had shown our concerns they could see a weakness in our armour and, as I am sure any competitive team would do, saw a chance to win and went for it.

As early as heat three PC momentarily lost control and very nearly crashed. We then made our feelings known. Our worst fears became a reality early in the meeting as on the first turn a crash involving Chris Pusey left him badly injured. Chris was rushed to hospital with a suspected broken leg. He had hit my old sparring partner Langfield's back wheel and careered into the fence, where he was struck by the other Aussie rider, Billy Sanders. Later it was discovered that Pusey had not broken his leg, but had chipped a bone and sustained other injuries.

The whole Lions team had protested greatly with the referee before the meeting that in these conditions someone would get badly injured. Sadly it had happened. A posse of British Lions were now making their way towards the referee: now would he see sense? Apparently not, he insisted that the meeting should continue. We had a team meeting and as a team we all agreed not to ride. John Berry had argued strongly in our favour that the meeting should be cancelled due to the dangerous conditions, but would not support a walkout. With the benefit of more years of experience, walking out of a meeting is never the answer, and it puts a manager in an untenable position. Unfortunately we wanted to walk out; I say unfortunately, because it was not the right thing to do. We were swept along with the situation. The emotion of Chris Pusey's bad accident fuelled the fire, and we were seriously threatening to walk out. It was not the end of the world, but it put a dampener on what was an excellent tour and drove an unnecessary wedge between the team and John Berry.

Berry later famously said: 'Speedway is a sport and we were not prepared to treat it as a war. There is an inherent danger and we all accept that. But the Sydney track went beyond the normal danger limits. I wasn't prepared to have a death on my hands.'

After a long delay we did return to race after Berry had told the Aussie authorities that we would not be taking any undue risks. We lost that Test Match 62-45, I scored just 5 points and PC, who was our leading scorer in the series, finished with just 2. I would like to be able to say I thought it all through and I knew exactly what I was doing, but I was the youngest in the team and at nineteen years old what did I know? I was swept along by it all. I can reflect on it now, and any walkout would have to be a unanimous decision including the manager or you ride, but it really should never happen.

We won the final test at Brisbane, 57-50, in what many described as the best match of the series. Malcolm Simmons replaced our skipper Pusey for the final Test. The Australians were making fast starts on their Street Four-valve Conversions, but we were still picking them off from the back. Once again the track was a bit wet early on, but as it dried out we got better and better and we won, taking the overall series 6-1. I finished the competition as the fourth-highest scorer in the Lions team behind PC, Doug Wyer and John Davis. Chris Pusey acted like a true captain, even with his leg in plaster and still suffering from the spill at Sydney. He was rallying round the lads at the last Test, doing a bit of spannering, and generally doing what Chris always did – feeding us with enthusiasm.

I should explain why Chris Pusey was christened 'Bushfire' very early on during the 1975/76 Aussie tour by Peter Collins. Bushfires are a familiar topic of conversation in Australia and had been a regular news item as the summer started to take hold in November, with many warning of the risks of bushfires and the precautions that should be taken throughout the summer months. Chris Pusey was partial to the occasional cigar, and as none of the rest of the team were smokers it was a source of amusement to the lads whenever we were at a social gathering watching Chris Pusey, the Scouser, trying to put on a posh act while lighting up a King Edward cigar, holding onto his Bloody Mary and generally not looking like the Pusey we knew. Sideburns were very popular in the mid-seventies and Chris Pusey was the sideburn World Champion! He had a face full of hairy chops, but not, I hasten to add, a beard. There was one razor-blade width under the chin that distinguished his facial hair as sideburns and not a beard. One night we were watching Chris attempt to light up his cigar in his usual style. As he sparked up the lighter PC commented, as the flame was licking around old Pusey's chops: 'Imagine if old Pusey's sidies caught fire, it would be like a bushfire!' That was it, a nickname was born. We were all highly amused and when Chris Pusey asked us what we were all laughing at, he saw the funny side and from then on he was called 'Bushfire'.

That Australian tour was one of the best experiences of my life. They were a gang of great lads that all got on well together and looked out for each other. It was a sad occasion when Chris Pusey died in October 2002 at a fairly young age (fifty-five) as he was the victim from years of drinking too much alcohol. Although he had been in the wilderness for years – I had certainly not seen him for over ten – the majority of that Aussie touring team attended his funeral to say their last goodbyes to a flamboyant entertainer whose never-say-die approach to racing was an inspiration to us all. I have lump in my throat as I write this piece, I think partly because it was a sad end and we just didn't see enough of Chris Pusey at his best.

At the end of the Australian tour, we had a few weeks and a few meetings in New Zealand before we went back to the UK in mid-February 1976. This meant a frantic few weeks getting ready for the 1976 season. During the past two years speedway had seen a steady development of the four-valve engine, initiated and highlighted by the superb results that Phil Crump and Neil Street were having with Neil Street's Four-Valve Jawa Conversion. Many conversion ideas were inspired by the Street version, but none could emulate its success.

Doug Wyer raced with us in Australia on a Swedish ERM Four-Valve Conversion and had some fantastic results – most notably at Sydney where he scored an unbeaten 18 points. He was riding the MK2 version as Sweden's Christer Lofqvist rode the MK1 in the 1974 World Final in Gothenburg and finished in eighth place with 8 points. They were all DOHC (Double-Overhead Cam) conversions of the Jawa and the ERM stood for Endfors Racing Motors. They were manufactured in Sweden.

All this had paved the way for complete four-valve engines. The Weslake four-valve had been making steady progress for the past eighteen months, and the Aussie tour had seen a mixture of two-valve and four-valve engines. What this mixture had proved was that the two-valve was dead, long live the four-valve. That was it; 1976 would see myself and many others on a Weslake four-valve, following the riders who had taken an early march in 1975. I ordered two engines from Weslake and built my 1976 season on Dave Nourish-tuned Weslakes – it was a wise move.

My relationship with Jackie had done more than just survive me going off to Australia for four months – it had blossomed because we decided to get married later in the year. This happy and memorable day would be two days after my birthday and we would get married on 24 July 1976, but before that I had some serious racing to do.

During the transition period while the sport was changing from two to four valves, riders using the former against the latter were at a distinct disadvantage. But 1976 saw all that change and it became a level playing field as everybody was using four-valve engines. It was now about racing and riding skills. Engine tuning would play a part, but to paraphrase George Orwell 'we were all equal, but some were more equal than others.'

As March 1976 rolled in I was ready to get stuck in. I had experienced some serious and tough racing Down Under, and felt that I had made progress with both my racing skills and my knowledge of equipment. My total focus would be on qualification for the World Final in Poland. My rationale was that if I concentrated on that level of performance my form for Belle Vue would benefit. The reality is that the majority of the time they complement each other.

1976 was a memorable year and for those of us who can remember it, it was a summer of sunshine. It was baking hot, there were hose-pipe bans, water shortages, the lawns at people's homes had turned a brown colour and all the usual things that are associated with a hot spell in Britain. The earth was parched and dry, with cracks appearing in the dried earth and even some of the tarmac on the roads was breaking up due to the heat. River levels and, according to some reports, reservoirs were dangerously low, and the wildlife was suffering too. There were doom-mongers who warned that it would never rain again – the end was close at hand and all that kind of stuff. All this was before global warming and the greenhouse effect had been discovered. Environmentally speaking, these were innocent days.

For a young, enthusiastic racer like me, it was an absolute pleasure to travel around Britain to meetings knowing that the beautiful weather meant that the meetings wouldn't be rained off. Rain is one of the sport's biggest enemies, and it seems that speedway is more vulnerable to it now than it ever has been. But there was a downside to all this hot sunshine because this meant that the tracks were often dry and slick, which wasn't good news for me as my abilities from the start were questionable to say the least. However, you make the best of it and get on.

It was also the year when Concorde had its first commercial flight – it is amazing to think that this supersonic jet is no longer in service. In addition it was the year when punk rock is said to have reared its ugly, though important, head, with bands like The Clash and The Damned. Anything that could put paid to the cheesy Bay City Rollers was fine by me! Unbeknown to me at the time, AC/DC, who had already captured my interest and admiration while in Australia, also made their first live appearance outside Oz with their now-legendary gig in the Red Cow public house in the Hammersmith district of London. *The Omen* redefined the horror genre on our movie screens and Lee Majors' hit TV series, *The Six Million Dollar Man* brought bionics to the world.

This was also a great time to be involved with British motor sport because Britain had virtually fallen in love with the playboy personas of 500cc Grand Prix motorcycle racing star Barry Sheene and the equally charismatic, though more of a public schoolboy, Formula One ace James Hunt. The fact that British speedway had some of the world's best riders wearing the flag of St George or the Union Flag, meant that speedway was able to capitalise on the increased awareness of the success of British motor sport. I believe it was this year more than any other when speedway in Britain really did establish itself as second only to football in terms of attendance figures. A combination of on-track success, great weather and super entertainment made it a super summer for speedway racing. Personally speaking, it would be especially memorable for my career.

As the season was getting underway my new equipment felt great. This was my first experience of the Weslake four-valve power – it was just what I had been looking for. It was the quickest thing I had experienced and it made all the difference for me. I could compete against anyone, anywhere and give them a race, and beat them; this was the first time I had genuinely been on equal equipment.

From before I started riding, I had since discovered that Jawa works' riders had been using superior equipment with options like Long-Track Jawa's, which were unbeatable on big tracks if you had a standard Jawa. There were also cylinder heads with large inlet valves – which became available to all through a company called Piper Engineering, but not until 1975 – as used by Malcolm Simmons in the 1975 British Final. The Piper Head helped me for a few months in 1975, but by that time the four valve revolution was well underway. I found it very interesting, one day in Australia, when we visited the former Sheffield star Jim Airey at his house, named 'Seven Seasons'. On his bench was an engine in bits that he had used during his time in England while riding for Sheffield. The cylinder head was sporting one of the said oversized inlet valves, and as he had finished in 1971 I discovered he was well ahead of the game. All this stuff is perfectly legal, but to be at the top you must have the best. The standard Jawa was a good, competitive engine, but your top guys were on better gear than that.

I was planning many things in 1976. As Jackie and I were getting married later that year we were going to need somewhere to live. Up to this point we had been living at our parents' homes, but we had managed to save up enough for a deposit for a house of our own. It cost £6,995; it was a new house, not yet built but it would be ready by the end of May: Number One, Paddock Close, Atherton, Lancs. We were on the property ladder, not bad for nineteen-year-old Partington lad, and a nearly eighteen-year-old Longsight gal. They said we were too young; 'they' may have been right but 'we' didn't care as we knew what we were doing. Besides, I would be much older by the time we got married… twenty!

My season had started well with high scores in the first few weeks of the season. I was feeling my confidence grow as we started to get near the start of the World Final campaign – which for me would be on Jackie's birthday, 18 May at Leicester in one of the British Semi-Finals. As May got under way I started to set my mind into a focused and determined condition. Once I was aware of the semi-final, I had a clear plan mapped out in my consciousness as I considered how I would qualify for my first Individual World Final. I knew that I now had to put my plan into operation. Having a plan makes it appear far easier than it really is. However, in my short career, I had discovered that my experiences had left me wanting and nothing would be left to chance. I went into May aiming to race every race to the full – which was what I did – but a racing incident sent a shockwave into my philosophy – something I wasn't ready for. It was not about to affect my progress, but it most definitely taught me a very important lesson.

It was 10 May 1976 and the lesson today was 'Motorcycle Racing is Extremely Dangerous'. We all know that and as a racer you accept and respect it. But did I? I do now, but before this day I only thought I did. It was a league match, Birmingham v. Belle Vue and the Brummies were keen not to lose their fourth league match on the trot. It was going to be a tough match for Birmingham against an in-form Belle Vue.

As we went into heat eleven, Belle Vue were ahead. I was off the outside gate with Alan Grahame (Birmingham) on gate three, my teammate Russ Hodgson was off gate two, and Alan's teammate was off gate one. Alan made a good start as I went for the run around the outside. I was gearing up for tough racing and they don't come much tougher than Alan; it was no quarter asked and certainly none given with him. I knew how tough Alan could be, but I was determined to give the outside run a try. It was looking like I would make the run around the outside and pinch the lead coming out of the corner. But Alan had other ideas and he stuffed me up against the fence. I was left scraping the kick board and just survived what was as hard a bit of riding as you will ever see – I would seriously question whether I should have been there in the first place. But it was a racing incident. What then followed was not.

I was incensed at his audacity and the anger welled up inside me. In a split second I had gathered myself and set off on a mission to teach the bastard a lesson! As we came out of the next corner to cross the line for the first time, I had gone from third place back to second and was planning my attack on Alan, who was out in front. We went into the second corner at the beginning of the second lap and Alan was about mid-track. I took the inside line and was in a position to cleanly pass him, but no, I had to show him that he could not stuff me in the fence and get away with it. As we came to the middle of the corner I let my bike drift from the inside to the middle of the track to where Alan was, and with venom I slammed my back wheel into his front wheel and catapulted him and his bike into the safety fence. I also slid off, got straight back up, and as I went to ride off, knowing I would be excluded, I looked at Alan all tangled up and all forlorn in the fence. At this stage I was not aware of his injuries, and was already feeling remorse. A little voice inside me said: 'Are you happy now?' The answer was 'no'.

Alan sustained a broken femur, probably one of the worst leg injuries you could sustain, thanks to me getting my own back in a rage. People may look at the incident and suggest it was a racing incident, but I would disagree. I know I was guilty of acting out of rage, which has no place in professional sport. Racing is dangerous enough as it is and anyone that races accepts that. But when anger and rage or any uncontrolled emotion becomes part of the equation it becomes ten times more dangerous. I am ashamed that I broke his leg, no matter what he did to me, when he stuffed me in the fence on the first lap he was racing and made a choice to close the gap. I suspected he may close the gap, but I also made a choice to go for it. What I did on the next lap when I knocked him off was out of anger and intent, and I know that. Had I been genuinely racing and the accident happened I would accept it as a racing accident and as the Americans say 'shit happens'.

I learned to control that anger and the quick bursts of temper very quickly, and channel the energy in a more controlled way. I would be hard where necessary, and occasionally I would be dirty, but never through uncontrolled rage, as your judgement will fail you as it did me that day. I reasoned that a speedway bike can be a lethal weapon – respect it. I learned my lesson well at Alan Grahame's expense, and I also nearly caused a riot that night. I had to have a police escort out of the stadium as I was not Mr Popular. I was always grateful that Alan never held that incident against me, or didn't seem to, and we went on to enjoy some more good, hard but more controlled races against each other. If you beat Alan, you will have earned the win. Occasionally we would also ride in the same team when we represented England.

I was ready for the start of my 1976 Individual World Championship campaign. Finally 18 May had arrived and we were racing at the Leicester track, situated in Blackbird Road. I enjoyed racing there, although I would not call it a favourite of mine. In my opinion, it limited your racing a little, but I did enjoy some good meetings there and I felt it was a fairly safe track that generated some excellent racing.

I always considered semi-finals as something you needed to just get through; I approached them by targeting to get a minimum of second places in each race. That way, with eight qualifying, 8 points should get you through, with enough room from five rides for an engine failure, or a fall, should you be unfortunate. I always felt planning in some way gave you a structure to your crusade.

Psychology within sport is what makes the difference at the top, and the psychology is a thread keeping you focussed on your goal through the whole of your being, from the initial preparation of equipment right through every meeting, every race, every practice session and every difficult moment you face. Many, many times I would have to dig really deep to keep the dream alive throughout my career, but without a plan you will crumble. Planning is part of the psychology, but you must always have an alternative plan at the ready.

I fairly comfortably got through this semi-final with 9 points. I would genuinely only go to qualify (winning a semi holds no esteem) but a British Final is attractive and provides some of the toughest racing you will ever experience. Before the British Final I had a warm-up in the Internationale, a prestigious individual meeting at Wimbledon on 31 May. This proved to be a superb test of my form as I finished in second place with 13 points. The in-form Malcolm Simmons was the winner with an unbeaten 15 points and a very young Michael Lee was third with 11 points – Lee was just seventeen and was the new wonderkid.

On to the British Final, and this was where it started to get ruthless. Not just in the racing, because for the Brits the route through to the next round, the Intercontinental Final, was through the British Final. However, only the top five scorers out of sixteen riders would progress to the ICF. As a country we were not alone in having rounds that were more like a culling exercise than qualifying. But hey, as they say, it's tough at the top. There was no room for any mishaps whatsoever. The British Final was where you had to start 'making it happen' and if you were not on the top of your game you would be knocked over in the rush. It was a big prize: qualify, and you would be riding at the great

Wembley Stadium in the Intercontinental Final, the last round before the World Final in Poland, but failure meant another year before you could have another go – an experience that would became uncomfortable with familiarity.

The day 2 June 1976 saw me take my place in only my second British Final. I felt that my form was good and I felt confident. Not cocky; cocky was not something I did externally, preferring to keep my energies contained. It was a strong line-up, but I knew what to expect from the previous year: keep focused on the dream, the goal, give every race your total concentration. It's different to league racing, a race win won't just happen – I had to 'make it happen'.

It was, as expected, a very tough meeting. There were top-quality riders missing out on the five qualifying places, but not me. Malcolm Simmons won the meeting with a maximum and he passed the British Final trophy to me to drink some of his champagne from as we stood on the winner's rostrum along with Doug Wyer. I had just taken second place from Doug in a run-off, as we both finished on 13 points. Simmo was in sparkling form all night and along with Peter Collins and John Louis we had survived the cull and were off to Wembley.

Wembley Stadium has passed into speedway myth. The Empire Stadium had an aura of being a very special place to watch speedway. I had been there to watch the 1967 World Final as a young lad. At that time I didn't really think that I too would be riding in this magnificent stadium. But here I was, in temperatures that reached 100° Fahrenheit, among sixteen of the best riders in the world who were just five rides away from qualifying for the World Final. That equates to just over five minutes of actual racing. If I stopped and took a look round the pits that night, I would have been astounded by the amount of talent on view. There was Ivan Mauger ('the Big I'), the defending World Champion Ole Olsen, 1974 World Champion Anders Michanek, my hero Soren Sjosten, the American Scott Autrey, PC, Simmo, 'Flyer' Wyer, Phil Crump and so the list went on. You could see why some people described it as a meeting that was harder than the World Final itself. As the youngest rider in the field, this would be a big test for me.

It is essential to get a good start in this kind of meeting. With only the top eight riders qualifying for the World Final, if you ran a last or even a third in your first race that meant that the pressure started to build. I knew I needed a good start, and faced three of my fellow countrymen in heat two in the shape of the in-form Simmo, John Louis and Doug Wyer. I took Wyer from the back for second and 2 points, and then pipped the Australian John Boulger for second in my second race. I then faced Mauger and Soren in my third ride. I had the same number of points as Ivan (4) while poor old Soren was having a nightmare of a meeting as he was experiencing clutch trouble with his bike and was on a borrowed machine for this race. Billy Sanders was the other rider in the race and he too had scored 4 points. The race went better for me than I could have hoped for as I passed Mauger for the lead and won the race – the crowd went nuts!

At the interval stage I had scored 7 points and found myself in joint-first place with Anders Michanek. At that stage, not only was I looking good to qualify for my first World Final, but I also had a chance to win the Intercontinental Final! Little did I know that only one of us would qualify properly for the final.

The meeting was incredibly tight. PC had recovered from a point-less first ride to win his next two races and I faced him in my next race. My other opponent was Olsen, who was in serious danger of failing to make the cut as he had just 2 points. He had been excluded from his first race and then he retired from his next race. As we made our way to the tapes, Olsen was desperate for points – just how desperate would be illustrated to me in less than two minutes. Dag Lovaas from Norway was my other opponent, but he was virtually out of the running on 1 point and wasn't looking comfortable in such exalted company.

From gate three I made a decent start. I exited the corner in second place and followed PC down the back straight. I knew Olsen was behind me and as I entered the first bend of the second lap he came roaring under me and took my line away and forced me wide. It was all I could do to remain on my bike, and his over-hard riding incensed me. Remembering my earlier experience with Alan Grahame I controlled my rage, but Olsen had pulled out a huge gap over me. I finished in third, and when I was on the slow-down lap and came by Olsen, I twisted the throttle, gassed it and sprayed him with a face-full of shale! The crowd loved it and I felt better too! He knew that I wasn't happy with his tactics and his actions had ended my hopes of winning the title that night.

Of course, looking back, he was using his experience and taking advantage of my naivety – remember I had never been this far in the World Championship before. As far as he was concerned he was saying: 'Welcome to the World Championship kid!' I had to wait two more races before my final outing and, after everyone had completed their fourth rides, I had gone from being a joint-leader to joint-fourth – all because of Olsen. Peter Collins, Simmo and Mauger had secured their places in the final on 9 points. I had 8 points and that should have been enough, but I was aware that there were eight of us that could still make the cut and I was in that group.

As I made my way to the start line and took up my starting position in gate two, I was cool and focussed. I was thriving on the atmosphere and was concentrating on making my dream become a reality. Now I really had to 'make it happen'. My parents, Jackie and Dave were all in the stadium on that balmy June evening, and they were probably more anxious than me because I was concentrating 100 per cent on the task ahead of me. I was up against the best Australian, Crump, and the best American, Autrey. The three of us had 8 points each. The fourth rider was a very experienced Swede, Bengt Jansson, who was in need of a race win. The Australian was on my left in gate one, the Swede was next to me on gate three with the American off gate four. The fidgeting and settling-down ritual was over. As I waited for the green light to come on that would put us under starter's orders, I knew that I required 10 points to be sure of a place in my first World Championship Final.

The green light was on, and my concentration on the tapes was pure and undisturbed. I made a good start, but Crump was just ahead of me in first place as we entered the first corner. Two points would be enough, but I could see Autrey was on a good run on the outside of the first corner. I needed the 2 points as I didn't want to leave my fate to other riders in the last few races. I made an instant decision to consolidate my second place. This was a policy I had used many times, consolidate, then chase to race. I let the bike drift towards the wire-mesh safety fence to claim my ground, making my intentions clear that there would not be room for anyone between the fence and myself as we raced down the straight. I timed my move to be clear, as fair as necessity would allow, and importantly leaving the American without the option to switch back inside me. He would have to follow me down the straight as I executed my move perfectly. As we came around to complete the first lap I had consolidated my second place. The chase was now on for first. A few lengths behind Crump, I pushed hard for the next three laps, only managing to pace the fast-riding Aussie. As I crossed the finish line and took the chequered flag for my incredibly valuable 2 points, my mental state changed: the noise of the crowd seemed to rush out from the stands to greet me in a wild frenzy of enthusiasm – 70-80,000 people at Wembley can make a lot of noise! I had just qualified for my first World Speedway final.

My mother rates this meeting as one of her most memorable. She says that Wembley was the only other track that could rival Hyde Road for that special atmosphere. In the following week's *Speedway Star*, Peter Collins, who won the meeting, said: 'Honestly, I couldn't be more delighted for Chris – he's really got what it takes and showed everybody tonight.'

All five of the Brits qualified for the final in Katowice, Poland, but all the drama was that Olsen had failed and Michanek only qualified as reserve. Ironically, Soren had also been unsuccessful and it seemed that my rise on the international stage had coincided with his sad demise. The following year he experienced a terrible season at Wolverhampton, and it was hard watching a rider I admired so much struggling to score points.

SIX

THE LEARNING CURVE

Like the majority of the summer days in 1976, 24 July was no different. It was hot and sunny, a great day to get married. And that's what Chris Morton and Jackie Evans did at St John's church in Longsight – less than a mile from the Belle Vue Speedway Stadium. Well, we did after a minor hiccup.

'You'll have to go round again, they're not here yet,' said the man to the driver in the bride's car! Meanwhile my best man, Dave Morton, was breaking the speed limit, not for the first time in his life and not by any small margin either! On this occasion he felt fully justified to be driving like a man possessed – not that you would have noticed a massive difference from his normal driving. In his role as the best man at his brother's wedding, it was his responsibility to make sure that the groom was at the church well before the bride. Any passenger, other than me, would have been scared shitless by his attempt to do a thirty-minute trip in fifteen minutes – seventeen minutes wasn't a bad effort, but it just wasn't good enough, we were late!

It all started the night before: Belle Vue were riding at Hackney in London, the club Dave was riding for, and it was also my stag night. Stag nights held the night before the wedding may be the traditional night for such a ritual, but it does introduce an element of risk to the following day's proceedings. As we were both riding, we travelled down together with a bike each on a trailer, with my mechanic Gary Miller kindly volunteering to drive on the way back because we planned to have just a few drinks.

After the meeting that's exactly what we did, and a few more – after all, it was my stag night. Gary attentively saw to our desire to do a London pub crawl, which took us to about two o'clock in the Saturday morning. Keeping up with tradition I was absolutely pissed – so was Dave – and the fact that 200 miles away I was getting married in twelve hours time was the least of our worries, as the alcohol had put the thought to the very bottom of the very last glass of the demon drink.

Thankfully, Gary had a rare but well-timed sensible moment and decided it was time to go home. As he was the only fit driver, we had to stop part of the way for him to have a sleep. Meanwhile, the clock continued to run down; not that we worried because in our blurry-eyed, boozy state, we were convinced that we had everything under control. Consequently we got home to Partington at 6.30 a.m. on Saturday morning and I was getting married in just seven-and-a-half hours. We desperately needed sleep. Unfortunately my brother needed too much. True to form, our timing did not leave any room for error. We worked out that, having done the trip many, many times, in order to be at a 2 p.m. wedding, if we left at 1.30 p.m. it would give us plenty of time, so we could sleep until 12.30 p.m. – it was six hours of much-needed slumber.

Mums are really good at getting you up, but not when you've got a hangover. However, my mother finally got us out of bed by 12.45 p.m. Now it was starting to get serious. I was getting married in one hour and fifteen minutes. I was now in a race against the clock. At 1.30 p.m. I was ready to go; in fact I had been ready for the last fifteen minutes. But Dave needed help and assistance from the groom, as he had been farting around with his tie for the last quarter of an hour! My Mum and Dad had seen that we were nearly ready and had gone. 'No point in us all being late,' was the comment, not much point being there without me I thought! I'm getting married in thirty minutes, or so I thought, but Dave was having problems fitting his tie and even with my help the clock seemed to have sprouted wheels.

We finally pulled away from the house at 1.45 p.m. and with fifteen minutes to go we had to cover twelve miles. It was going to be very tight to get there on time, never mind before the bride.

'Was that an advert for fruit pastels?' Dave recited his favourite witticism as we drove through yet another red light as he tried to fulfil his best-man duties.

It was pedal to the metal, foot to floor, running red lights, green light, go, go, go! We were travelling at breakneck speed and of all the races that I had been in at that point, this race against the clock was the most important. It's a good job I wasn't on a two-minute time allowance because I would have been excluded as we arrived two minutes past 2 p.m., just as Jackie was on her third drive around the block! We may have been late, but we had been busy and we arrived to a rousing cheer from all the speedway supporters who were around the church grounds. Fortunately the rest of the proceedings went without a hitch, and that night Chris and Jackie Morton went home to their new house in Atherton, Lancashire.

My main focus was to get myself organised for the 1976 Individual World Speedway Final at Katowice in Poland on 5 September. It was the second time that Poland had staged the World Championship Final at the Slaski Stadium – in fact it was only the third time that Poland had held the final. On the previous occasion, the Poles saw the crowning of their first World Champion in the shape of the shock winner, Jerzy Szczakiel. Since then he had never qualified for another World Final and faded into virtual obscurity. When the venue recently returned to the Grand Prix calendar – the stadium had been closed for redevelopment – the sport's organisers, BSI (Benfield Sports International), retrieved Szczakiel from the mists of time as they tried to re-establish the stadium's speedway credentials. But despite that brief moment in the limelight, he remains the sport's forgotten champion.

The Slaski Stadium would play a major part in the history of the sport's premier competition, and this time I was going to be performing my small part. The sport in this nation is still very popular, and I firmly believe that years of Soviet oppression has prevented the Poles from supplying more than one World Champion. Poland in 1976 was part of the Soviet Union, an outpost of Communist Russia, and heading to that country for my first World Final I got the sense of East meets West. Going behind the Iron Curtain, while the Cold War was on, felt like a page from a Len Deighton novel. Katowice is situated in an industrial area in the south of the country.

I now know that I approached my first World Final in the wrong way. I had achieved the first part of actually making the World Final – you've got to be in it to win it – but I was young and inexperienced. Unfortunately I knew this and viewed it as a valuable opportunity to increase my experience. In short, I only went along for the ride. It was certainly not my style not to give it my best shot, but as I have already said, at this level it was ninety per cent psychological and my mind was on gaining the experience for the future and not on putting my stake in the ground – which is what I should have been doing. I scored 6 points, which was pretty crap, but I had already accepted that as being okay before I went!

The World Final was won by Peter Collins with 14 points. He deserved to win it and rode well. Peter seemed to have a lot of pressure to win the World Championship because so many people had tipped him to be a champion. In 1975 his chances were ruined when a fan decided to water the track just before PC's third ride. I was happy that he won and, if nothing else, it made me even more determined to follow in his tyre tracks. Little did I know that I wouldn't get another chance for a few more years!

All that self-criticism aside, it was a fantastic experience and I fell in love with Poland. Many people found Poland around that time a little basic, and that may be true, but the people were extremely helpful with great enthusiasm for speedway. Initially, I found the contrast, compared to our own life in the West, surprising, but it's the people that give a country its culture and despite the difficult times it had endured it still had a charm and passion for life. I had a close family following that went over on a coach trip, and they still talk about it to this day with great delight.

At the end of the 1976 season in the UK – it had been my best season so far and Dave also enjoyed one of his best seasons at Hackney, with an average of over 10 points – I had been invited to freelance in Australia for the close season from mid-November to early February 1977. I was going to ride in Adelaide at Rowley Park every Saturday night in the solo handicap races. On a Saturday night, Rowley Park would run a programme that consisted of stock-car races, sidecar races and solos – this was a great way to have a three-month holiday. This trip would be different to the two previous years as Jackie would be coming with me, and we would stay settled in Adelaide for most of our time there. When we left in November Jackie was almost three months pregnant. We had discussed flying with our doctor as Jackie would be almost six months pregnant by the time we flew home, but the doc said that it would be okay.

We had a fantastic time in Adelaide. A motorcycle shop called Sandy Martins sponsored me, and a real livewire called Leith Mitchell owned the establishment. On hearing I would be based in Adelaide, he offered to sponsor me with bike maintenance, a trail bike for on the road and his services as a mechanic on race night. Leith and his family looked after us really well, along with a sidecar rider he also sponsored called Kym McConnell. Kym was crazy on a bike; sidecar racing Aussie-style is something to behold. They are barmy, often fighting after frightening race manoeuvres. When they crash they are the clumsiest of machines and cause some horrendous injuries – I never missed a race because it was all action. My bike was based at the track, and our only form of transport was the 175cc trail bike that was on loan to me from Leith, which was great fun for me, but not too great for Jackie – and injury was not something we wanted to risk. Our accommodation was eight miles away from the town and the track, so it wasn't long before I negotiated with the promotion the use of a car for the duration of our stay. The promotion was very understanding and helpful and they came up with a Hillman Hunter.

Race nights were great fun as it was a new experience for me, being in handicap races. There was a big variation in performance levels, and they had a progressive system that gave you a greater handicap the better you were. Races had six riders at different starting positions around the track and were run over three laps. A race layout would have looked something like this: a novice was off scratch at the normal starting tapes, one rider was off fifty yards, two riders started from 150 yards, one rider was off 250 yards – it was usually the up-and-coming Rob Maxfield – and starting from 300 yards from the scratch line/tapes were me and John Boulger. We had some tricky scraps, because as with any handicapping system they are set up to give the underdogs a chance. But a victory was achievable for the best riders and, as the best riders caught up with the 'underdogs', the last half-lap was when it got really dodgy! There were occasions when I had not shaken John off, or John had not shaken me off, and we were trying to beat each other and negotiate a number of slower riders while racing. I am sure it made for exciting racing, but it does mean you are among riders who are still learning – which can be risky.

Leith Mitchell saw himself as not just my mechanic but my motivator as well. He would take great pride in seeing me beat John Boulger on his home soil. I would be sat on my bike ready to race for the big final and Leith would put his arm around me. Into my helmet he would growl in his strong Aussie accent this motivational chant: 'Right Mort, you know what to do! Hold the barrrstard flat bloody biscuit mate!' So that's what I did, held 'the bastard flat bloody biscuit,' and it worked – the man was a genius. Well, maybe. Leith had a basic understanding of racing, and that was the foundation for his motivational technique… basic. His enthusiasm was infectious and added a lot of fun to what was a working holiday.

While in Adelaide I was invited to a match race against Phil Crump at his home town in Mildura. Mildura is a small town about 260 miles from Adelaide towards Melbourne – through some pretty basic and isolated Aussie country. It was going to be a great adventure, and I was given the loan of a trailer and a willing mechanic from England whose name sadly escapes me. We hooked the trailer up to my trusty Hillman Hunter – was I mad? A Hillman Hunter in the Aussie outback? You must be joking! Even on a bright spring day in England a short motorway jaunt would have the damned thing boiling up. What was it George Michael said? 'You gotta have faith.' Well, I obviously had plenty of that.

We were well equipped with an eskey, (Aussie coolbox) full of drinks, that we thought would be most essential, and so it would prove to be. About sixty miles out of Adelaide it was getting hot, well into the forties in centigrade and getting hotter when, just like any self respecting Hillman Hunter would do, it boiled up. The engine temperature went off the scale so we pulled in at the road side in the middle of nowhere – literally miles from anywhere. We knew that behind us was sat at least thirty miles to civilisation, but ahead we did not know. So off came the radiator cap, but, talk about disorganised when you consider what we were travelling in, we did not have any water! What were we going to do? The situation was a little desperate and just a tad scary.

Traffic was not something you could rely on because there wasn't any! Hours and hours could pass before you would see another vehicle. The only thing left was to get the eskey out in the sun to melt the little bit of ice that was inside with our drinks and that was what we used. The melted ice and the drinks that were left generated about three pints of liquid. After about an hour had passed the engine was cool enough to put our precious liquid into the cooling system. Then we set off at a very respectful pace – this Hillman Hunter was demanding some reverence if it was going to get us to Mildura. If we didn't get to some sort of civilisation soon we were in for a difficult time because the only liquid we had was now in the radiator! It was a very tense time with the both of us watching the temperature gauge more than the road. It was maintaining a steady needle just below the red band, and after about half an hour at 30 mph we were rewarded with a little village with a fuel station. Of course, we stocked up with gallons of water and plenty of drinks, topped up the radiator, maintained a steady pace and arrived in Mildura with time to spare.

Mildura is an excellent race track and is more like some of the small UK circuits at around 300 metres in length. If you ask anyone in Mildura when the racing starts the answer is simple: when the sun goes down. As the sun starts to go down, its blinding light makes it impossible to see as you face the sun. So they wait until it has set and then start the meeting. I had a match race with Phil Crump in his own backyard, but needless to say he beat me. After all, it was my first time around the place, but all in all it was a good, but testing journey.

Over the past few years during my trips to Australia I had struck up a good friendship with Billy Sanders and his wife Judy. Judy had recently given birth to Dean, and with Jackie also pregnant, we had plenty in common. We had a Saturday with no racing, so we planned a trip to Sydney to take Billy up on his offer to go and stay with them for about ten days at his parents' place. We were really well looked after, but it was back to basics Aussie style! Billy's parents had a trailer (caravan) in the back garden of their house, and it was old and I reckoned it had not been used for years. I dread to think what sort of creatures we were sleeping with during the nights, and stories of black widow spiders and funnel-webs didn't sweeten the dreams. During the days we had a fantastic time, mainly water-skiing, and helping Billy build his new speedboat, which he had named *Shattered*. Water-skiing was Billy's passion; he was a gifted water-skier and had just mastered the art of barefoot skiing.

Toilet arrangements at the Sanders' residence were what the Aussies called 'the Dunny,' which was a basic outside shack with a 'dunny bin' inside. The 'dunny bin' was a bit bigger than a five-gallon drum, on top of which a toilet seat was placed. The 'dunny bins' were called 'Black Diamonds,' a kind of official title, on account of them being painted with a black pitch. The 'Black Diamond Collectors', who would take away your full black diamond and replace it with a nice clean one, regularly collected these – and the whole cycle rolled on.

We got back from Australia in early February in time for me to get my equipment ready for the 1977 UK speedway season that started in mid-March. 1977 was another memorable year as it was the Queen's Silver Jubilee, and I can clearly remember street parties and celebrations. It was also the year that Elvis Presley died suddenly on 16 August. Musically speaking, it was the year when Meatloaf released the epic *Bat Out of Hell* album, a record that became a huge seller and grew to classic status.

I was all set to build on my success of 1976 and felt sure that I would experience another good season. Peter Collins's younger brother, Les, had joined the Aces full time that year and we were expected to be a major force after finishing runners-up to Ipswich the previous season.

But it didn't quite work out like that. As the reigning World Champion PC was in great form, but the record shows that his average did slip a bit. Nonetheless, having the World Champion riding in your team was great, but it also meant that every club wanted to lower the Aces' colours, and we slipped down the league that year. Having had the experience of one World Final behind me, I was eager to qualify for another one and have a real crack of taking the crown from PC.

As the months passed by, and the due date for our first child got closer we made our preparations. A bag of essentials had been packed for a week or so when, on 7 June, I arrived back from Wimbledon at 2 a.m. and Jackie said: 'I think it's time to go, the contractions are getting regular.' We very calmly drove down to Bolton General Hospital where Jackie was going to have our first baby. The plan was that I would be present at the birth. After a while the contractions stopped, but they decided to induce. As it got late in the night the nurse in charge said to me: 'It will be some time yet. Why don't you go home and when it is getting nearer we will give you a call so you can be here at the birth?' It sounded like a sensible thing to do; but it wasn't. Jackie gave birth to Emma Louise Morton at 9 a.m. on 8 June, while I still lay in bed waiting for the call. The shifts had changed and my request had been forgotten.

The call finally came to me from Jackie's mother who had called the hospital to see how she was, and found out it had already happened. I rushed to the hospital, where I was taken to a room just off from the delivery room. They would be a few minutes getting Jackie sorted out, and then the nurse brought me my daughter, who was less than an hour old. Fresh from the birth, she was still wrapped in the blankets that were used and were showing the remnants of the natural battle that had taken place in bringing her into the world. I was overwhelmed with some brand new feelings. For a few moments I sat there all on my own, looking at her bright eyes that seemed to be trying to make some sense of what had happened, while it all made perfect sense to me. Becoming a parent triggers an inbuilt set of reactions that seem to come complete with instructions – although they are a bit vague. This was a new chapter in my life – in our lives – and I felt surprisingly confident that I would be able to deal with this brand new baby. Or was that just my enormous sense of pride? Being a father is something that no amount of victories on a speedway bike can replicate. Certainly at that moment, there was nothing that could even come close to that magic sense of joy.

SEVEN

IT'S A LONG WAY TO THE TOP

'Hard luck Chris. Don't worry, you'll do it next year.' It was a genuine effort by a supporter to console me and make me feel better, but I can remember thinking, unfairly in my irritation: 'What fucking good is that sort of comment? They have no idea the pain and frustration I'm going through.' My year was over and next year may as well have been 100 years away. At the time I was walking back to my van, having just got changed after the 1979 British Final. I had failed to progress any further in the Individual World Championships for another year. It was destroying me. After qualifying for my first World Final in 1976, I failed to progress past the British Final in 1977, 1978 and 1979. I refer to them as 'the drought years'. My form was good enough, but my gating ability – or lack of it to be exact – was in question at Coventry, where it was difficult to pass. However, whatever the reasons, I considered that it was now becoming a psychological problem for me to get past this round at Coventry as the 1980 season started.

As I believed that I could have a psychological issue I decided that, rather than just apply a positive approach to the subject with a straightforward positive mental attitude, I would have to completely eliminate any possibility of me being intimidated or affected in any way by the Coventry track, or the fact that I had stumbled at this round for the last three years. I knew what I was looking for; it was some kind of psychological dynamite, some way that I could gain full control of my mind. I was, by this time, using 'positive mental attitude' techniques to apply to my racing, but this problem needed something more. I contacted a hypnotist called Doctor Lorenzo, but I wasn't looking to be hypnotised into winning – if only it was that easy! No, I wanted help to get into my psyche and gain greater control, not to be controlled by a hypnotist, but to learn that sort of control for myself. He had an immediate understanding of the help I was looking for, and over a period of about three months he taught me the technique of self-hypnosis.

This is not about being in a trance, but in fact the opposite as you achieve a heightened awareness. Basically it is meditation, where you go deep into your sub-conscious mind and, during that process, focus on what it is you are trying to achieve. It was not about 'I want to win that particular meeting', but involved more focussing on the practical parts of winning by concentrating on the basic fundamentals of racing: the concentration level required, and the pure focus on the job you are trying to achieve by visualising winning and what I would have to do to win. You would then apply that formula to each individual race. Whether I could have qualified through those rounds without this psychological tinkering I don't know, but I was certainly not willing to take that chance in 1980.

It seemed that my first race in the British Final was always jinxed, as in 1977 I was excluded from my opening race and found myself chasing a qualifying place again. At this level you can't afford to give anything away as the quality riders in the field just take advantage of your misfortune and make you pay. I had fought hard throughout the meeting and even took John Louis from the back to win my second outing and finish on 9 points. But I found myself in a run-off with Swindon's experienced international Bob Kilby for the reserve spot in the Intercontinental Final. I won the run-off, but being reserve at a top meeting like that is merely the consolation prize – your only hope is that one of the qualifiers has to pull out of the meeting for some reason. You're not really part of it, and you can only watch as your rivals are racing for a World Final spot.

Although the World Championship had been a frustrating and disappointing experience, I had not gone through those years without any success at all. It was at White City in 1978 where I won the Grand Prix series. I hadn't won a single round on the way to the Grand Final, but I rose to the occasion. I wasn't the favourite to win it; that was Gordon Kennett, who was the home rider, and he was leading the qualifying points as we entered the Grand Final at White City. Peter Collins was actually leading the scorers, but he had to withdraw from the finale because of a World Long-track qualifying round. Entering the meeting I was 8 points adrift of Kennett on 21 points. We had all raced in various qualifying rounds throughout the country and accumulated points that would be added to our final scores in the Grand Final at White City – but it was in the final where the big points would be scored.

I battled hard throughout the afternoon and drove inside Kennett in heat six to take second place after I had been left at the start. Then I passed John Davis round the outside in heat twelve. I finished the meeting as the winner with 13 points, but more importantly I was awarded 50 series points that gave me overall victory with a grand total of 71 – 5.5 points ahead of joint-second-placed Malcolm Simmons and John Louis.

It was a memorable occasion, not least because of the presence of the girls known as the Penthouse Pets, but also the fact that the madcap comedian and entertainer Freddie Starr was presenting the prizes. Starr was a familiar face on the speedway scene as he had struck up a friendship with Sheffield's Reg Wilson. Later, Starr sent Ipswich's Tony Davey a cheque for £1,000 when the rider pleaded poverty in the *Daily Mirror* newspaper after finishing fourth in the Grand Prix series. Davey said that he would have to sell his car to get a new engine for his bike, but Freddie came to the rescue. It was a warm sunny day and Freddie Starr was wearing an expensive-looking jacket that had all the style and the flamboyance that you would come to associate with show business. When he got onto the parade truck with us, I can remember him removing this garment and casually slinging it into a dirty corner of the truck as if it was nothing more than an ordinary jacket he had picked up from a local store – the trappings of fame!

This victory gave me a tremendous boost of confidence before the British Final that year – 1978 was a bit special because it was the sport's Golden Jubilee season and the final was held at Wembley, so every British rider wanted to be there. This was the final when PC failed to qualify and it was later discovered that he had sugar content in his fuel. The press made a big deal about his machine being sabotaged and it blew up into something a lot bigger than it was because it made a good story. But despite my success at White City, it was another disappointment at Brandon Stadium and I failed to qualify for the prestigious night at Wembley. I was very close, but it wasn't enough. I was in another run-off with Gordon Kennett and Steve Bastable after we had all finished on 10 points. I was in this position because of a mechanical breakdown in my first race. If I had managed to get just 1 point from that race I would have qualified. As Shawn Moran used to say: 'Could've, would've, should've' – hindsight is such a wonderful thing.

The winner qualified for Wembley, second was reserve for the big night and for third you were rewarded with nothing but the bitter taste of failure. Although I came out of the first bend in second place, Bastable had a moment of inspiration and roared past us both on the back straight and took the lead. Perhaps it was his sheer excitement at the prospect of being in a position to qualify for his first World Final, or maybe it was just the momentum of his speed, but he made a mistake and Kennett regained the lead. Unfortunately there was no way through for me and despite my best efforts to get on terms, the chequered flag signalled the end of my dream for another year. What made it even worse was that I had a brilliant season in 1978, averaging over 10 points a match for Belle Vue.

Our season was dealt a dreadful blow when our captain Alan Wilkinson crashed badly during our match at home to Swindon on 1 July. I saw Alan go down and from the pits gate where I was stood – which was the opposite end to where the crash happened – it didn't appear to be a bad accident. Like everyone else, I expected he would just get up, but at that distance I didn't realise the force of the accident. As I always did when a rider went down, I would be there on the scene if any help or assistance was required. How Wilkie was handled that night after the accident has been discussed many times. But it's clear that had the crash happened in 2005, there are strict procedures to deal with this type of accident that are far more advanced. Had these happened in 1978, the outcome may have been different.

Wilkie was a good captain and he was the type of rider you wanted on your side: a tough, consistent rider who rode to his average, something that I feel was a measure of the true value of a rider. You know when it gets tough and tight he will deliver to the best of his ability and sometimes more when it really mattered. Alan Wilkinson had that. This was an incredibly bad accident that saw a great rider paralysed. Unfortunately, danger is a part of the sport and the risk is something that you have to square up with yourself as a rider.

There has been a lot of talk about how tough and cut-throat the modern speedway Grand Prix is, but the old qualifying rounds from the British Final were just as hard and you could liken them to the modern-day Grand Prix. The British Final was one of the toughest rounds because the British riders were among the best in the world at that point and, of the sixteen who qualified, two-thirds of the field were at least of international standard. There wasn't another country in the world that could say that at that time. So having only the top four or five riders qualifying for the next stage was extremely difficult when surrounded by so many good riders. It only took one bad ride and your dream was over for another year. At that point the disappointment was hard to take, but when that supporter said 'hard luck' to me after the 1979 British Final, I knew that I had to do something, anything, to turn my fortunes around. It wasn't as if I hadn't been in a World Final as I had, so I knew, or I thought I knew, what it took to make the World Championship Final. Some very good riders never make a World Final – Reg Wilson was one that springs to mind – and others are happy just to be in one final. But having tasted the big time, I wanted a second, third and fourth helping. Furthermore, I had to be in a World Final to be World Champion and I firmly believed that I had the ability to become World Champion. But it would never happen if I couldn't make the final.

Nonetheless, I was getting a fair number of potentially lucrative bookings on the Continent at the weekends and these meetings often turned into little adventures. On one particular occasion we had been racing in Germany at the weekend, which was a regular jaunt during the UK season in the 1980s.

'We' consisted of Peter Collins, Les Collins, Dave Morton and myself, with four mechanics. It was quite a van-full. All eight of us had been squeezed in this van coming back from Germany for the past twelve hours or more. PC and myself would have had a meeting at Belle Vue on the Saturday night then flown over to the grass-track meeting while the rest of the riders, mechanics and equipment, would have driven over on the Friday. Tim Harrington was PC's Continental mechanic. He lived around the West Midlands and did most of the driving. My mechanic at the time was Steve Cooney, who was excellent and a good companion with a sharp wit. On our way back home to the North-West we would drop Tim off at his house in St Neots, but before this we made an excursion from Dover to Hastings – the home of the Weslake factory – to get some much-needed spares. I needed various bits and pieces, but very importantly I needed some special ends that go on the push rods, which push the valves open, called nipples. I had left Steve to sort this out.

When we arrived at Tim's house – three hours later – we all rolled out of the van. Tim kindly invited us in for a cup of tea, where we were all introduced to his wife, who was a schoolteacher and the exact opposite to Tim, who was a bit rough and ready. Anyway, Tim's wife treated us extremely well with tea in china cups and biscuits. This was all a bit of a change from the rowdiness of a gang of lads on a trip; we were now sat like good little boys sipping tea. You could feel the unease in the air. It had a tension – not unpleasant, just slightly uneasy. Tim's wife certainly did not intimidate us, but we were just over-respectful; a silence seemed to have descended on us as a group that just heightened the nervousness in the air.

In my slight discomfort I thought I should say something to break the silence and ease the tension – a good idea but was I up to it? I thought in my head that I would ask Steve if he got the nipples while we were at Weslake. Simple little statement, the problem was I didn't process it correctly. It went something like this: I subconsciously thought: ask Steve if he got the nipples and send this message to the mouth. But on the way my alert conscious mind said, in a state of alarm: 'Stop! You can't say "nipple"!' Unfortunately I had already started saying it and it came out like this: 'Steve, did you get those Nnn Nnn Nnn Nnnnipples?' I couldn't have given the word 'nipples' a greater fanfare if I had tried. Steve had a look of shock and alarm on his face but managed a stifled 'yes'. They were the only words spoken, and greatly appreciated by everyone I am sure. It was not a great example of the art of conversation, but a good lesson: if you are going to speak make sure it has been processed before you open your big mouth!

The World Speedway map was changing and the World Championship qualifying rounds reflected the changing face of international speedway racing. The Swedes were not the force that they once were – only Jan Andersson could be judged as a truly world-class racer – and they were replaced as giants by their near-neighbours Denmark. Ole Olsen's performances had influenced a new generation of riders from that little country, beginning with Finn Thomsen, Mike Lohmann, Bo Petersen and Hans Nielsen; and they were followed by Tommy Knudsen, Erik Gundersen, Jan O. Pedersen and John Jorgensen – these riders would form the basis of a successful national side that would go on to dominate the international scene during the mid-to-late 1980s. The USA had also re-emerged as a major force again, with Scott Autrey and Bruce Penhall leading the young talent of Dennis Sigalos, Ron Preston, the Moran brothers (Kelly and Shawn) and Bobby Schwartz, with more to follow. These nations, combined with strong representation from Australia, New Zealand and, to a lesser extent, the then-Eastern Bloc countries of the speedway-crazy Poland and Czechoslovakia – now divided into the Czech Republic and Slovakia – signified a peak period of talent that began in the mid-1970s and would last for the remainder of my career. The standards were high and the competition was always hard. If I wanted to be a major player, I would have to step up my game and continue to strive to remain competitive with both my fitness and new developments.

Speedway was breaking new ground; none more so than our tours in the winter of 1978 and 1979 when a troupe of British riders went on a short winter tour of the Middle East. Reg Fearman and Terry Chandler were responsible for putting these meetings on through their company Speedway Developments Limited, and they also had sponsorship from Rothmans and then Craven A – during this period tobacco sponsorship was not only allowed, but very active in motor sport.

I was pleased to be one of sixteen British lads chosen to go on the Middle East trip to Kuwait. It was a forerunner to a three-week tour of the Middle East that would be run the following year, but this initial trip to Kuwait in November 1978 was to test the water. Myself, Dave, PC, John Davis, Reg Wilson, Jimmy McMillan, Les Collins, John Louis and Neil Middleditch were among the sixteen riders who raced in a two-day event held at the Royal Kuwait Sporting Club, which was the national football stadium at the time. Twelve bikes were shipped over and were to be shared by sixteen riders. We all had to help each other out. Some of the soldiers from the nearby British Army barracks helped out in the pits. They were probably pleased for something different to do because Kuwait was a very religious country and there were no pubs, nightclubs or bars, so you had to make your own entertainment.

Peter Collins won the event with his brother, Les, in second place, while I scored 21 points and finished fourth. The racing wasn't as competitive as it would normally be for a British League match, but there was a matter of pride at stake and the locals seemed to enjoy it. To say that it was an experience just doesn't do the whole thing justice. The heat of the desert, the culture, the amazing wealth that was on show and the enthusiasm of the locals made the trip an unforgettable encounter for all the riders who went out there.

The following year the tour was spread over three weeks – with a week and two meetings in each of the three cities of Kuwait, Cairo (Egypt) and Abu Dhabi (Saudi Arabia). When we arrived in Kuwait – the venue for our first two meetings – it was late at night and we would have been staying at the SS Santa Paula that was permanently moored and converted into a hotel. But it had not been booked until the following night, so for the first night we would be back at the hotel that we had stayed at during the previous year. It was after midnight when we started to get into our rooms. About six of us ended up in one room and turned on the television to find the Sex Pistols blasting out *God Save the Queen*. We all immediately responded by dancing the pogo, a punk dance which is quite simply jumping up and down straight-legged to the music. We had an instant party that, unfortunately, did not impress the holidaying couple in the room directly below who had been woken up by this pogoing mob! A really irate bloke in his dressing gown was showing his disapproval at what was happening by ranting like a man possessed and obviously not really believing what he was seeing...Johnny Rotten would have been impressed though.

The next day we moved into the Hotel. In the evening a special event was put on to launch the tour, organised by the sponsors Rothmans. No social do in Kuwait would be complete without the inclusion of camels. When the end of the evening came, I was outside with Phil Collins, watching the camels being taken away after being on show for us. The vehicle was a standard Ford Pick-Up truck, not a big one, just about the size of a Ford Sierra. You may think, like we did, how do you get a camel on a little pick-up? Well this truck had a winch attached to it, which was going to be essential. The camel was encouraged to drop down on its belly with all four legs bent at the knees, which were then tied in their bent position. The winch was then used to lift up the camel and place it as far onto the pick-up as possible. This left the animal with his back quarter hanging over the back of the tailgate – which obviously could not be closed. The winch belt was then taken off and it looked like the job was done as the driver then got into the vehicle and drove off. But oh no, after he had travelled about twenty yards, he jammed on the brakes as hard as he could, shooting the camel forward. Then the driver calmly got out, went to the back of the pick-up and coolly shut the previously obscured tailgate. He then got back in and drove off for the second time with his camel settled in his little pick-up! So that's how you get a camel in a pick-up – it was the most entertaining part of the evening.

Speedway took the Middle East by storm during that three-week tour. We raced in front of 20,000 people during the first round of the Craven A Masters at the Zamalek Sporting Club. I won all three meetings to win the series – Dave finished second – but there were also other meetings too, such as the Cairo Championship that I won, the Craven A Premier Award, which was won by PC with my brother second, and Reg Wilson won a similar event at Abu Dhabi.

There were massive crowds at Kuwait and their enthusiasm for speedway racing was palpable. At Cairo the over-excited fans invaded the track during the presentations and PC and myself were suddenly hoisted shoulder high by the crowd. It was frightening but also a bit embarrassing too, because the Egyptians congratulated us with kisses. We eventually managed to fight our way back to the safety of the pits, where the security guards slammed the gates shut to keep the crowd back. The next day the riot squad were encamped on the infield to ensure that public order was maintained. They were an intimidating sight, and not one that you usually associate with a speedway event. Although the locals were just as enthusiastic, this time they remained in their seats, which was just as well as more people were locked outside the stadium.

In November 1978 Jackie, Emma and I moved into 15 Gainborough Close Wilmslow – this would be our new bit of space for the next five years. It was a new house on a new development. We made plans through the winter as to what we would do to the house and garden over the next year. My main priority was to fit out my workshop and set up a special area for cleaning my bikes, which could cope with all the shale and crap without blocking up the drains. This was the first job, it was done during the winter and I also got the workshop sorted.

One of the plans for the summer of 1979 was to build a brick barbeque – a kind of permanent feature. This would be my project, and it needed to be ready for the sunshine – if we had any! The main reason for me telling you all this is to set the scene for one summer day in 1979 when a strange thing happened.

At the time, Steve Cooney was working full time for me as my mechanic, and it was a Saturday with a meeting at Belle Vue that night. I planned my day well: my bikes were ready for the meeting with just a few jobs to do in the morning. Then I would be clear to do some bricklaying on my barbeque, which was behind schedule.

Steve arrived in the morning and at the time I had an old Ford Escort van we used for running around – saving my Citroen Safari for the professional work. However, we needed a trip to the dump to get rid of some rubbish, so me and Steve loaded up the old Escort van with some old tyres, an old battery and general boxes of junk and went to the dump, and dumped them. Simple, job done.

I now had to run in one of my engines for the meeting that night. This required more than just starting it up. It needed five to ten minutes of warming up – not very popular on an estate. So, being a good neighbour I would always take my bikes over onto the spare ground away from the houses – which was what I did on this occasion, bunging the bike in the trusty old Escort that had just served us on the trip to the dump. We went onto the waste ground and warmed up the bike. As Steve was checking the bike over, I sat on the back of the van floor where the back doors were open and we chatted for a few minutes. Satisfied, we loaded up the bike and made our way back. I said to Steve: 'I think the floor on the van has a hole in it, the carpet is wet and I have a damp bum.' Steve was slightly amused and we thought nothing more of it. Time for lunch and for me to plan my bricklaying; we were ready for the meeting at Belle Vue that night and it looked like a good day for bricklaying and speedway.

While we were having lunch Jackie said to me: 'Have you got fleas? You keep scratching your bum.' It was true, my backside was a little itchy, but there was no time to worry about that as I had some bricks to lay. After an hour or so I was doing well: I had laid about forty bricks, even though my backside was driving me crazy. 'Maybe', I thought, 'I have got fleas in my old jeans'. I was concentrating really hard on my bricklaying, but I noticed that I was feeling colder around the crotch and bum. Suddenly I became aware that there was a lot of laughter coming from Jackie, Steve and the neighbours. Then I realised they were laughing at me. Disturbed from my concentration and aware of the need to yet again scratch my backside, I realised I had no cloth around my bum, just threads of rotten seams! The whole backside and crotch of my jeans and undies had vanished, and I was left looking like some gay cowboy in nothing but his riding chaps. It must have been a wonderful sight, watching me laying bricks with my red raw bum hanging out! The wet patch on the van floor was acid from the old battery we took to the dump that morning! Some of us are just born to entertain!

As 1980 came round, a new decade and a new era, I had put many things in place. I had two reliable mechanics in Steve Cooney and Ged Blake, a good sponsorship package, and a new psychological approach. At one stage I had even wanted to move away from my beloved Belle Vue and Hyde Road, as I thought that a change of home track would represent a change of fortunes. Some people thought that it was because I was fed up with racing in the shadow of Peter Collins, but it wasn't that. Peter was the number one and how could I expect to be the number one if my record didn't compare? I asked for a transfer because I felt a bit stale and I thought that a change would boost my confidence. But despite it all, I remained an Ace and 1980 would be a memorable year.

After helping out with bits and pieces in 1978, Steve worked full time for me in 1979. He was a truck mechanic and he had worked for Soren Sjosten, but it was through my fan club secretary, Linda, that Steve got to hear that I needed help and he joined me. We got along really well; he was experienced and we had some great times together, but not all of them were at the track. As strange as it is, it's the little things that you always remember. Steve would come round to my workshop to work on my bikes and his mischievous sense of humour would often kick in. One day when he was cleaning the bike, some Jehovah's Witnesses came round. But before they could get into their spiel, Steve coolly told them that he didn't live there and pointed them in my direction! As I was fairly well known in the area, occasionally fans would stop by and collect an autograph from me. We had been messing around and Steve had told me a really stupid joke, so I was laughing in a silly manner to reflect the lame nature of it. While I was doing this Steve could see this woman walking up behind me. So there I was, laughing in a silly way, not my normal laugh, when I heard this voice ask: 'Can I have your autograph please?' I reacted with a slightly embarrassed reply of 'Oh, sure' – I had made a complete ass of myself.

Another story that Steve often tells was when I got up early to put up these shelves in the garage. The garage had an up-and-over door, and I could get into the garage through the kitchen. I had an idea to put these shelves up and I spent all morning doing it. When I had finished I had put all my various bits and pieces on them and was very pleased with the job I had done; it looked smart and tidy. I was busy admiring my work when Steve turned up and knocked on the garage door and he said: 'Hi Mort'. I opened the door, but it only travelled eight inches to a foot before it went 'bang' and stopped dead. I had made the shelves too close to the door. All that Steve could hear from the other side was an embarrassed 'Oh.' I wasn't feeling so pleased with myself now!

Even though the World Championship was a disappointment in 1979 as I failed to progress beyond the British Final again, I still had a very busy racing schedule. It became apparent that I needed someone else to help me when Steve went abroad with the bikes for open meetings on the Continent. I knew Ged Blake as he worked at Belle Vue on race nights and we would often talk during the meeting. I asked Steve what he thought about Ged helping us out, and he said that he thought that he was all right. He was a car mechanic for British Leyland and a very infectious and enthusiastic character. We would share many adventures together.

I had been in good form and, looking back, it was at Wimbledon in a Test Match against the Americans when my season really kicked off. I was promoted from reserve when DJ (Dave Jessup) was ruled out through injury and I scored 12 points and top-scored as we drew the first Test Match 54-54. The England team managers at that time were Eric Boocock and Ian Thomas and it was the latter who said of me after those dozen points at Wimbledon: 'The little Belle Vue tiger was the hero and it was the Test that made Chris Morton's season.'

There was a lot of gamesmanship going on in this series against the Americans, that included the Yanks arriving early and nicking our pits at Hull. I rode in all five Tests but we lost 3-1, although I was selected for the World Team Cup squad at King's Lynn. I dropped just 1 point as we won the qualifying round and put one over the Yanks. The meeting had been a two-horse race between us and the Americans, as Australia and New Zealand didn't really make much impression. We provided ten race winners of the sixteen races and I dropped my only point to Bruce Penhall. England took the lead in heat two and we never looked back.

I was feeling really confident when the British Final came round at Brandon. However, this time I avoided a run-off and qualified for the next stage at Wimbledon with 7 points. Following my performance at Plough Lane in the First Test against the Americans, the place held no fears for me whatsoever when I returned for the Commonwealth Final of the World Championship. This round included riders from Britain, Australia and New Zealand only.

The track at Wimbledon is a small, tricky race strip and not at all like the wide-open spaces of Hyde Road. Only the top nine qualified and I made the cut with 9 points, but to illustrate how awkward the place could be, PC scraped through and grabbed the last qualifying spot with 7 points. Following the frustration and disappointment of the past three years, I left the stadium at Plough Lane with the knowledge that I was just five rides away from qualifying for my second World Final. The 1980 season was shaping up to be a memorable year for me.

EIGHT

MAKING IT HAPPEN

I always found that the track at the White City Stadium, London, encouraged good racing. Although it was quite flat, it was always prepared with areas of grip that were there if you searched for them. It would change significantly throughout the meeting so it needed a watchful eye on how it was changing as the meeting progressed – just in case you needed to exercise a passing manoeuvre to gain a few important extra points.

This was where the 1980 Intercontinental Final was being held. It was the first time I had qualified for this stage since that balmy evening at Wembley in 1976. I had a good support team in the pits with Ged Blake and Steve Cooney as my mechanics. I was always very comfortable with either one of these in my corner, as they both understood me well. I had total faith in their ability – this situation can be likened to the role of a professional golfer and his caddy. A good caddy knows his golfer well enough to advise, not necessarily on what club should be used, but what club he should use to suit 'his game'. It's about intimate knowledge – I enjoyed a similar relationship with both these lads, and they worked well together. I also had with me Keith Rushton, who was the managing director of Coldshield Windows – they were a successful double-glazing company in Manchester – and they had been my main sponsor for some time. Keith was in charge of keeping an up-to-the-minute programme, and keeping a general eye on proceedings. In these meetings it was essential that nothing was left to chance. An incident or passing manoeuvre in a race may provide important information for me, so I liked to have someone there watching what was going on just for me. Another essential member of my team was Ted Howell, who had been tuning my engines for some time and his tuning skills had produced some very fast engines. Ted was my engine-tuner for most of my career and, although occasionally I would try other tuners in search of something different, Ted was the one who did my best engines.

Practice on the Friday had gone okay. It never really ever went better than okay because I always found it hard in practice to really put myself through my paces. I needed the reality of the meeting to get into racing mode, but it did give me a chance to feel how the track was riding – although more than likely it would be different on race day, usually watered more, and usually this provided more grip. Practice would often confirm for you which bike to ride, or at least which one to use in your first race. All that done, I was ready for the Intercontinental Final, the last hurdle. If you qualified from this round you were in the World Speedway final: ten qualifying places out of sixteen riders were up for grabs. Easy? Try telling that to the bottom six!

When it happened I was running third in my second ride, I had finished a fortunate second place in my first ride, which would have only been a third but for Peter Collins having an engine failure. As I desperately tried to improve on my poor third place during my second outing, a strange sense of horror over-whelmed me. Horror that, if I continued like this, I would not take one of the qualifying places for the World Final in Sweden; this race was a lost cause and third was all I was going to get. Something had tripped a panic button in my head during that race and as I rode back to the pits after the race had finished, I had the vivid realisation that I had waited three years for this opportunity and if I continued in this vein I would fail. Failing was not an option; and in the time it took me to ride back to the pits I had reviewed and redrawn my plan – I had put all that had gone before well and truly behind me.

I then spent the time I had before my next ride sat down in the pits and I practiced all I had learned from Dr Lorenzo to clear my mind: focus and concentrate solely on my next three rides. I did not look anything like a contender in this meeting after my first two rides: this was going to be a test of my own 'make it happen' approach and Dr Lorenzo's mental control.

Ged told me later that, after I had passed Scott Autrey to win my third ride, he had said to my sponsor Keith Rushton 'he won't be beaten again tonight'.

Winning my next two rides required all my racing skills, determination and previously mentioned up-to-the-moment race-track knowledge I had in me.

The meeting itself was a tough one – as these meetings always were. Autrey didn't make the final; and neither did the reigning, record-holding World Champion Ivan Mauger, or Ole Olsen. Little did we know that a new era was beginning and I would be at the head of it. The journalist Richard Bott later described the meeting as an 'afternoon of damaged reputations'. In fact, it could be argued that I was one of the main reasons for their elimination as I defeated both Mauger and Olsen in my fourth ride.

My 12-point tally put me in a run-off with Bruce Penhall for the title of Intercontinental Champion. Normally 12 points wouldn't be enough to win a meeting of this calibre, but Denmark's Hans Nielsen had ridden a superb last ride to pip Penhall on the line for a vital win that secured the Dane's first World Final appearance. Bruce and I tossed the coin for gate positions.

Unless there is an outstanding advantage from an inside gate I would always take the outside gate if I won the toss. This was not because I like to ride the outside, but for other tactical reasons. If you gate from the outside you can control your opponent on the first corner. However, if you don't make the start from the outside you have options – unlike if you miss the start from the inside. Then any good-quality opponent will trap you inside him around the first corner, thereby controlling you around that first corner. I won the toss and took the outside gate.

I made the start! Yes, I did make some starts, and won the race to take the Intercontinental title and my long-awaited place in an Individual World Final. Four years since making my World Final debut in Poland, I had signalled my intent with a victorious performance that had some people – including my mechanic, Steve – predicting that I could win the World title that year. When you look at the list of world-class riders who have won the Intercontinental Final – before and since – you can see why some people described this meeting as harder than the World Final itself. With my name on the roll of honour, I was alongside some of the great names in the sport. To be crowned Intercontinental Champion was a very proud moment, but it also proved that the work I did with Dr Lorenzo had not been in vain.

We were all elated; it had been a long but very successful day – arguably the most successful in my career to date. As we journeyed out of London, northbound on the M1, Jackie suggested we get a bite to eat at the next services – the famous Watford Gap on the M1. We had already avoided the last service station because it was too busy, but these were also busy. However, we needed some well-earned sustenance, so this was the place. Ged was carrying Emma – who was just three years old – as the five of us walked into a very hectic restaurant area considering the usual 'sausage, egg, chips and beans'. Although at the time I was aware that there would be some speedway supporters in among the truckers and the like, I was certainly not prepared for the reception that followed.

As we walked through the door the whole place erupted with cheers and applause and a spontaneous standing ovation from a full motorway services restaurant. It was one of the most rewarding moments of my career. As I write this now, it still fills me with pride that what happened that night at White City Stadium, London, could generate such a spontaneous response from a few hundred people in a service area halfway up the M1 – hours after the event.

With a fifth place in the semi-final at Judek, West Germany, I had also qualified for the World Long-Track Championship final. I also lifted the prestigious Golden Hammer meeting at Cradley Heath that had assembled a world-class field of riders and won a qualifying round for the Berger Grand Prix at Sheffield with a maximum. Leading up to the World Final, my form for Belle Vue had also been good and included 19 points at Swindon in the Knock-Out Cup that ensured that we progressed to the semi-final at Cradley – more about that later.

Belle Vue's season had suffered an early setback when Mike Lohmann sustained serious injuries early in the campaign. It happened at Hyde Road on 25 May, during the second half of our 43-35 win over Halifax – Lohmann's former club. When I saw the crash I knew it was a bad one. Mike was a tough racer and always seemed to put all he had into his racing. He was dicing for position, got involved in an incident and lost control halfway around turns one and two. It seemed like bikes and bodies were bouncing and landing very heavily.

I ran to the scene from the opposite end where I was watching from the pits. Whenever there was a bad accident I always liked to be there as quickly as possible in case the St John Ambulance people needed any assistance. Although we had very experienced and capable medical staff, at a lot of tracks they don't understand how to remove a crash helmet and I have seen injured riders getting distressed while someone tries to clumsily remove their crash helmet. I liked to see injured riders were handled correctly, and I was the first on the scene along with the St John Ambulance crew at the Mike Lohmann crash.

The aftermath of the accident really was horrific – it was the worst I had ever witnessed. His full-face crash helmet had not really helped him and there was a horrible sound like a warbled sucking and blowing. His helmet was removed to reveal something from a horror movie. It was very clear he had not just broken his jaw; it had been smashed into pieces! Teeth and bits of bone were lying on his face from the impact, which, maybe fortunately, had ripped his throat.

1. Innocent days, my brother Dave and I. (Morton Family Archive).

2. Racing around our home-made track where we would ride until the fuel can ran out. (Morton Family Archive)

3. On board my Villiers 197cc bike, which I defeated Peter Collins with for the first time after I did some special tuning on it. (Morton Family Archive)

4. An Ellesmere Port Gunner in 1973. (Wright Wood Collection, courtesy of Ian Somerville)

5. Dave and I at Belle Vue in 1974. Dave was guesting for Reading. (Morton Family Archive)

6. Leading Nigel Wasley and Wayne Hughes on my way to the British Junior Championship at Canterbury in 1974. (Morton Family Archive)

7. With my father, the Peter Craven Memorial Trophy and my JAP bike. (Morton Family Archive)

8. British Lions Touring Squad 1974/75. From left to right: Wally Mawdsley (team manager) Jimmy McMillan, Kevin Holden, Nigel Boocock (captain, on bike), Doug Wyer, Reg Wilson, Chris Morton, Eric Broadbelt. (Morton Family Archive)

9. Dave and I after we won the first ever British Grass-Track Pairs Championship in 1975. (Morton Family Archive)

10. Consolidate and then chase to race: Inside Phil Crump during the race that clinched my first World Final appearance during the 1976 Intercontinental Final. (Mike Patrick)

11. Next to Malcolm Simmons while on parade at Katowice, Poland for my first World Final, as it starts to spot with rain. (Mike Patrick)

12. Going for it during the 1976 World Final at Katowice, Poland. (Mike Patrick)

13. I never wanted to ride for any other club. Here I am riding for Belle Vue on the inside of Hackney's Keith White. (Mike Patrick)

14. With the entertainer and comedian Freddie Starr after I had won the 1978 Grand Prix Championship. (Morton Family Archive)

15. Grass-Tracking was where I started racing.
(Morton Family Archive)

16. The body language says it all:
disappointment at the 1978 British final as an
engine failure puts my place in the next round
in doubt. (Mike Patrick)

17. A winner in Kuwait City in 1979 when the Middle East went speedway crazy. This was round two of the series, which I went on to win and I am flanked by my brother Dave (right) and third-placed Dave Jessup. (Morton Family Archive)

18. A pits discussion with Ged. This is one of his favourite photographs. (Ged Blake)

19. Yes! I've done it! This was a pivotal moment for me as I punch the air in triumph after I had defeated Bruce Penhall to win the 1980 Intercontinental Final. (Mike Patrick)

Above left: 20. The 1980 Intercontinental Champion – I enjoyed an impromptu standing ovation at the Watford Gap Services on my way back home which was a very humbling experience. (Mike Patrick)

Above right: 21. Grand Slam winners 1980. England had clinched the Grand Slam by winning the World Team Championship. Here is that victorious team standing on top of the world: Michael Lee, John Davis, Chris Morton, Peter Collins and Dave Jessup. (Mike Patrick)

22. A long-track race: When you hit the front on a 1,000-metre circuit, it was one of the most exhilarating feelings in the world as you peeled off flat out into the wide sweeping turns at over 100 mph – it truly was sensational. (Mike Patrick)

23. On parade at Wembley in the 1981 World Final with Tommy Knudsen behind me. This meeting was one of my biggest disappointments. (Mike Patrick)

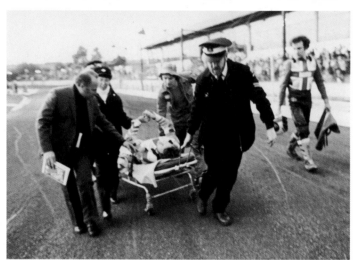

24. This was the first time that I was stretchered off, after my big crash at Hackney in the 1982 British semi-final, but against better judgment I carried on and qualified for the British final. Unknowingly I had broken a bone in my neck. (Morton Family Archive)

25. One of the highlights of my career: British Champion, 1983. Also in the picture are Michael Lee, second (left) and Andy Grahame, third. (Mike Patrick)

26. Leading Bobby Schwartz during a Test Match against the USA at Swindon in 1983. I was always very proud to ride for my country.

27. Discussing conditions and tactics with my mechanics at Belle Vue, Ged Blake (left) and Steve Cooney. I had total faith in their ability and they both understood me well. (Morton Family Archive)

28. This is the race when I set the track record at Belle Vue of 66.4 seconds during the Northern Riders' Championship on 29 July 1983. Along with Erik Gundersen, we are the fastest riders around Hyde Road – it is one of my most valued accomplishments that can never be beaten. (Morton family archive)

29. Heading for glory in Italy: Peter Collins is on my outside as we race away for the World Pairs title. Although we never discussed it, PC and I always had a unique on-track understanding. (Mike Patrick)

30. Erik congratulates me on the rostrum with Peter Collins after we had won the 1984 World Pairs Championship. (Mike Patrick)

31. Celebrating my 100th cap for England at Cradley in 1986 with teammates Kelvin Tatum (left) and Phil Collins. (Mike Patrick)

32. Leading Hans Nielsen during the final staging at Hyde Road of the 1987 British League Riders' Championship. Racing against Hans was always a challenge and it took a decisive move from me to defeat him and win the 1984 BLRC. (Ken Carpenter)

33. Passing Lance King on my way to a maximum at Bradford in a Test Match against the USA in 1988. England team manager Eric Boocock said afterwards: 'Chris is like fine wine, he gets better with age.' (Mike Patrick)

34. Vetlanda, 1988: It's all smiles from me, Ged and Dave after I had snatched qualification from the jaws of elimination to qualify for my seventh World Championship. (Mike Patrick)

35. 1993 Northern Riders' Champion at Sheffield – which was my last competitive speedway meeting. (Morton Family Archive)

36. Chris Morton MBE, an incredibly proud moment. (Morton Family Archive)

37. My family. From left to right, back: grandson Jake, Emma, Jackie, Charlotte. Front: grandson Cameron and me. (Morton Family Archive)

I say fortunately because this was where the strange sound was coming from, because as his mouth was smashed to pieces, he was at least able to breathe through the hole in his throat.

As you can imagine there was a lot of blood, but it was apparent that no arteries were severed – it really was a most shocking sight. I am able to deal with this type of thing fairly well so I helped where it was needed, but I have to say that the St John Ambulance crew and the track doctor did an excellent job that night and probably saved his life. It was amazing to go and see Mike in hospital and, although he was very lucky to be alive, they had marvellously put his jaw back together and within weeks he was up and about again.

We covered for his absence by using a combination of the rider-replacement facility and pulling riders from the club's assets who were racing in the National League. This seemed to work out just fine at Hyde Road, but away from home it was PC and myself who scored the majority of the points. Critics said that we were top heavy, but our team manager, Eric Boocock, did well to inspire his team to step up their game and we remained well inside the top half of the league table.

I was rated at 14 to 1 alongside Billy Sanders – who was third at White City – for the World Championship. Dave Jessup was the hot favourite at 11 to 4 and had been in brilliant form all year. He won the British and Commonwealth titles, the Internationale, the World Pairs with PC and had been flying for his club, King's Lynn. Bruce Penhall was rated next at 4 to 1 while Mike Lee – Jessup's teammate – was 5 to 1. Peter Collins had also qualified and although he was probably displaying the kind of form of that brought him the World title in 1976, he was rated by Corals at 8 to 1.

The World Final was held at the Ullevi Stadium, Gothenburg in Sweden. With Ivan Mauger out of the final, it was certain that a new World Champion would be crowned that night. I was hoping it would be my night too. My equipment for the World Final was on its way to Sweden with Ged and Steve in charge. At the time I was at home cleaning a bike I had ridden in a league meeting at Leicester, when tears started rolling down my face as I was overcome with a strong sense of sadness. A matter of days ago my brother Dave's son, Jamie, had died after a fall down the stairs – he was just three years old, just a few months older than my daughter Emma. Dave was devastated, as were all the family. The death of a child is such a cruel and sad loss and it always seems so unfair that they should miss their chance in the world. Jamie was always smiling, full of fun, and was clearly a happy lad who enjoyed his short time with us. I was able to attend the funeral before flying out to Sweden for the World Final practice.

Ullevi is a great-looking stadium, with the curving roof of the main stand that looks like a giant eyelid. The track is quite a large circuit but, with very little banking it was very difficult to pass on – gating was going to be of paramount importance.

In my first race I was off gate two with local favourite Jan Andersson off the inside. Jan made the gate, but using my old adage to consolidate, I resisted the temptation to try a run around the outside of him on the first corner because I knew that if it failed I could find myself at the back. I tucked myself in tightly behind Jan around the first turn and I was feeling some pressure from the third-placed Egon Muller. I knew that it would be no use this early in the meeting to move an inch from the inside line. As we raced into the second corner for the first time, I was as tight as you could be to another rider without touching. One mistake from Jan and I would be through like a shot. But he didn't put a wheel wrong as we exited the second corner for the first time. I launched myself inside him as we hit the straight and I found a rut that gave me extra drive coming out of the corner. When we crossed the line for the first time I was alongside him, albeit half a wheel down when he dropped it across me as we entered the first corner for the second time. I continued to apply the intense pressure, hoping for a mistake, but his knowledge of this track and his close-control riding skill meant that if I was going to pass him I could not rely on a mistake.

As we exited the first corner for the second time I found an extra bit of drive that again got me alongside him down the straight. But yet again it wasn't enough for me to dominate the entry to the next corner. I was riding incredibly close to him, ensuring I didn't lose any of my momentum. So, as we came out of the corner to start the third lap, I realised that I could use the grip I was finding that was just six inches inside the line he was taking to make the pass. We raced onto the straight; again I got alongside him only to be chopped off as we entered the corner at the start of the third lap. This was one of the most concentrated and pressured races I had ever had. I was managing to do what could be considered the impossible on this circuit, especially this early in the meeting, but Jan continued to maintain a tight hold on the inside line. He was riding perfectly as we entered the back straight for the third time. Again I was alongside him, but I knew my best chance was on the second corner. As we roared onto the home straight, the intensity and the immense concentration that had gone into my efforts to pass Jan Anderson caused me to make one of the biggest mistakes of my whole career!

As we came off the fourth bend and onto the home straight for what was the end of the third lap to enter the final lap, I had exercised an heroic and successful attempt to get ahead as I raced to the line. We crossed the line to start the last lap and I was level, but I thought it was the end of the race and shut off the throttle, to suddenly realise we had one lap left!

I had got myself into the perfect position to take the lead as we crossed the line heading for the next corner – if only I had just carried on. I recognised my error almost instantly, but I had lost valuable yards, which left me with only the rest of that lap to catch up lost ground – so I ended up finishing a close second to Jan Andersson in my first heat. But as you can see from my recall it left an indelible imprint on my mind.

Ole Olsen, who had obviously watched the race intently and seen the error I had made, said to me with surprising concern: 'What were you doing? You had him beat. You cannot make that sort of mistake in a World Final.' Of course, I have to agree. It is sadly ironic that knowing the level of concentration, determination, physical effort, gathering of skills and experience those three laps squeezed out of me, they were, I consider, the nearest I got to a race that saw the ultimate of my physical and mental skills. I was absolutely 'on it' for three laps. Ged still regards this as one of my best races because of the way that I worked the track even though it was so slick. I have had a fair few races that I am proud of but this race got the most from me for three laps – unfortunately I am not proud of it.

My draw saw me off gate three in my next ride – the outside gates were proving very difficult to make a good start from, and I was no exception. I only managed a third place and 1 more point. Now on 3 points from two rides, my third ride was 'make or break' to stay in contention. This time I was off the outside gate and I knew it would be a tall order to get a good start, but I needed a race win and rode out of my skin. But a third place in this race saw my World Championship hopes go out the window; three races and 4 points – out of contention. I had two rides left to retain my dignity.

After all the riders had completed three rides each, there then followed a short interval. At this stage it was clear who the contenders were – Michael Lee (8 points), Jessup (7), Billy Sanders (7) PC (7) – and who was out of it. Bruce Penhall was inconsolable, having failed at this point. The future would show that whatever lessons he picked up from his first World Final appearance would be put to good use in twelve months' time. I was in the first race after the interval off the inside gate. I made the start and, for the first time in the meeting, I had a free run to express my frustrations. I recorded the fastest time of the night in that race as I defeated Penhall and Finland's Kai Niemi to win the race. Obtaining the fastest time of the event of 74.4 seconds was a very small consolation for finishing in eighth place in my second, and long awaited, Individual World Final.

To give you some idea of how slick and smooth it was, all the first four races were won from the inside gate. Michael Lee won the World title with 14 points with Dave Jessup second and Billy Sanders third. I finished with 8 points and won my first World Final race, but I have to admit that I expected to do better because I had been riding so well. Steve Cooney thought that my form was good enough to win it, but the track was just too slick for me and I had to race very hard for the points I scored. I wasn't the only one to complain about the slickness of the Gothenburg track and it wasn't good enough for a World Final. But this was the way that things were heading.

Individual World Championship disappointments were put aside as I was one of the England World Team Cup squad. As a team we had qualified for the final at Wroclaw in Poland, and my form in this event was something I was proud of. But we were up against it if we were going to beat the in-form American team.

I was fuelled by my disappointment in Sweden and still hungry for more success in that season. As a team we worked extremely well together, with good management in Ian Thomas and Eric Boocock, who earlier in the year had taken some stick for their team selection. Therefore, as a team, our desire to win was ubiquitous, which was a credit to our management.

Lee's victory in the World Final meant that England were in place for a unique achievement if we could win the World Team Cup Final. If we were successful, then as a nation we would hold all the major World titles: Individual, Pairs and Team. This had never been done before.

We faced America, the hosts Poland and Czechoslovakia. Earlier in the season we had to qualify through the semi-final stage, the Intercontinental Final, which was held at Vojens in Denmark. Olsen constructed this track and England faced the Danes, the Swedes and America – only the top two teams qualified. Sweden were passengers as it was a three-way scrap between us, the Yanks and the Danes. Vojens seems to attract more than its fair share of rain and this occasion was no exception. Despite the fact that we had won the UK Qualifying round at King's Lynn and PC and Jessup had won the Pairs, the team were still getting a lot of stick from the press. Furthermore, the Americans continued to needle us over the fact that they had beaten us in the Test series. We were determined to qualify by winning.

However, the weather had caused havoc with the track, but the Danes, or more accurately Olsen, their captain, who happened to be the promoter too, wanted the meeting on at any price. The rain was persistent and heavy and it seemed that there was no way that it could go ahead. The referee, Gunter Sorber, called the meeting off at around 5.15 p.m. and that should have been the end of it. But he was under pressure from the Danes and he had a meeting with all the managers, and somehow Olsen convinced him to put the event back on.

It did stop raining, but the parade was half-an-hour long, which was ludicrous when you consider how dark and heavy the clouds were. We got on with the job, but if it wasn't for that long parade we could have made it through the rest of the meeting without any further rain. As it happened, it was pouring down with a couple of races to go. We had done enough to guarantee that we qualified for the final, and it was just a matter of determining first and second place – and we wanted first.

Locked with America on 30 points, Dave Jessup stormed around in the spray to defeat Penhall and clinch a win – Denmark were out. But the Danish shenanigans were not over yet. We were asked to go out to the pit gate and wait for the presentation ceremony. It was raining and there was no sign of the Danes, and we got fed up and walked to the rostrum. Hammering down with rain, we waited, but then Ian Thomas got cheesed off and handed out the medals! Eric Boocock handed out the medals to the American lads, Brian Larner ran up to the commentary box and found a record of the national anthem and put it on. When we returned to the pits the Danish riders were just coming out! Then there were arguments over payments and the Danish officials wouldn't let one of our vans into the pits. It was unbelievable; their attitude was disgraceful because they lost. Furthermore, there was no champagne, only a bottle of grape fruit juice – between all five of us!

For the final at Wroclaw, we knew that we would face a tough challenge from the Yanks, who had been strong all year, but we also realised that we couldn't rule out the Poles on their home track. They included some experienced riders like Edward Jancarz and Zenon Plech. We recognised that the Grand Slam was on and that no one had done it before, but we were confident of winning the meeting.

In front of a sell-out crowd of 55,000 people, Bruce Penhall got the meeting off to a good start for the Americans by winning the opening race and then I won my first race by rounding Scott Autrey. Peter Collins won heat three and, with Dennis Sigalos at the back, we were in front. In my first World Team Cup Final, I would have a big say in this historic achievement, as not only did I finish as joint-top-scorer with 11 points, I was the rider who clinched the gold for England in heat thirteen. I faced the USA's Sigalos and, typical of his style, he jetted from the start and into the lead. Unlike Gothenburg, Wroclaw was a track that was constructed for racers and I shadowed Siggy and passed him for the victory and gold. Later, when I watched a video tape from ITV's *World of Sport* coverage, commentator Dave Lanning said: 'Outside or inside, it doesn't matter to him!' This memorable phrase is one that typified my performance that day and the way I approached my racing.

Ian Thomas later described my performance as 'fantastic to watch, nerve-racking at times'. But then he described me as the 'revelation of the season'. It was a proud moment to be a part of speedway history and it was one of the highlights of what had been a memorable season.

Although I had been enjoying a good season, it wasn't quite as good as Dave Jessup. Jessup had won the British Championship, the Commonwealth Championship, the World Pairs – with Peter Collins – the Internationale, was runner-up in the World Final and of course he was a member of that triumphant World Team Cup side. He was the man in form and, to be honest, he should have won the World Championship that year – under the GP system he would have been the champion. In August he had defeated Hans Nielsen for the Golden Helmet and I was announced as his challenger for September.

At the time the weekly newspaper *Motor Cycle News* sponsored the Golden Helmet and it was a very prestigious trophy. Its tradition went back to the post-war years when Jack Parker held it for so long that it was dubbed 'Parker's Pension' and the list of holders reads like a who's who of speedway. In 1976, the helmet was presented to the family of Sweden's Tommy Jansson, as he was the holder of the trophy when he was tragically killed in a meeting in Sweden.

It was a match-race competition where two riders – the holder and the challenger – would race against each other in the best of three races. One leg would be at the holder's track and the other at the challenger's track. If, after these two legs, they were tied, then the two riders would race a decider at a neutral venue. I faced DJ in the first leg at Belle Vue and won 2-0. I was quite confident when I went to King's Lynn for the return and to my delight I won there as well, 2-1, to win the helmet for the first time.

My first challenger was Denmark's in-form Bo Petersen. Petersen had been sensational all year for Hackney, who were experiencing one of their best seasons, as they chased Reading for the British League Championship. I was keen to finish the season as the winter holder of the Golden Helmet, but I expected a tough challenge from Petersen because it was the first time that he had raced in this competition. It went to a decider at Leicester but Petersen's fast starting meant that he went into the close season as the holder.

On 10 October 1980 I was supposed to be racing at Hackney, but Jackie was in labour with our second child. If I was going to make it to Hackney Wick for an 8 p.m. start I would have to leave by 3.30 p.m. at the latest from Wythenshawe Hospital. Having missed the birth of Emma three years earlier, I was not going to miss this one. To avoid being disciplined for not turning up at a meeting I was praying for rain and was getting it. Although Jackie's labour was progressing by 3 p.m., it was clear that if I was going to be at the birth I wasn't going to be at Hackney. So I called the track to let them know I would not be there, and they told me that the meeting had been postponed due to rain. I witnessed the birth of Charlotte Jayne Morton. It was another extremely proud moment; our family was complete. I went home to celebrate with Steve Cooney instead of racing around Hackney Wick.

1980 was quite a successful year for me, but a very busy and long one. Belle Vue had qualified for the Knock-Out Cup final against Cradley Heath, but it proved one too many meetings for me. Belle Vue had won the home leg 67-41, but although we were confident of holding on to our lead, we knew that it was going to be a tough second leg at Cradley Heath for us to win the cup.

Due to bad weather the meeting was postponed as Cradley were struggling to get the track in a race-fit condition. But pressure from the authorities meant that the meeting was put back on and both teams started a meeting that shouldn't have been run due to the conditions – and in a cup final you just have to go for it. In my second or third ride I had an horrendous crash. Steve Cooney tells me that as I lost control the bike pitched me off and I went as high as the lamp standard. As the bike and I bounced down the track, it missed me by a whisker each time it bounced. Unfortunately I had taken a serious blow to the head and, although I foolishly tried to ride in my next race in an attempt to keep our hands on the cup, I was in no fit state as I was suffering from double vision! Peter Collins also suffered an injury early in the meeting, so a great season finished on a bit of a downer. But I had enough positive experiences to take forward into 1981, and a well-earned winter's rest.

On 8 December 1980, John Lennon was shot dead – he was shot four times in the back by Mark Chapman, who had asked the former Beatle for his autograph only hours before he laid in wait and killed him. He said he had heard voices in his head telling him to kill the world-famous musician. Chapman pleaded guilty to gunning down Mr Lennon and is currently serving life in Attica prison near New York. In October 2004 he failed for the third time to secure his release. I heard the news as I travelled along Washway Road in Sale, Manchester; it was a shock and I remember thinking this was incredibly sad and unnecessary. Like many, I was a John Lennon fan and feel bitter towards Chapman for wasting a great life for no reason whatsoever. Future works from John Lennon that many would delight in discovering would never be.

Meanwhile, Trust House Forté had put Belle Vue up for sale and, although at the time we didn't know it, this was the start of the great stadium's, and, more to the point, the great track's demise. I say we didn't know it was the start of its demise, but there was a general feeling that, as the new owner Stuart Bamforth had made his money out of demolition, it was just a matter of time before he would demolish the place. Sadly, seven years later, this suspicion was proved correct.

Peter Collins had decided to concentrate on racing on the Continent, and retired from British League speedway. Our new boss displayed great enthusiasm for his new-found sport, and also the team that came with his new purchase. True to his responsibility he was keen to see the team do well. As PC had moved on I was given the role as captain, which really was a great honour considering that eleven years earlier I was a spectator on the terraces. Peter Collins was going to be a very difficult man to replace, but the man brought in for that role was a New Zealander from Wimbledon, Larry Ross. He was a very capable rider who did an excellent job and really enjoyed his team racing.

With no PC, the Aces' team had a fresh look about it. I was the captain of a side that now included Ross, Louis and Peter Carr, Jim McMillan, a new Danish signing in Peter Ravn, Mike Lohmann, Larry Kosta and riders like Robert Maxfield doubling up from the National League. We missed PC and, although Ross and I scored a lot of points, the team wasn't strong enough away from Hyde Road to live with Cradley – who won their first league title that year – Ipswich and to a lesser extent Coventry and Swindon. Peter Collins made a comeback late in the season, but by then it was too late. With the Carr brothers and Ravn there was a lot of potential, but the American Kosta experienced a difficult season and he wasn't able to maintain the form that he had shown the previous year. Mike Lohmann's shocking injury had taken away much of his confidence and this was reflected in his scoring. We finished fourth, which wasn't bad, but a vital cog was missing – as the saying goes, the best was yet to come.

In 1981 the World Individual final was held at Wembley. Of all the finals, this was the one to be in – on your home soil. History would show that this final would take on extra significance, a final for the purist, a classic, a memorable meeting that has speedway fans throughout the country still talking about it to this day! Following my performance in the 1976 Intercontinental Final at Wembley, and combined with four more years of experience, I felt that I had good reason to fancy my chances – I just had to be in it. To book my ticket there would be required, as usual, some serious racing and several tough qualifying rounds to get through. As ever it was an exciting challenge.

I started my fitness-training regime during the winter months – you need to be very fit to ride a speedway bike at full tilt for five races, three or four times a week – but I always felt that there was an added benefit from fitness training as it sharpened up my mind and helped me to focus on winning. I did a lot of weight training, and while I was working out I would also be concentrating on winning. In my gym, where all the focal points were for the various exercises I was doing, I had written on the wall or ceiling 'First place,' and that was what I focused on while I was training. I felt it was a constant reminder, a subliminal message linked to exercise – it helped to get the most out of me.

I drew Sheffield for my British Semi-Final – my first Individual World Championship qualifying round hurdle. Sheffield was one of my favourite venues and I finished in a comfortable second place behind Les Collins. Then it was on to where the going gets tough: the British Final at Coventry. I felt that I had successfully exorcised my demons from this place the previous year. Having said that, it was an incredibly hard meeting to get through and really does sort the men out from the boys and, consequently, British Champion was quite a prestigious title – but one that was not going to me that year. Instead it went to Steve Bastable, who was crowned British Champion after a run-off with the Halifax duo of Kenny Carter and John Louis. I finished with a comfortable qualifying score of 10 points, which meant I was through to the next round.

In 1981 the FIM introduced a new qualifying round called the Overseas Final. This was largely to increase the number of qualifiers from the American round, as up until this point the Yanks had only two qualifiers progressing from their national qualifying round. But with the new Overseas Final, America's allocation was increased to four. It was staged at White City, which saw the Brits meet up with not only the Americans, but also the Australian and New Zealand contingent. On my old hunting ground at White City, I finished in a very comfortable second place with 13 points behind the winner Dave Jessup, who was on top form again.

But then it just got a bit tougher as we travelled over to Denmark for the Intercontinental Final in Denmark's back yard, Vojens. As often happens at Vojens it was raining the day of the Intercontinental Final. Ole Olsen had done all he could to keep the rain off the track, but unfortunately for us riders it was pouring down and really the meeting should not have been on. But Ole cajoled us into riding after long debates about the importance of the meeting and how it would be a lottery – and that was exactly what it was. Fortunately I pulled out the right ticket and got myself through this round to qualify for the World Individual Speedway final at Wembley Stadium. This would be my third Individual World Final appearance and my first at Wembley. My team and I were in a euphoric mood – we were off to Wembley.

My form had been good all year and I was building on the success I had had in the previous year. I was a regular choice for England and we were defending the World Team Championship. We had battled through the qualifying rounds for the final, which was in Germany at a town near Munich called Olching. This was a fantastic race track, although like a lot of the continental tracks it was flat. It didn't have any banking on the corners, which helps racing off the inside line. What this track did have though was plenty of dirt, which did help with the racing if you were brave enough!

There were some changes to the England team from the previous year. Peter Collins was taking his year off and Michael Lee was suffering from some illness and had gone to Spain to recuperate. The team was myself, Dave Jessup, Kenny Carter, John Davis and reserve Gordon Kennett. Michael Lee's absence was going to be a big gap to fill.

Events were set to conspire against us, though. In order to win any sporting event at the highest level you have to be at your best and firing on all cylinders. But without Michael we were a bit disjointed and Gordon Kennett – whose form at Eastbourne had been good – had been brought in at the last minute. Unfortunately our team manager, Len Silver, was only due to get to the track a few hours before the start of the meeting as he was preparing the speedway track for the Wembley World Final.

To make matters worse, he missed the ferry to Germany and nearly ended up with a reckless driving charge as he ignored a ferry official as he desperately forced himself on board a second ferry. In the end he arrived just before the start of the meeting to take over from travel organiser Tony Francis who had been standing in for him. I don't think any of this helped our title defence.

As it happened the Danes were in the ascendant, and saw our weakness as the perfect opportunity to start their climb up the ladder. Denmark put in a first-class performance to win with 36 points, leaving England with 29 points and battling against the hosts Germany, who scored a credible 28 points. The USSR made up the numbers with just 3 points. There was some consolation for me in that only I dropped 1 point, to Hans Nielsen, to finish with 11. This meeting also produced one of my most memorable rides that typified my 'never say die, it's never over till it's over' approach to racing.

Heat twelve looked like Denmark had got it sewn up. I wanted to make sure that we didn't let the Germans beat us for the second-place spot. Erik Gundersen was on the favoured inside gate, while I was on gate two with top German Egon Muller on gate three and Valeri Gordeev had the outside. Erik made a good start off the inside and I tailed him around turns one and two as Muller, with his track knowledge, rounded the pair of us as we hit the back straight and tore away from us like he was on a different planet.

I tried a wider line than Erik on turns three and four, but only succeeded in losing more ground. As we started the second lap, I was running a bad third with Muller steaming away with it. I tracked Erik's line for the next lap, but still made no ground. By the third lap, I was nearly the length of the straight behind the race leader, Muller, and half the straight behind Erik. I decided to venture into unknown territory and take a wider line into some deep dirt – now we were getting somewhere!

I found something out there to work with, and my engine bit into the dirt and the traction nearly pulled my arms out. I caught Erik up within half a lap and by the time we started the last lap I had passed him, and caught Egon on the back straight resting on his laurels. As I crossed the line for the win, I had pulled out forty yards on Muller to beat him by the same length as I was behind him as we started the third lap. I have watched this race many times on the ITV coverage, and it is the only time I have heard Dave Lanning struggling for words. If you like racing, it's worth a look. I have an oil painting that was commissioned for my testimonial meeting and it is a stunning and imposing picture that was unwittingly taken from a photograph of that race – it is something I treasure and the photograph appears on the front of this book.

My form was good as we led up to the Wembley date and I had justified my confidence that I could be a contender in this World Final. My team of Ged, Steve, my wife Jackie and myself had an expectant air that was going to be dealt a severe blow. The 1981 World Final, won by Bruce Penhall, and considered to be one of the best Individual World Finals ever, turned out to be one of the worst times of my life. Whatever the reasons were for why I performed so badly and scored only 5 points can be debated and disagreed or agreed upon, but to give such a poor performance compared to great anticipation of something far, far better than what was delivered, was incredibly hard to deal with. I had dealt with disappointment before, but this was not going to be shrugged off that easily – maybe I felt I had dealt with my quota of disappointments and this was one that just sneaked up on me? I think the truth was I was embarrassed at how bad I was. It still riles me now.

After the meeting I was driving away from the venue to our hotel and I was clearly unhappy as I left the Citroen in first gear and screaming in protest under the high revs. Steve Cooney was with me and he remembered that it was best not to say anything due to my disappointment, but as he put it: 'The bonnet had dents in it where the valves were trying to get out!'

For the first time ever I qualified for the British League Riders' Championship at Belle Vue. All the top average riders from each British League team qualify for this meeting, and each team had only one representative. Previously, Peter Collins had always pipped me to represent Belle Vue, but this was a chance to redeem myself at the end of the season. After a tough meeting, it was the lover of the Belle Vue race track Kenny Carter who was the champion. I finished second after a run-off with Shawn Moran.

My second place in the BLRC saw the end of the 1981 season. After another busy year riding in over 100 meetings, myself, Jackie, Emma and Charlotte left for a three-week holiday in Florida for a well-earned rest. While I contemplated my plans for the following year, I had been granted a testimonial in 1982 by Stuart Bamforth for ten years of service at Belle Vue.

Those ten years had flown by, and the last two had been very successful. I had realised a childhood dream by racing for Belle Vue, racing for England, winning a World Championship at team level, performing in race meetings all around the world, racing inside the awe-inspiring Wembley Stadium and qualifing for three World Finals. While all this was great and I was really proud of what I had achieved, as the Florida sun warmed my tired body and limbs and I felt the warm feeling of pride sweep over me as I watched my family, there was still this frustration of unfinished business.

Ten years was significant; a milestone, and while there was much to celebrate, there was still no World Championship. I had the experience and the knowledge; but I was disappointed with my World Final record. For whatever reason I had underperformed on the big night, but I still felt that I could win a World Final.

Stuart Bamforth had developed a taste for speedway racing and, as we started the 1982 season, the rest of the team, like me, felt it was time Belle Vue – after being so close over the last few years – should be League Champions again. Peter Collins was back in the side after a year out of British Speedway, completing what looked like a force to be feared, with myself, Larry Ross, Peter Collins, Louis Carr, Peter Carr, Jimmy McMillan and Peter Ravn. When this team was firing on all cylinders we were awesome.

Current World Champion Bruce Penhall would be defending his title on home soil, the Individual World Final would be staged in Los Angeles in America, and they had already begun their promotion of the event with all their razzamatazz before the 1981 World Final. But when Penhall won the title, their publicity machine went into overdrive.

Like any other World Final, my ongoing quest was to get myself in the line-up and have a crack at the title. My form for Belle Vue was as good as ever, and with PC back in the side and Larry Ross fulfilling the other heat-leader role, we had a strong spearhead; with no weakness in the back-up from the rest of the lads. But it was not going to be plain sailing. My World Final campaign would start at Hackney – where there was no room for error.

NINE

THE PAIN AND THE GLORY

I was laid out on a stretcher in the Hackney Wick Stadium ambulance room. This was the home of the Hackney Hawks, but tonight it was hosting the British Semi-Final of the 1982 World Individual Speedway Championship. A most frightening crash had just happened in heat three, and it involved me. It was always difficult in the early heats from gate four. I had made a good start, but as we went into the first turn I was at the end of a four-rider tussle and I was hit really hard by Rhodesian (now Zimbabwe) rider Mike Ferriera, which sent me completely out of control and heading upright towards the fence.

At Hackney you had very little room for a mistake. I went into the fence, head-first at full speed with the bike behind me. I could feel the tremendous force compress my neck as my crash helmet burst through the wire-mesh fencing. I knew this was a heavy one. I had not suffered concussion, but the pressure my neck had received was giving me cause for concern. As is often the case in heavy crashes you are completely stuffed. But I knew it was a bit more than a heavy bang.

Apparently the track doctor at Hackney would never come out onto the track to assess injuries, he preferred to let the St John Ambulance people do their work and get the injured rider into the ambulance room where he could attend to you.

As he was talking to me in the ambulance room, the implications of not competing in this meeting were just too hard to accept. I would do whatever it took to qualify for the next round, which was the British Final. My target was to qualify for the World Final in America – a further two rounds after the British Final. I gave the doctor all the right answers, as he needed to believe I was fit to ride. I thought that if I could just rest here for a while, I would be okay. Ged was looking at me, knowing I was in trouble. We both knew that I was in the rerun as it was all four riders back. But we also both knew that I couldn't make that – I was in trouble.

By this time, about ten minutes after the crash, my neck had completely seized up and the muscles were stiffening up like my body was protecting a problem. I asked Ged if my bike was okay. 'Nothing we can't deal with,' came the answer. I told him that my neck was a problem but I wasn't going to tell the doctor because he would stop me from riding. He gave me the 'are you sure about this?' look. Fortunately my next heat after heat one wasn't until heat eight, which gave me about twenty minutes to half an hour to prepare myself mentally for one of the most difficult and, probably, the most stupid things I have ever done.

I have stated previously that I genuinely approach semi-finals with the intention of doing just enough to qualify. Just enough to qualify from this situation was going to test how much the World Championship really meant to me. Ged and I discussed the situation as I lay on the stretcher in the ambulance room. I had four rides left. Eight points will usually be enough to get you through as the top eight out of sixteen progress to the British Final. Easy. All I had to do was get second places in each race – minimum.

I got myself upright at about heat six to prepare myself for my second heat. The pain was really bad; my neck had completely seized and would not move at all. It was like a stiff neck, but 100 times worse! At that stage I didn't even think about what the problem was, as long as I could stand up and put my helmet on this neck problem wasn't going to stop my World Final quest. I rode in the meeting and I scored 8 points. It was a very strange feeling as I rode as gently and as fast as I could, but not once did I move my neck – it was completely rigid. I knew at the time that I should not be doing it, that another accident in that condition would have been incredibly dangerous but, most importantly, I had qualified for the next round.

As you can imagine, when I woke up the following day I was in a mess. I couldn't get out of bed at first and I could not lift my head off the pillow. I had to roll my body out of bed and finally lift my head up with my hands to stand upright. I went straight to my own doctor, who gave me a quick once over and decided I had damaged the muscles and gave me a collar to wear for a couple of weeks. I didn't ride for fifteen days, then I came back and rode with what I thought was a stiff neck for a few more weeks. I would only wear my collar at night and when it was aching.

A few years later in 1988, I had a serious accident at Wolverhampton where I suffered concussion and swallowed my tongue. Swift action from the track doctor saved it from being a more threatening problem. However, I was taken to the hospital out of routine although I was feeling okay. Again out of routine, the hospital doctor had my head and neck X-rayed. He stuck the X-ray on his light screen to study it. 'When did you break your neck?', he asked. 'I haven't,' I replied 'Yes you have,' he said. He showed me on the X-ray where one of the vertebrae had repaired itself. 'It is clear from this, Mr Morton, that, at some time, you have broken your neck.'

My short rest after my British Semi-Final at Hackney was followed by a need to get into some serious racing. Onto the British Final: a hurdle that I cleared to take me into the Overseas Final. This was staged on one of my favourite hunting grounds: White City, London. But nothing worked right for me on the day and I was devastated to be eliminated at that stage – no American World Final for me.

It was a day that saw Bruce Penhall lose some favour with the British fans when, in heat nineteen, observers said he appeared not to try in a race that included three of his American colleagues – his actions of finishing at the back meant more Americans could qualify for the next round. It caused a bit of a furore, but I wasn't really bothered about all the fuss. Having scored only 5 points it didn't affect me and I was wallowing in my own disappointment.

England had also been eliminated from the World Team Cup at Vojens, giving way to Denmark and America at the Intercontinental stage. There was only one competition left for me to get some honours out of this season – we had to win the British League title. I had never won this and I was feeling a strong desire to achieve this at least once in my career. We had been close a few times and so I knew it wasn't easy or a matter of course.

Stuart Bamforth was proving to be a passionate manager and walked out on us at Wimbledon as we lost, 38-40, in a meeting that perhaps we should have won. Tensions were running high with Bammy feeling the frustrations and he had a big row with most of the team and stormed off threatening to quit. I chased after him, realising that if he walked out now and went home it would create a rift within the team between him and some team members and ruin the work he had done. The team had great respect for him, but too much pride can undo a lot of good work. I spent twenty minutes in the car park reasoning with him that he should come back. Did he want to win the league or not? Knowing all the time that that was what his outburst was all about, I knew this team could do it, but really not without Bammy because he topped up the drive and passion needed to complete the job. I convinced him that he had to ride this sort of setback and deal with it in a different way.

Something changed; we had an horrendous performance at Sheffield on 29 July, losing 50-27, which was incredibly poor for us. Bammy must have decided to take the bull by the horns and try a different tack. He summoned us all to a meeting and read the riot act. Anyone who was not up for winning this league should leave now. It was not a frustrated loss of temper, it was a controlled passionate and frank talking to, a bit Churchillian.

But it did the trick, as the Belle Vue team didn't lose another match until 17 October, and that was a challenge against Halifax after we had clinched the British League title at Reading, which saw us win in a hard-fought 40-38 battle. Belle Vue had won the league for the first time in eleven years, and it was the first time for me, having joined the year after they last won. Stuart later paid me this compliment in *Speedway Star*: 'He has been very helpful and an excellent captain. He's given excellent advice from the start, and acts as mediating force to keep us all together.'

Winning the league was some consolation for my exit from the World Championship. I had a hard-working team of people working on my testimonial fronted by my fan-club secretary Linda Cairnes, and my manager Tony Francis. They worked hard arranging the events throughout the year, leaving me to get on with my racing.

Speedway can be very dangerous and the risks were made all too clear in 1982 when American Denny Pyeatt and Australian Brett Alderton were killed in action. In both cases, memorial meetings were hastily arranged and I raced in Alderton's, which was staged at his home track of Milton Keynes.

Milton Keynes was a National League track and the line-up for this meeting was a big draw as it gave the supporters a chance to see some of the top international riders of the day. I was one of those top riders, but let me tell you, do not let it go to your head as you can soon be put firmly in your place by your public.

During this meeting, I was in the riders' standing area for watching the racing with Phil Crump and a couple of the American lads, Bobby Schwartz and Bruce Penhall. The four of us were watching a race and chatting. In the supporters' enclosure next to where we were standing was a supporter by the fence, and he was shouting 'CHRIS! CHRIS! CHHHRRRIS!' It was clear he wanted me, but I was watching a race and planned to go to him after it had finished. However, having not got the result he wanted he tried again: 'CHRIS! CHRIS! CHRIS! CHHHRRRIS!' I looked over to acknowledge him and saw that he had an autograph book, so I mouthed 'in a minute'. I carried on watching the race, then after a few seconds I heard 'CHRIS! CHRIS! CHHHRRRIS!' I had already acknowledged him so I just carried on watching. The race finished and straight away I heard: 'CHRIS! CHRIS! CHHHRRRIS!' Always happy to oblige, I walked over to him to sign his autograph book. He thrust it at me and as I went to sign it he said: 'No, I don't want yours. Will you get me Bruce Penhall's autograph?' Having been firmly put in my place I did as I was asked.

Another extremely exciting and controversial World Final was staged in Los Angeles on 28 August 1982, which saw a race between Bruce Penhall and Kenny Carter that caused endless debate. And I will put my 'rider's view' in the pot.

In order for me to make my point I will go back to an incident during the 1973 World Final that saw a little recognised injustice occur, or in my opinion it was an injustice. The World Final was staged at Katowice, Poland and the eventual winner was an unknown Pole, Jerzy Szczakiel, after defeating Ivan Mauger in a sensational run-off. The outcome of this World Final may have been different if the slightly lesser known Russian, Grigori Chlynovski had been dealt with less harshly. Grigori was having a storming World Final and looked in great shape as he met up with the Polish hero, a young Zenon Plech in heat nineteen. At this point I must make it clear that as this is a World Final hard riding is expected. Not necessarily dirty riding, but hard riding where no quarter is asked or given. In World Finals riders do not want to give up their position, even when they know it is lost. Zenon Plech was leading the race for a couple of laps while Chlynovski was all over his back wheel looking for the break.

As they exited the corner onto the back straight of the last lap, Zenon Plech left a gap and Chlynovski seized the opportunity and got alongside Plech on the inside. As he passed him they drifted towards the fence. Chlynovski closed the gap and, from my riders standpoint, Zenon Plech knew the gap would be closed. But as he desperately did not want to give up his winning position, he did not yield and drove himself hard into the fence, and predictably came off in an untidy fashion.

Now this may have been six of one and half a dozen of the other, but as a racer I know that Zenon Plech made a racing decision not to yield even though he knew he was on a loser. This all happens very quickly, but I can also tell you that as a highly adrenalin-charged and motivated sportsman, your reaction to all this is electric. So, whereas it may look like a rider is brought down, he has more than likely made a choice to stay and keep going. Incidents where riders are brought down and given no choice are clear – this was not one of them. As you can imagine the Poles were in uproar as one of their own had seemingly crashed because of the Russian. It was a highly emotional scene and unfairly, I believe, Grigori Chlynovski was excluded from the re-run and this wrecked what was up to then a good World title attempt.

In the final analysis, after many arguments and a long wait, the referee came to a strange conclusion. He gave first place to Peter Collins, who was third at the time of the incident, excluded Chlynovski, and gave second place to Plech, who was battling with Chlynovski for first place. Had Plech won he would have been in a run-off with Szczakiel and Mauger, or had Chlynovski won, he would have been in the run-off instead of Plech. The referee was a West German called George Transpurger and his handling of the final was not good at all. My main point is that although it is not always clear, and riders sometimes appear to be brought down, very often the fallen rider had a choice but he just didn't want to give it up.

This brings me to the Bruce Penhall and Kenny Carter incident at the 1982 World Final. This is a higher-profile situation, as both riders throughout this race were at it with each other and it was as tough and cut-throat a race as you will ever see. When Kenny finally came off he didn't want to give it up and made a choice to keep going, knowing that Bruce was not going to give him the room – he kept going until he ran out of track. Although the Kenny and Bruce incident was a bit tougher, it was a similar situation with opposite decisions. I feel that the Chlynovski and Plech decision was wrong, but the Penhall and Carter decision was right. Bruce Penhall went on to successfully defend his World crown to become the 1982 World Champion, but then shocked the speedway world by announcing his retirement from the sport to embark on a career in showbiz – and getting himself a part as an American motorcycle cop in the TV series *CHiPS*.

Having missed out on the 1982 World Final I was keen to continue my quest in 1983, with the World Individual Speedway Final being staged for the first time in Germany at a little-known place called Norden. As usual, the slate was wiped clean at the start of the World Final campaign that saw all the participating countries hold their domestic qualifying rounds to slowly but surely reduce the qualifiers from approximately 1,000 speedway riders around the world to just sixteen to compete in the World Final.

My first round, the British Semi-Final, was at Leicester. I routinely got myself through this round with a steady 10 points – I say routinely but this plays down how it can be a fine line between qualifying or not. With only the top eight out of sixteen qualifying, it only takes one engine failure for it to start to get tight. So although these meetings were approached with the expectancy of getting through, nothing was left to chance.

I was riding well for Belle Vue and we were, of course, defending British League champions. As the title holders all the teams wanted to beat us and with a name like Belle Vue, teams did lift their game when we were in town, and we had some great battles with the Midlands clubs Cradley Heath, Wolverhampton and Coventry. This tough club racing was good for keeping you on form for the higher profile international and World Final calendar. Having got through to another British Final it meant that I had three more extremely hard meetings to end up in the last sixteen at Norden. As is tradition, the British Final was in early June. In 1983 it was 1 June.

As always, the first priority at a British Final was to get one of the eight qualifying places with an eye on the chance to take the title if it should present itself. After two rides I was safely applying my qualifying formula, having secured two second places. Like all British Finals this meeting was cut-throat, with no riders dominating and everyone dropping points.

As I went into my third ride – which was the last one before the interval – the riders in this race were the last four to complete their third rides and, consequently, it was the first real indication of who the winners and losers would be. Therefore, out of a possible 9 points, the highest anyone had scored so far was 6. As I began my preparations for this important race, I had scored 4 points and knew that a win would put me on 7. My opponents were John Davis – he could reach 7 as well – former British Champ Malcolm Simmons (who had 3 points) and Sean Willmott, who had just 1 and was desperate for points if he was going to qualify.

This was a pivotal race in many ways and I let myself sniff the title opportunity. I was off the unfavoured gate two starting position, but I wouldn't let that bother me as the chances were that Mavis (John Davis) would make the start, but I knew that I could outwit him on the track. I had decided that, one way or another, if I was really going to have a chance at the World title this was the sort of situation where titles were won and lost. A win in this heat was not the real test; the real test would be how I responded to the pressure of being in the driving seat with two rides left.

As expected, Davis did make the start with Simmo alongside him. As we exited the second turn, I was in third and eager not to let either of them get away. I passed Simmo and then set about Mavis. I managed to get some drive off the fourth bend and closed on JD as he crossed the line for the start of lap two. Davis positioned himself mid-track, but I had the momentum and the power to surge around the outside of him as we came off the second turn. From then on I just kept my head down and screwed it on. I felt good, my bike was fast, and there was no way that anyone was going to catch me.

With that heat-twelve victory under my belt, I was now at the top of the leader board with 7 points. But I had three riders snapping at my heels on 6 points – Davis, Dave Jessup and Simon Wigg. Jessup, though, was out of the running after a crash with PC in his third ride that saw him taken to hospital with a shoulder injury. The very reason why these meetings are so tough caught me out in my bid for the British title when I faced Andy Grahame – the defending champion – who had only scored 4 points and was desperately looking for a win in his fourth ride. He got it by beating me into second place, leaving me with 9 points after four rides. I had to battle my way through to second, passing Les Collins and Gordon Kennet and, although I got close to Andy on many occasions, he just had the edge. If only I had had another lap! Nonetheless, I had to be content with 2 points from that race.

My fifth and last ride was in heat twenty – the last race of the meeting – so I would know exactly what was needed. I had managed to hold onto my slender 1-point lead, but as the final round of races unfolded before my eyes it quickly became apparent what would be required to win the British Championship. Grahame had won his final outing to bring his final tally to 10 points. Michael Lee had recovered from a poor opening ride and easily won the penultimate race to finish with 11 points. I had 9 and needed a win to clinch the title, but I faced two very tough riders who were looking for points.

Kenny Carter had been on formidable form all night and, but for a surprise last place in his third ride, he could have been level or ahead of me. If Kenny beat me and I was second it would force a three-man run-off for the title with the two of us and Lee. Simon Wigg, who had suffered from mechanical problems, needed the win to get in the top eight and qualify for the next stage. The meeting reserve, Kevin Hawkins, came in for the injured Jessup. This was a tough race, and my opponents were not going to make it easy for me because they all had something to gain. I was off gate four and this really was a test of my resolve. I knew this was the biggest pressure test that I had had for some time. Not only did I have to make the start, but I also had to clear my rivals and stamp my authority on the first turn. If I didn't make a good start, I was sure that I would be shoved wide. So I knew how important the gate would be as I felt that I would not get another chance to pass the in-form Kenny.

I made just the start I wanted and out of the corner of my eye I noticed a bit of trouble as I rounded the first corner. I hit the back straight only to see the red lights come on to stop the race… all four back! Having passed the test I had to do it all over again! I gathered myself, thinking: 'Concentrate and keep focused, win and I will be British Champion.' I wanted it; it was in my grasp and I wasn't going to let this go. I made another magnificent start and gave it my all for four laps to become British Champion. What meant far more to me was the fact that I had successfully delivered in the face of a very important physiological test that was both internal and external. I had not dominated the meeting, so I had to go and get it and make it mine. At the time I did feel that I was the in-form rider, but to win such a prestigious title was one of the highlights of my career. I had beaten the best that Britain had to offer, and when you look at the riders that didn't qualify from that round, Dave Jessup, Gordon Kennett, Simmons and Wigg, you can see how hard these meetings at Brandon were. In *Speedway Star's* match report they said: 'Everyone must have been delighted for Chris Morton, the most genuine British racer of his generation.'

Although I felt that I was on form, the England team manager Wally Mawdsley did not pick me for the World Pairs and I was disappointed. At the time I felt it was because I had a disappointing night during the Third Test at Poole against the USA. I had only scored 3, but I had finished as England's top scorer in the first two Tests at Wimbledon and Swindon.

That was a great series and England won 3-2 after a tremendous final Test at Sheffield. It was a fantastic meeting in front of a huge crowd and I remember it being a match that was talked about for the rest of the season. America had taken the initiative in heat two and, after the sixth race, they had established a 6-point lead. We clawed our way back to level the scores by heat nine, and I managed to swoop inside Dennis Sigalos to win heat fourteen and put us 2 points in front. With three heats to go we had a slender 2-point lead. But although I managed to keep Bobby Schwartz behind me, I couldn't find a way past John Cook and this put the Yanks level with us on 48 points with just two heats remaining.

Neil Collins, who was the fourth Collins brother, teamed up with Carter to score our first 5-1 over Sigalos and Lance King. Then PC and Mike Lee registered the same score over the Moran brothers, Shawn and Kelly, to round off a dramatic win. It was particularly satisfying, not only because of the last-gasp way that we grabbed the victory, but also because America had completed a clean sweep of all the major trophies in 1982.

It was while I was away riding for England that Shawn Moran broke the track record at Hyde Road. He was standing in for me while I raced in Abensberg in a World Team Cup qualifier and it had been set during a Knock-Out Cup match against the Halifax 'Flukes'. At the time the record was held by Hans Nielsen at 69 seconds. When I first started to go to Belle Vue as a kid, the record had been set by Peter Craven in 1958 at 69.9 seconds (for the purists, it was actually calculated at 69 and four-fifths) during a match race against Barry Briggs. This stood for twelve years until Ivan Mauger had reduced that slightly, in late October 1970, to 69.6 seconds. Peter Collins then lowered it to 69.4 seconds on 31 May 1975 and then, over a year later, he cut 2.4 seconds off the record to lower it to 67.0 seconds. That was the way it stayed until the track was reshaped before the 1983 season.

During the close season of 1982/83, Hyde Road was allocated the Overseas Final of the World Championship, which was an FIM event. Therefore, changes were made to the stadium to make sure that it came up to FIM standards. Among these was the reshaping of the inner line of the track and the drainage system. Later new lights were to be added and there was also talk of Belle Vue holding the World Final in the future as Wembley was no longer an option.

This did not affect the length of the circuit, which remained at 382 metres (415 yards), but the width had been narrowed slightly. However, someone had decided to wipe the track-record slate clean – although in reality PC's record still stood. So during our opening meeting of the season against Cradley Heath, I set a new track record of 69.8 seconds, but it only stood a week before Hans Nielsen claimed it by scorching around in 69.0 seconds.

In this match against Halifax, Hans Nielsen's record was equalled four times and then finally beaten in heat thirteen by Shawn Moran, a Belle Vue specialist. He set a new record of 68.8 – shaving off two-tenths of a second. The Belle Vue track was not easily giving way to the progress of machinery. It was clear it was throwing down a challenge.

As I walked around the track on 29 July I considered it to be well prepared for a record attempt. It was not grippy all over – if a rider wanted an easy ride he could find one – but he would be unlikely to win. If a rider picked the right line though, some fast racing was on the cards. This prospect was enhanced by the fact that we were staging the prestigious Northern Riders' Championship and Moran was the defending champion. Only riders contracted to the northern teams could participate and this meant that the field included my brother, Kenny Carter, Doug Wyer and Shawn Moran as well the top Aces' riders – and fast racing was illustrated by the opening three races.

Heat one was won by Peter Collins in 68.4 seconds, taking four-tenths off Shawn Moran's time of 68.8; Kenny Carter, another Belle Vue specialist, went out in heat two and won in 67.4 – taking a full second off Peter Collins' new record. My challenge seemed to be a chance to get around in the quickest time I had ever done, but Kenny's time of 67.4 seemed a tall order. I gave heat three everything I could, using all my knowledge of ten years of racing and ten years of watching at this fantastic race track, and it rewarded me well as I won heat three in 66.4 seconds. Amazingly I took a full second off Kenny Carter's stunning marker in the previous heat. Furthermore, I had taken six-tenths of a second off the time set by Peter Collins during his championship-winning year back in 1976. There was no disputing the fact that I was the fastest rider around Belle Vue. I went on to win the meeting, but far more significant was that one of my greatest challenges had been achieved. I was the Belle Vue track-record holder.

The track record at Hyde Road is one that will never be beaten, since they knocked it down and put a bloody car auction there. The final programme from Hyde Road reads: 'Track Record: Chris Morton and Erik Gundersen 66.4 seconds.' Although I would have preferred that the track had been able to stay open for the track record to have been a target, I do feel a strong sense of pride in that I hold the track record at the old Belle Vue – the best speedway track in the world, and to hold it jointly with Erik just swells the honour. Erik equalled the record, about a year after I had set it, at a Northern Riders' Championship. Very often tracks where records are broken are accompanied by complaints that a track is either too rough or too grippy, but that is why records get broken because tracks with grip take a bit of riding. So you have to adopt a more aggressive approach or the bike will be difficult to ride. It's not supposed to be easy. It is one of my most valued possessions that can never be beaten, only equalled – well done Erik!

As British Champion I made hard work of qualifying through to the World Final at Norden, being the last qualifier at both the Overseas Final at Belle Vue and the Intercontinental Final at White City. I felt there was a need for some starting tuition in order to improve my gating technique. I went straight to the top: who better than Mr Ivan Mauger?

I was very grateful that Ivan was willing to give me the time. Leading up to the World Final we had a few sessions at Belle Vue. My gating saw an improvement at club level, but carrying it through to the World Final would be the real test. One of the most noteworthy comments Ivan made during our gating sessions that gave an insight into his approach was: 'You either have to be scientific in your approach to gating, or cheat!' He wasn't being flippant, as you only have to watch some of the races from the early seventies when rolling at the start was rife.

But the reason Ivan was so good was that he made starting a skilful scientific art. He was masterful at using rolling techniques, coupled with anticipation, sometimes psychologically taking control of the start and the referee. All this linked with his natural ability to get the bike to drive forward from the start would often see him more than a bike length ahead of his opponents as he entered the first turn. Ivan had many tricks and techniques up his sleeve that he would bring out and use, whatever was appropriate for the time.

I was not averse to anticipating or rolling. I was just crap at it! So I tried to be more scientific, keep it simple. My brother, Dave, was a good trapper. He was a master of anticipation, often knowing how long each referee would tend to hold the tapes for after the green light had come on, and it would go something like this: 'Stay back from the tapes, green light comes on, move slowly forward counting 1, 2, 3, GO!' Using this method he was very often successful, although sometimes he would have to duck under the tapes. Occasionally – and some-times very occasionally – he would break the tapes and get excluded. I always had two issues with this method. One: I was not very good at it, and two: break-ing the tapes at club level I could live with, but in qualifying rounds it could spell the end of the road, so I decided to work on the science. It would not be long, as the sport progressed into the 1980s, until we would see the starting procedure cleaned up, rolling would become a thing of the past and touching the tapes would result in an exclusion.

Germany had taken some stick for staging such a high-profile event as the World Final, that they had campaigned hard for, at the relatively unknown venue of Norden. For many of the international riders who had qualified for the final at Norden, this would be the first and last time they would ride there – which was an illustration of its obscurity as a World Final venue. To be fair to Germany, a lot of money had been pumped into the stadium and the whole event. However, it was never going to live up to the potential that some of the other stadiums that Germany had to offer as prestige venues.

But this was the first indication of what was to come. Wembley had already closed its doors to speedway racing and the sport in Britain was rocked to its very foundations by the news. England was due to stage the 1984 World Final, and the prospect of it being anywhere other than the Empire Stadium was just too odd to contemplate. The Speedway Control Board manager, Dick Bracher, was exploring all sorts of different venues from White City to Hampden Park – although the prospect of holding the World Final at Belle Vue was, for me, most appealing. Like many I was disappointed with the choice of Norden as the venue as it sent out the wrong message about the sport. It was, financially, a safe bet, but it missed an opportunity to promote the sport in a national stadium. I know there will be many reasons why it had to be there, but I do not believe that if given a choice anybody except the stadium owners would say 'let's have the World Final at Norden'.

I was pleased with my build-up to this event and my form was okay, although I was aware I would have to lift my game. I had five rides to get it right. I started strongly with a second place in my first ride after some hard and tough riding; I felt that if I created the right breaks I was riding well enough to pose a threat.

After a disappointing second ride, running third, I came back with a classic four-lap battle with New Zealander Mitch Shirra and took the win to put me on 6 points – my best position to date in a World Final at the interval stage. My desire for a World Individual final appearance to be proud of was ruined as I only scored 1 point from my last two rides – local hero Egon Muller eventually won the final.

I was bitterly disappointed with my own performance, but you become immune, somehow resistant to the emotional pain it can inflict by reserving the right to use the experience to stoke up the fires of determination. After the meeting, Norden was the host of a grand celebration as Egon Muller had just been crowned Individual World Speedway Champion for 1983.

Having enjoyed some German hospitality we had just left the reception and were making the eight to ten-mile journey back to our hotel in my Ford Transit van. I had a full van: myself, Jackie, mechanic Ged, daughters Emma (aged six) and Charlotte (nearly three), Peter Collins and his wife Angie. Ged had offered to drive but I said I was okay and was sat in the driving seat. The road back to the hotel was through the countryside around Norden and it became very dark as we drove away from the lights of the town to our country hotel. After about five miles we came to a sign that seemed to indicate a bend in the road, but as we neared the bend it was in fact a t-junction. Frankly, I was going too fast and I realised that my braking was not going to be good enough and we were going straight on. I quite calmly said: 'We are going in the field.'

I was wrong, because before the field was a standard German countryside ditch, which was about six feet deep and ten feet across. That was where we landed, nose down at the bottom of this ditch. Fortunately, by the time we got there, I had scrubbed off most of the speed so it was just a sudden jolt as we hit the banking on the opposite side of the ditch. Everyone was all right, but we were in a pickle. The van was at a forty-five-degree angle down this ditch with the rear wheels just about at the top of the ditch – it was going nowhere without some serious assistance.

Therefore, we had a discussion between the men! It was decided that PC and I would ride back to town on my speedway bike to get some help. Unloading a bike out of the back of a Transit at forty-five degrees is a bit of a task, but we managed it after a bit of huffing and puffing and effing and jeffing. We also retrieved the fuel can, torch and the toolbox to take the right-hand footrest off so we could negotiate the right-hand bends on our quest for much-needed assistance. Ged filled up the fuel tank as we did not know how far a full tank would take us, and we also planned to take another fuel can with us.

As we were getting ready to start on our intrepid mission, we saw a light in the distance. This could be someone with excellent timing, our knight in shining armour. It was better than that. It was the American Cavalry in the shape of Lance King and his army of fine men, with special guest star John Wayne! You may think I'm joking, but it was speedway's equivalent, the one and only Bruce Penhall – Bruce was a match for John Wayne as part of the Cavalry on this occasion.

They took over the situation and hooked some straps to the back of my van from the back of Lance's van, and he took the strain with his Transit while the rest of us got down in the ditch and pushed with all the grunt we could muster. Among the gang in the ditch were Bruce Penhall who, as the defending World Champion, had been a special guest at the after-meeting proceedings. In true American Cavalry style he was still in his white suit and he was in there with the boys, with all the damp, mud and splatter. After two or three attempts it was dragged and shoved out of the ditch to great celebration. We were all incredibly grateful and this book gives me a great opportunity to say thank-you in style to Lance King, Bruce Penhall and the rest who were on duty that night. Although PC and I were looking forward to the ride into town on my speedway bike I think, with the benefit of hindsight, it turned out for the better.

Although our situation looked quite grim, with a poor World Final and a smashed-up van in need of repair, the situation was about to improve for at least one of my crew. It was clear that we would need at least a radiator for the van if we were going to get home, so the following morning we set ourselves the task of finding a Ford dealer. On hearing of our plight at breakfast the following morning, Barry Briggs offered the services of himself and his car to drive us around to find our much-needed parts. It really is a credit to our sport the way people rally round in times of need. Barry Briggs was Ged's childhood hero and, although Ged had probably been in his company during our time together, he had never spoken to him. It was like a *Jim'll Fix It* situation for Ged. I got in the back of the car so I could watch as Ged came face to face with his all-time hero. I gathered a whole load of material to tease him with as he relived Briggo's career with a range of 'I remember you winning this' and 'I remember you winning that.' Ged was like a big kid. Briggo was enjoying the self-focused reminiscing as we drove around the suburbs of Norden. By the way, we found a radiator thanks to his help.

England's challenge in the World Team Cup was always going to be a tough one with the final being in Denmark's own back yard, Vojens. It turned out to be too tough; although we took a gallant second place ahead of the USA. So the rest of 1983 had little to offer.

Although British Champion was a big tick in the box, I had experienced a good season for the Aces, finishing at the top of their averages with a figure of 10.30. We relinquished the league title to an impressive Cradley team who we had defeated at the start of the season in the Premiership. We also won the League Cup by defeating Coventry, which went some way to making up for the disappointment of finishing fifth in the table. Furthermore, the Aces had unearthed a most promising rider in the shape of Andy Smith who, at the time of writing, has just rejoined Belle Vue after a long and distinguished career.

Stuart Bamforth was eager to see that the Aces remained one of the top teams in the country. Sadly, Leicester had closed, but this allowed him to snap up one of the great emerging talents of the period in the shape of former British Junior Champion Mark Courtney. Courtney had just completed his second full season in the top flight with Leicester and had overtaken Les Collins at the top of the club's averages. Meanwhile, Louis Carr left and was replaced by another promising rider from Scotland, Kenny McKinna. On the eve of the new season we were being touted as potential League Champions again.

I was keen for a winter's rest to recharge my batteries for the 1984 campaign, which was going to be a very important one for me and England. I always entered into riding for England with a strong sense of patriotism and sometimes felt that I performed better for my country than I did for myself.

As the England squad was put together at the start of the 1984 season, the new England team manager Carl Glover appointed Kenny Carter as captain – a good choice as Kenny's commitment to England was total. Our first meeting for England was against a strong USA side in what was now an annual Test series. As the series progressed, England lost Kenny Carter when he broke his leg riding for his club at Cradley and Dave Jessup took over as captain for the remainder of the Test series – which the USA won 4-1, making England look second best. As my form improved I obviously impressed Carl Glover because he handed over the role of captain of England to me for the Test series against

Denmark, which we won 2-1. To be given the role of captain of your country is an enormous accolade of which I was immensely proud. It was a position I would take very seriously.

Many British League clubs had foreign riders in their teams now and this was to be expected, because Britain was the best speedway league in the world. There was no doubt about it; if you were serious about being an international rider and mounting a challenge for the World Championship then you had to ride regularly in the British League. Naturally these riders became crowd favourites – like Soren Sjosten was to me – but many supporters took to cheering their club riders when they were representing their country – whether it was Denmark or the USA – when they raced against England.

John Davis had already spoken about this and I did so when we defeated the Danes because the national side was under a lot of pressure to get results. We expected to receive the support from the terraces in Britain, especially when we were doing well, but this was not always the case. Denmark were at the top of the tree and this victory was a significant one. Under my captaincy I was disappointed to see so much support on the terraces for the opposition coming from the Brits.

This was a very busy period of the season with international and World Championship engagements coming thick and fast. I was chosen, along with Peter Collins, to represent England in the World Best Pairs event. The qualifier was at Pardubice in Czechoslovakia. Peter and myself had never had this opportunity before and our team riding for Belle Vue had developed into an almost telepathic understanding of each others' riding technique – this was backed up by a strong friendship from being children. We never discussed this event a lot, other than the strategy for the meetings and individual races, but we both had an unspoken understanding that we had an equal and overwhelming desire to lift this title. We qualified from Czechoslovakia by winning the meeting with an unbeaten score to seal our place in the final on 17 June 1984 at Lonigo in Italy.

But before that meeting I had also qualified for the British Final. As the reigning champion I was looking forward to making a successful defence of my title. I had qualified from the semi-final at Poole with 13 points in second place, but in the other semi at Oxford there was a courageous performance that grabbed all the headlines.

Speedway, like other forms of motorcycle racing, has many stories of riders displaying extraordinary courage by defying medical advice and overcoming their injuries to race in the important meetings. Love or him hate him, you had to admire the sheer determination and daring of Kenny Carter. Weeks after breaking his leg he rode in the semi at Oxford with the aid of a special boot, and qualified for the British Final by scoring 8 points. I had some heroics of my own to perform, although far more understated, in that they had longer consequences. In order for you to understand the significance, I need to fast forward to Oswestry Hospital on 8 October 2001.

Mr James Richardson, the orthopaedic specialist at the hospital, was talking to Jackie just after my hip resurfacing operation. He said: 'The operation has been successful. It certainly needed doing, it was in very bad condition.' I was in the recovery room waiting to start my recuperation from this long-awaited major surgery that would return me to a pain-free active life again.

Seventeen years and a couple of months previously, I just had the first sign of a problem – although at the time I didn't realise what the problem was. It was 1984 and Carl Glover, England manager, had been taking some criticism for selecting me for the World Pairs along with Peter Collins because I was not a 'Trapper'. Making starts helps, but speedway racing is over four laps with the winner being the one who passes the chequered flag first! Peter Collins was the title holder as he had raced to victory in 1983 with Carter.

Practice went okay; Lonigo was a track I had always enjoyed racing on. I did, however, have one anxious incident in practice when I hit a hole in the middle of the third and fourth corner opposite the pits end. My left leg was knocked back, sending an excruciating pain down my left thigh. It was so severe and sharp that it took my breath away. I chatted with the track doctor, Gioacchino La Rose, who suggested it was muscular and for the meeting I should strap up my thigh muscle. This sounded like a sensible thing to do.

The following day, the day of the meeting, out of a desperate need to eliminate any possible problems that may stand in the way of PC and myself winning this World Pairs Final, I followed the doctor's advice. I had my whole thigh strapped up with three-inch sticky-backed heavy crepe bandage. Against my better judgement, I just let the doctor, who must have been a masochist, wrap about two yards of this very sticky bandage around my bare and hairy thigh. I thought no more of it, and got myself leathered up ready for action!

Lonigo was a relatively new venue having been constructed just seven years before at a cost of 800 million lire. The town is a wine-growing town and the San Marino Stadium – to give it its official title – was holding a World Championship Final for the first time. Later it would go on to stage other World Championships including the Grand Prix – it has just been returned to the GP calendar after a seven-year absence.

The line up for this event reflected an experienced group of riders. Some of them had yet to show the achievement that would elevate them to greatness, while others had already established themselves among the elite. New Zealand illustrated this point with Ivan Mauger – who needs no introduction – and his partner, Mitch Shirra, who at the time had only one World Final behind him.

Denmark, with Ole Olsen now retired, chose Erik Gundersen and Hans Nielsen, two very fast riders who would go on to dominate the sport for the rest of the decade. The USA had paired double World Pairs Champion Bobby Schwartz and the World Long-Track Champion Shawn Moran – amazingly neither had qualified for a World Individual final at the time. Australia had finished second to us in Pardubice and Billy Sanders and Gary Guglielmi represented them, while Czechoslovakia chose the experienced duo of Ales Dryml and Jiri Stancl. Finally, the hosts were represented by the then-largely unknown Armando Castagna and Armando Dal Chiele. Italy were the final's only weak partnership because of their inexperience that, as the meeting unfolded, would be cruelly exploited by this top-class field.

The Venetian sun beat down on this June day and baked the riders on the long parade. There was no escape from the heat for the capacity 15,000 crowd, but a full house that afternoon gave the event a proper 'World Final atmosphere.'

My own form at the time was pretty good. It couldn't have been better really: I had qualified for the British Final and was leading at the top of the British League Averages, I had scored a paid maximum against Halifax and was relishing my role as England skipper by scoring 11 points as we took the series by beating the Danes at Halifax. The Pairs final was the first meeting in a crazy schedule that saw three big meetings in six days. After this we travelled back to England to ride in the British Final, and then headed to Mariestad, Sweden for a World Team Cup qualifier. It was hectic; there was no room for error, or injury.

As form had gone that year we were not the favourites by a long way, and when PC pulled out of his last two rides at that Test at Halifax because, like me, he had already sent his best machines to Lonigo for this meeting and he was riding his brother Phil's spare bike, most people favoured the Danes or the Americans over us. But what form had not taken into account was history and a need for glory. Other than the issue with my leg giving me some mysterious pain, the practice had gone according to plan for both PC and myself.

One of my mechanic Ged's regrets is that he was not at this final. The reason why not I cannot recall, but for that trip I had on loan Simon Wigg's mechanic Greg Williamson. He was a very competent mechanic and served me well. Before the meeting we discussed tactics between team manager Carl Glover and ourselves. We decided to take whatever starting positions would give the best result as we exited the first and second corners. This worked really well and as the meeting progressed I was finding a line tight on the inside that everybody was missing. PC was gating pretty well off the outside gates, and on most occasions as we hit the back straight we were there in front together.

A crucial heat came for us in heat five when we met Denmark's Erik Gundersen and Hans Nielsen. These guys were on form and had begun the opening race with a 5-1. They made the start on us, and as we hit the first turn I was surprised to see Hans Nielsen rush into the corner and miss the tight run around the inside. Having seen his mistake I was quick to capitalise on it, and made a perfect run around the inside to take the lead as we hit the back straight. Meanwhile PC had been shunted in the first corner and had a battle on his hands. He fought like a demon to overhaul Erik Gundersen, but Hans Nielsen was gone. But we came away from that heat with a first and third, which was what made all the difference in the final analysis.

During our third race, Jiri Stancl put on a determined display and kept the pressure on PC and myself at the front. This was in stark contrast to his opening race in heat one when he trailed off at the back. It wasn't until later that I learnt that the Danes had loaned Jiri one of their Carlisle tyres for the race against us. Our only race without a win was against the in-form Mitch Shirra for New Zealand. Peter and I filled the vital second and third places, but after all the nations had completed four outings we were equal-first with the USA, Denmark and New Zealand with 17 points. Moran had all the journalists scribbling away when he produced a tremendous turn to pass the Aussie duo and join Schwartz at the front. We faced them next.

But before our race with the Americans we knew what we had to do because Nielsen had defeated Shirra and Mauger. The 'Big I' had made a good start but Gundersen was unable to find a way through and they had dropped points to the New Zealanders too.

More importantly, a drawn heat was just the result we needed, because a heat win against the Yanks would give us the advantage. As I came out of the first bend in front, I looked across and PC was there and we sped away for a vital 5-1. The Danes, though, were not going to give in and they too walked away with maximum points over the Americans.

As we entered our last heat against Italy we needed at least a 4-2 to seal the victory. We delivered and crossed the line together to beat Denmark into second place by just 2 points. It was an unbelievable feeling of emotion. I know we both felt that it held a lot more significance over and above winning the World

127

Pairs Final for England: it was also the day two lifelong friends who used to ride on old bangers of motorbikes as kids beat the world. Of course, PC had realised the ultimate dream when he won the World Individual final in 1976, but it was clear this was a very special occasion for us both, as the crowd at Lonigo saw, when these two helmeted figures jumped off their machines at the end of the race and embraced each other with sheer joy.

The meeting went like a dream. The critics were right, I wasn't a trapper, not that day, but I came out of most of the first corners in front with PC alongside me. We understood each others' riding so well we were telepathic. It was, as the Italians say, 'magnifico' and *Speedway Star*'s headline summed it up perfectly when they wrote 'England's Pair of Aces'.

I was now in the showers after the meeting letting the bandage on my thigh get wet. I had a little tug at it before getting into the shower and, realising it was not coming off easily, I decided that getting it wet would help. I finished my shower and sat down to take the bandage off. After ten minutes I had got about an inch off – in considerable pain I might add – or so I thought. Czech rider Ales Dryml ('Officer Dribble') was watching me fart about when he said: 'No No No! Like this!' Immediately, he grabbed hold of this puny inch I had carefully removed, and then ripped another three inches off! I hit the ceiling in absolute agony. Now it's my turn. 'No No No!', I scream. 'Yes Yes Yes', says Ales calmly. I know I really have no choice, so I let him rip this bandage off three or four inches at a time while I'm in excruciating pain, so much so that I have to make him stop halfway to gather myself. I'm no wimp, but this was really painful. Job done; and I actually thank Ales for ripping off all my hairs and, in places, my skin, but what does all this matter anyway? Peter Collins and Chris Morton were the 1984 World Pairs Champions.

Later that year I found that I had a bit more of the same problem, experiencing pain in my leg while riding, and discovered it was my hip joint. An X-ray revealed that my hip had suffered from erosion of the cartilage around the joint, and was already creating a bone on bone reaction, which would cause more and more problems. There was no cure for this condition. Maintaining mobility was my only hope if I was to carry on riding. Life has a strange way of tapping you on the shoulder and saying: 'What are you so pleased about?'

I was on top of the world as the British Final came into view a few days after the World Pairs victory. I had every reason to be confident: my form was good and I was World Pairs Champion. I just needed to get through another British Final and continue my progress to the World Individual final in Sweden. I am sure that speedway, like any other sport, requires confidence. But sport does not allow complacency because there is always someone else waiting to beat you. I say this because complacency is not something I allowed into my psyche with regard to the opposition, but something close to this happened at the British Final and taught me a massive lesson.

Conditions at the British Final were absolutely appalling. The track was not fit to ride on, let alone race on. Any other meeting would have been called off, any other referee would have called it off, but there was pressure on the referee Lew Stripp to get the meeting on. The referee had some very significant support to get the meeting on from Kenny Carter, who had already achieved an outstanding feat by getting to this final with his broken leg in a special cast. Kenny's only focus had been this next round towards the World Final; he was motivated and could see the situation created a chink in his opponents' armour. He was up for it, no one else was.

Lew was trying hard to convince the riders to ride. The discussions started to get heated as Lew wouldn't budge and Kenny was backing him up. It was the usual and often valid argument from the riders that it was extremely dangerous in these conditions, which were only exaggerated by the importance of every point available. At one stage we nearly had a fight between PC and Kenny Carter as we had passed the discussion stage and got to verbal abuse. This was the final straw in a strained relationship that was often described as a feud. The situation was calmed by Lew Stripp, who said 'let's just give it a try', assuring us that if it wasn't fit he would call it off. It was agreed that the meeting would go ahead to the consternation of most of the riders.

I entered into, on reflection, a really stupid mindset that I had never done before. I believed that after a few races it would be called off as conditions were too bad to stage a British Final – how wrong I was. I had never let myself think in this way before, and would never again. I entered my first race intending to give it a go just in case the meeting did go ahead. Unfortunately on the first corner I got completely obliterated by wet shale, all five sets of goggle rip-offs got filled in and I couldn't see a thing and had to pull off.

Convinced that they really could not run a World Championship qualifying event in these conditions I, like many other riders, tried to speak to the referee to get his agreement to stop the meeting if conditions were not acceptable, but he would not speak to anyone and continued with the meeting. I had made an enormous error of judgement and learned a valuable lesson to keep focused on racing. I scored a miserable 5 points and completely blamed myself, but maintain that the meeting should not have been run and the majority of referees would have respected the riders' opinions and the meeting would have been rearranged.

For me, Kenny Carter in this situation was another matter. I have to take my hat off to him for firstly riding in his condition with a broken leg, recognising a way of enhancing his chances, then going out and winning the meeting. I handed over the title without a challenge, from hero to zero in two high profile meetings.

I was incredibly disappointed to be out of the Individual World Championship hunt. My form was good, and I really fancied another crack at Ullevi in Sweden. That opportunity was gone, so I concentrated my efforts at club level, which saw Belle Vue pipped by the successful Ipswich Witches in both the league and the Knock-Out Cup.

As the season drew to a close, I had topped the Belle Vue averages, which meant I had a place in the British League Riders' Championship meeting at Belle Vue. It was a chance to finish what had been a great year – although no Individual World Final appearance – with another individual title that had eluded me so far. This meeting always had a line-up that was the cream of the speedway world, and one that everyone wanted to win. The dominating Danes would be there; current World Champion Erik Gundersen, who had won the title for the first time in 1984 in Sweden, and his biggest rival Hans Nielsen.

The only points I dropped in the meeting were to Erik Gundersen and Hans Nielsen in my second ride where I met both of them together. Erik won with Hans second and me third. Determined to keep my chances alive in what I knew was going to be a meeting that would provide further chances of these two dropping points, I won my next three races and finished with 13 points along with the Danish duo. Therefore, it would be a three-man run-off for the title.

I was off the outside gate with Hans Nielsen next to me off three and Erik was off the inside. In his keenness to make a good start, Erik touched the tapes and got excluded. It was just left to Hans and I to battle it out. As is usual so late on in meetings, the outside line was becoming the line where you would get grip. We both knew the start was crucial to gain domination of the grip on the outside. Hans, being the prolific starter that he was and incredibly hungry for some consolation title after losing the world crown to his great rival Gundersen in Sweden, made the start.

As I expected, he predictably took the outside line right up by the fence believing I would be trapped and have nowhere to go. As he moved off past the normal racing line to block where he believed I would be, I quickly switched back inside him and had to perform a fairly hard and ruthless manoeuvre. As we exited the first corner, I pulled alongside him and dived for the only bit of dirt and drive available and left him no choi0ce but to let me have it. It was then just flat out for the rest of the race to become British League Riders Champion for 1984 – a great way to end a year that saw me become England captain and World Pairs Champion along with my old pal Peter Collins.

TEN

BLOOD, SWEAT AND TEARS

It was late October and it was cold; it had been cold for a good month. King's Lynn at that time of the year can be pretty bleak. It was an open individual meeting with all the top riders, a good line-up including Michael Lee, Billy Sanders, Bo Peterson, Dave Jessup, Dennis Sigalos etc. It was a run-of-the-mill, late-in-the-year kind of meeting. Many riders have a problem called 'vibration white finger' caused by the vibration from a speedway bike through the handlebars. It affects the blood vessels and in the cold they close up, restricting the blood flow to your fingers and turning them white – hence 'vibration white finger'. This was a problem I suffered from quite acutely as the season in England was drawing to a close from late September to the season end in October.

As you can imagine it was difficult to ride with dead fingers, so I had a very simple way of keeping my fingers warm. I had a little tobacco tin three inches square that I would put a little bit of methanol in and light - unlike traditional motorcycles speedway bikes don't use petrol fuel. Methanol, being an alcohol fuel, burns very slowly and is comparatively safe compared to petrol, which is quite volatile. This simple little fire was sufficient for me to keep my white finger under some sort of control.

This was a particularly bitter night and other riders were using methanol, burning in a similar contained and sensible way, to keep warm. With riders huddling around little methanol fires, to an onlooker the scene must have resembled a panoramic view of the soldiers' fires burning in their camps as depicted in that Oscar-winning hit *Gladiator*.

Now Ged, being an inquisitive little mechanic, had noticed that as my little tobacco tin of methanol ran out, the flame would go smaller and smaller into one corner of the tin and finally fade away. I would then put some more in and light it. This had got Ged's mind going. He thought that as the small flame faded away in one corner he could top the tobacco tin up before the flame went out with a quick little tip from the gallon methanol can, and so keep the flame going without having to light it again. He had mentioned his little theory to me a few times that month and I had told him it was a stupid thing to even consider – but what do I know?

Later on in the meeting the rider pitted next to me, Billy Sanders, had fortunately packed up and gone early. It was now the interval and the riders were all hanging around freezing to death, or huddling around little fires to keep warm. My tin was running out with a tiny flame in one corner. Ged saw this as a perfect opportunity to test his theory and he was in there like the wizard's apprentice before I could stop him.

My methanol can was a standard-type tin gallon can, which Ged was now using to top up my little tobacco tin before the flame in the corner finally faded away. It happened just as I and many others would have guessed – his little trick was unsuccessful. As he tipped the planned little bit of methanol into the tin, it generated a mild, although it was slightly alarming to Ged, woofing sound. At first it appeared to have been a sloppy but successful attempt, with just a few little drops of methanol at the side of the tobacco tin on fire – not a problem. My gallon can had about two-thirds left in it, and what Ged soon realised was that the mild woofing sound was the methanol inside the can setting alight. He was basically holding a live bomb! By now he was holding the can at arm's length and starting to panic when basic science took over. As the oxygen inside the can ran out, the can threw up half its contents all over the pit wall and roof like a flame-thrower. Then, in a natural act of panic, Ged dropped the can like you would. Some of the remaining contents then spilled over the floor of the pits. This didn't look good, as a large section of the pits was on fire while the can was lying on the floor, semi-exploding every few seconds as the burning methanol demanded more air.

It may not sound like it, but methanol is a very safe fuel and although the pit area looked like it was on fire it wasn't. As methanol burns slowly at a low temperature it tends to burn out and not set things on fire. Fortunately that was what happened in this case. As the methanol burned out on the wall and ceiling it left nothing burning. We attracted a lot of attention, with all the riders gathering around my twitching fuel can getting themselves warm. Michael Lee congratulated Ged on producing a decent fire for such a cold night. As the final embers died down Martin Rogers came into the pits from the centre green wondering what all the activity was. 'Just keeping warm Martin,' we said, as we stood around a now-little fire. He had no idea that ten minutes earlier his pits were on fire!

Early in the 1985 British speedway season I was, like many others, deeply shocked by the news of the death of Billy Sanders, who was a good friend, a great racer and an excellent ambassador for the sport. Just a week before he took his own life on 23 April, I was the Golden Helmet-holder, having taken it the previous week from Bobby Schwartz. I had to defend it at Ipswich on 18 April, where I lost it to an in-form Billy Sanders. Only a week later the sad news of his death shook the speedway world. Bruce Penhall flew in specially to attend the funeral and gave an emotional speech before a packed audience of mourners. I always enjoyed racing against Billy; I loved my tussles with him around the old Belle Vue and he told me he loved to race around the place. His scores reflected that because he was one of the best visiting riders. He was a big loss to speedway.

The 1985 season saw the World Final return to England. This time it was scheduled to be held at the Odsal Stadium, Bradford. Every Englishman wanted to be there – including me. After coming so close to winning the league in 1984, Belle Vue were hoping to go one better and Stuart spent some serious money on signing Carl Blackbird from Ipswich for £20,000 and Andy Campbell from Exeter for £15,000. Mark Courtney and Peter Carr found themselves moving to King's Lynn and Sheffield.

The league had shrunk as Eastbourne, Exeter, Newcastle, Poole and Wimbledon all elected to join the National League where the costs were not so high. This was the confirmation that many experts had sought; speedway racing in Britain was not such an attractive proposition anymore. With only eleven teams in the top flight, it was the lowest number of teams since the British League was launched in 1965.

Speedway's fortunes were not helped by a very wet summer. I had qualified from the British Final after scoring 12 points at Cradley Heath, but the original staging was postponed due to the inclement weather. When it was restaged a fully fit Kenny Carter retained his British title with a 15-point maximum. I successfully negotiated this round by scoring 8 points and was looking forward to the next round, the Overseas Final, at Bradford – which was also the venue for the World Final.

Bradford was a good racing track. It was a track where you could have a good blast around the outside and most riders enjoyed riding on it. But things just didn't work out for me on the day. I had gone there hoping for a place on the podium but I finished up losing a run-off to Phil Collins for the reserve spot at the Intercontinental Final. I was bitterly disappointed.

Although a World Final place had gone for another year, the World Team Cup Final was being staged in America for the first time. It was being held at the Veterans Stadium, Long Beach and all the reports were that the track was a good circuit. The thought of riding for England in sunny California was very appealing.

I have always enjoyed representing my country and considered it an honour to wear the Cross of St George or the Union Flag. As a sportsman, few things are more fulfilling than standing on the top step as your national anthem *God Save the Queen* is played. The pride you feel as you're standing there as a winner is tremendous.

Therefore, being England captain meant a lot to me and I took the role seriously. John Berry was appointed as the new England manager and I expected he would review the situation and perhaps hand the captain's role back to Kenny Carter, who was appointed skipper prior to breaking his leg. But I found what actually happened a little bizarre as John Berry announced to the squad that he was not nominating a captain. It seemed to me at the time, as the current captain, a poor way of handling a team. I was ready to accept it going to another justifiable member of the squad, but to take it off me and not appoint anyone else made it clear he didn't rate me as a captain or anyone else. I am still not sure whether the idea of not making anyone else captain was a way of trying to soften the blow of taking it off me. Whatever the reasoning, I accepted his decision. Rightly or wrongly I felt I had earned my place as an England World Team Cup rider – providing form justified it. I was disappointed to be put in at the reserve spot for the WTC qualifying event at Bradford. I felt that John Berry lacked confidence in having me in the team, and for whatever reason he did not seem to rate my riding.

In 1982 Berry was briefly joint-England manager with Eric Boocock and during a Test Match against the Americans at Swindon he pulled me out of my scheduled third ride and replaced me with Alan Grahame. I had always gone well round Swindon, and the Yanks were flying that day and were fired up after losing the First Test. At the time his decision didn't feel warranted as I had scored a paid 3 points from my two rides, and I expressed my disappointment to him. We had an exchange of words, nothing serious, just enough for him to display that superior attitude of his. My mechanic, Ged, wasn't very pleased with him either, but I put it behind me and finished the meeting with a paid 11 score. He seemed to have some sort of issue with me. Whether it was about ability or personal, I don't know. But looking back, that small incident at Swindon could have been the start of it.

On a trip to one of the qualifying rounds for the World Team Cup in 1985 we were in Germany. The hotel we had been booked into was a little poor, and there was a better hotel further down the road. A discussion was had and the riders all wanted to move, but we had to wait for John Berry as he was coming later. I felt that we should wait for John to arrive first, but it was decided that leaving a message would be sufficient. What happened after our move was about to prove significant.

We settled into the new hotel and the whole group of riders and mechanics were sitting having a chat when John Berry appeared and aggressively confronted me for moving the team to another hotel without telling him and he went on to say, in his anger, how I was out of order. His approach was, in my opinion, completely unjustified. His outburst may well have been understandable towards the whole team, but to direct it at me was completely wrong. I had not moved us, we had moved, I don't know why it was directed at me – but it seemed to speak volumes. After he went to his room it was discussed between the lads that he was completely wrong to humiliate me in that way. 'What has he got against you?' someone commented, not to mention that he got his facts completely wrong.

Unfortunately for John Berry and consequently for me, being a successful British League promoter does not make you a good England team manager, something that John proved to me on many occasions. I have been fortunate to serve under many England team managers, and through this experience I can say, without doubt, in 1985 John Berry was the worst manager I had ever ridden for. He was a different man to the one I rode for in Australia in 1975/76. His unjustified attack on me in front of not just the other team members, but the team of mechanics and helpers as well, was nothing short of disgraceful. I fully understood his frustration at his team moving hotels that had him struggling to find us, but to launch an attack on me without knowing the truth made it clear I was to be the centre of his frustrations. The truth was that I was suggesting we waited until he arrived, but the rest of the team wanted to move straight away. Moreover, in an attempt to help him find the place, I left the new details with the place we were leaving.

I am not a difficult person to deal with. His general treatment of me I found demoralising and disrespectful. I started from a point of respect for one of the British League's most successful promoters and ended up in a situation where I refused to ride for England as long as Berry was the team manager in order to retain my dignity. His outburst said far more about him and his attitude towards me than it did about the situation. I was not given the chance to defend my World Pairs title as he said I was not a suitable partner for Kenny Carter as we were not on speaking terms. This was not the case at all. He should have tried talking to his riders because I did not have a problem with Kenny; we may have been rivals, but we both rode for England. It was one of the most difficult decisions not to ride for John Berry as it meant not riding for my country, which was one of my passions.

All in all, 1985 was a disappointing year on the international stage, not only for me, but for England too. Kelvin Tatum was England's sole qualifier for the World Final as Carter crashed out of the title chase on a rain-soaked track at Vetlanda in Sweden and broke his leg. Erik Gundersen went on to win his second World title after a three-man run-off with Hans Nielsen and the American, Sam Ermolenko. Furthermore, England was whitewashed 3-0 in the Test series against the USA and were mere passengers in the World Team Cup Final at Long Beach where they finished third behind Denmark and the hosts. I took no pleasure from seeing England so far down the international ladder and I felt confident that we would be back.

However, a new season brought new enthusiasm, and I was keen to get picked for the England team squad and put last year's memories behind me. Eric Boocock, my old team manager at Belle Vue and one half of the managerial duo that orchestrated England's Grand Slam success in 1980, was back. Colin Pratt, Cradley team manager and another ex-international rider, formed the other part of the managerial team and with such experience at our disposal I felt confident that the disappointments and problems of 1985 would be well behind us.

It was very much the start of a turbulent period for British speedway in 1986. The sport's authorities brought in a one-tyre rule for the British League and it was Barum who won the contract to supply the tyres for all British competition. Meanwhile, at FIM events, you could still use one of the other makes such as Dunlop – which many riders preferred. Halifax closed and the team and promotion moved to Bradford's Odsal Stadium, but their initial enthusiasm of having a new track and stadium to race in quickly turned to sadness in May.

As often happens with bad and sad news, you have instant recall as to where you were. On this occasion I was sat at Hilton Park services with my mechanic Ged on the way home from a meeting. It was in the late hours of the night when a supporter came over to us and said: 'Kenny Carter has died.' We were deeply shocked; details of the circumstances have been widely documented so I do not intend to go into this. I can comment, however, on his contribution as a speedway rider. Although he was an abrasive character, some say you either loved him or hated him, but I believed it then and I believe it now that he was great for speedway. The ITV *World of Sport* presenter Gary Newbon was a 'nobody' until he discovered Kenny Carter, and his passing was a sad loss to the sport in tragic circumstances. [1]

At Cradley Heath in an England Test Match against Denmark a milestone in my career was reached when Stuart Bamforth, as Head of the British Speedway Promoters Association, made a presentation to me for my 100th cap for England – a very proud moment. In actual fact I went on to complete 128 appearances for England – second only to Peter Collins. This was further proof that I was viewed as a valued member of the national squad by most of the national team managers of that period.

This achievement is not likely to be equalled in the future, as the modern speedway rider just does not have the same number of opportunities to represent his country as I did. It is much harder to find suitable dates to stage Test Matches and tournaments because a successful rider in the new millennium not only races in the British League but also in the Swedish, Polish, Danish and German leagues. The successful modern speedway rider is, as the phrase goes, 'a speedway nomad'.

It is difficult to separate the passion I had for both Belle Vue and England. That choice was decided for me as the England selectors rightly had first choice over your club. One thing I would not do was turn down a chance to ride for England for a more financially lucrative private international booking. There was often some contention with riders – including myself – over the rates of pay for riding for your country, which was usually less than you could earn when riding for your club and certainly less than some international open meetings. All that aside, for me the pride and opportunity to represent my country was more important.

Some time in the mid-1980s I had a bit of a 'rock 'n' roll moment'. I was at an open meeting in the beautiful city of Copenhagen and there were a few of the lads booked into this bed and breakfast hotel. As was usual we were well looked after by the local speedway people.

The following morning I was due to fly back to the UK quite early, so with this in mind my hotel bill was settled the night before. I rode in the evening meeting and it was arranged that I would go for a drink with some friends, so we hit the town. I was introduced to Elephant beer. It's powerful stuff, especially when later on you are introduced to the Danish bitter Gammel Dansk – a bit like the German Underberg and with an appropriate nickname of 'North Sea Oil'. I finally got to bed in the early hours and I was much the worse for wear.

Sure enough, not long after laying in bed half asleep, my stomach decided to strike 'North Sea Oil' – I was going to be sick. This room was fairly basic, but it did have a sink. It was a simple room about four metres square, with the bed in one corner near the window and the sink on the opposite diagonal corner near the door. Being a considerate customer I staggered to the sink to erupt the contents of my disagreeing stomach. I was amazingly diligent in my drunken state, or so I thought, as I turned on the tap to swill away the disgusting contents that my stomach had now deposited into the sink. Feeling incredibly relieved, I got back into bed and fell into a satisfying sleep.

When I awoke in the morning I was strangely aware that something was not right. How astute I was… I could hear water running; I had left the tap on for what must have been hours! I jumped out of bed and straight into a three-inch deep, four-metre square pool! I was horrified at my drunken stupidity. When I got to the sink I found my sick had bunged up the sink and the water had just been pouring onto the floor. As the door had a small step up and the room was on the ground floor the water was going nowhere, but I was. Fortunately my bag was on a chair and my clothes were on the bed with my trousers dangling an inch from the rising flood. What else could I do? I had paid my bill, so I just left in a hurry! Very rock 'n' roll'! At least I didn't throw the TV out of the window - not that there was one!

As you may have noticed, rock and roll, or music in general, has played a significant part in my life. There was an album released by Wishbone Ash in 1972 titled *Argus* and it was a concept album – the type of which was in fashion at that time. This album was a constant companion throughout my speedway career. If I had a bad meeting, it would lift my spirits; if I had a good meeting, it would enhance my celebrations. I play the guitar a bit and speedway – motorcycle racing in general – does seem to have the knack of attracting characters to the sport who like to enjoy themselves. There are many who spring to mind, and a good number were world-class racers.

One of these was the American Kelly Moran, whose exploits on the track were only matched by his legendary off-track tales. He was one of the sport's likeable characters, but I would also like to add that he was one of speedway's most gifted riders. There are few who could match his talent on board a speedway bike and, when he was on form, there weren't many riders who could beat him. Along with his equally talented younger brother Shawn, there are many stories of their rock 'n' roll moments and Kelly was about to expose me to one that almost ended in tragic circumstances.

We were on a tour in Poland that was organised by JMS All Stars. We had finished a meeting and the whole touring gang were at a well-organised party. It was a few hours after the meeting and we were on the schnapps, shouting 'nastravia' ('cheers') and throwing the glasses into the fireplace. We were all well oiled as the various groups were starting to break up and make their way back to the hotel. Jackie was with me on this trip and we decided to get a taxi back to the hotel along with a few others.

As our group walked into the hotel reception there was a bit of a fuss going on at the reception desk. Kelly Moran was trying to sort something out with the girl on reception who was trying her best to understand what he wanted. Jackie and myself were definitely drunk, but Kelly was a few steps up from us – he was completely pissed and was not making much sense. We suggested he should go to bed, but it turned out he was trying to get his room key. So we found his room number, got his key and Jackie and I agree to take him to his room and join the others in the bar in about ten minutes.

Off we went up to Kelly's room and the three of us were pretty merry. We got to his room and Jackie unlocked the door. As we went past the bathroom on the left, there was a second door that had a wooden frame surrounding a plain glass panel. We walked through this door and into the bedroom. As we got into the bedroom, Kelly flings his arm back, saying: 'I don't wanna go to bed' – he certainly got his request in spectacular fashion.

He smashed his arm through the plate-glass door panel and the glass shattered loudly and splintered everywhere followed by a fountain of blood, which squirted from his arm like a jet, spraying blood on the ceiling and the walls. It seems a bit sick to say this, but it looked like Spiderman when he projects his web from his wrist!

Kelly was flapping his arm around like a loose hosepipe spilling its liquid for fun, but there was no fun here. I grabbed hold of him and threw him on the bed and pinned him down. He had a look of fear in his eyes, and I had a hold of his arm, which was pumping blood out at an alarming rate. On the inside of his wrist through the shimmering red river the wound was an absolute mess, flaps of jagged skin and other severed bits that looked like they might be quite important, it looked like his arm had exploded from inside. Prominent through all this mess and sticking up out of the wound was what looked like an open pipe – like a windscreen-washer hose that was purposefully pumping out its contents, and draining the life out of Kelly. He had severed a main artery.

I had, thankfully, suddenly become stone-cold sober from being pretty pissed less than a minute ago. My body had kick-started me with an adrenalin rush that gave me amazing clarity. Jackie had rushed down the stairs to call for an ambulance and some help. I stopped the flow of blood by moving my hands down Kelly's arm and applied pressure with my thumbs as near to the wound as I could until the flow of blood stopped. Kelly looked at me and said: 'I've fucked up this time haven't I?' I saw the look of shock and fear in his eyes, and he looked scared. Was he thinking 'I could have picked a better place than Poland to do this'? I certainly was! Poland was still a Communist country and certainly wasn't as developed as Western Europe. I said: 'You'll be all right Kelly, just keep still. Jackie's gone to get help.'

Jackie got reception to call for the ambulance. She met Graham Brodie, our tour referee, and told him what had happened and Graham came upstairs to support me. By now word had got to the bar that Kelly had had an accident, and Graham kept everyone informed while we waited for the ambulance. Jackie came back after a few minutes, to let us know the ambulance was on its way and that she would wait at reception and bring the paramedics up as soon as they arrived.

After about twenty minutes the paramedics arrived, but their English was non-existent, and my Polish was limited to 'nastravia,' which I decided was pretty useless in this situation. The main paramedic indicated for me to move out of the way. At this stage they had no idea what the problem was. I gestured to Kelly's arm, but the paramedic again just wanted me to move. So I reverted to international sign language and visual aids; I released the pressure on the wound, which sent a jet of blood splattering up the wall! Both paramedics emitted a loud 'A-AHH!' and they then proceeded to put a tourniquet on Kelly's arm to stem the blood flow.

Kelly's was given some basic treatment and was then put on a stretcher and taken downstairs to the waiting ambulance. We followed the paramedics with Kelly down to the street. But hang on, where was the ambulance? A quick scan of the immediate area and there was no sign of the ambulance. Instead, to my astonishment, they walked over to this beat-up Lada Estate car! This was the 'ambulance'? The paramedics' street cred' was completely blown. We had been quite impressed up to then. As they bundled Kelly into the back of this Lada Batmobile/safari type of vehicle like a failed novice throwing his old speedway bike in the back of his car, Graham and I looked at each other in utter amazement – but now we were getting scared. A bad situation had just gotten worse. We hastily got a taxi to follow this 'ambulance' to the hospital.

We arrived at what must have been the Accident and Emergency department. It was fairly quiet and Kelly was put on a wheeled bed for the doctor to look at him. There only seemed to be one nurse and one doctor on duty – not at all like an A&E department in England, where several staff would rush to assist in an emergency. Admittedly it was the early hours of the morning, but things didn't look great. The doctor had a look at Kelly and planned to do some repair work straight away – at least to the severed artery. While the doctor was working on him Kelly may have been a bit delirious or the last of the booze was starting to kick in, but he started fighting the doctor off, not letting him help him. At this stage the only thing stopping the blood was the tourniquet applied by the paramedics. As Kelly was putting himself at greater risk by shouting and fighting the doctor, the doctor said to us in his best English: 'I cannot help if he does not stay good.' I spoke to Kelly, who was not really aware of what was going on and didn't want anything doing. The scene was getting emotional, and I was pleading with Kelly to let the doctor do his work. I was starting to get angry with the stupid bastard; the emotion, the booze and the shock all seemed to catch up with me as I started crying while I was negotiating with Kelly to let the doctor fix him up. At last he finally agreed. He was taken into what looked like a theatre for the doctor and the nurse to do some work on him. It was clear that microsurgery would be required to sort out some of the severed tendons. That would be done back in the UK. The target for tonight was to make him safe.

Graham and I finally sat down after what had been an hour and half of trauma and waited for some news. He said to me: 'If I have a crisis like this I want you to be there to look after me,' just as a Polish speedway supporter walked in who had been down at our hotel being very friendly earlier. He chatted with us, and pointed out that my shirt was covered in blood. He was right and it was my favourite shirt – the one you always like to wear and it feels good. He said: 'I take this shirt, I get it washed, I bring to hotel in morning.' As he was saying this he was taking off his shirt for me to wear, this crappy, sweaty Polish shirt, but it seemed like a noble gesture under the circumstances. We swapped shirts and he put mine on. It fitted him well and I thanked him. I never saw my favourite shirt again, the opportunist bastard!

After about twenty minutes the doctor explained to us that he had only been able to plug the artery, but he had dressed the wound and, rather strangely, he had put a plaster-of-paris cast all over Kelly's forearm. It was clear that it would need more serious attention as soon as possible in the UK and he was kept in overnight.

As we boarded the coach the following afternoon, Kelly was there bright as a button with seemingly not a care in the world – although he was overwhelming with his gratitude towards Jackie and myself. He was concerned that someone in the hospital had taken his riding fees out of his pocket, so he couldn't even buy me a new shirt! Later, blood was leaking from his cast and it was a good job that we were returning to the UK where he would get some more effective treatment.

Since I had that initial problem with my hip in 1984, I had become more aware of what the issue was and I was working with a local physiotherapist, Judy Ainsworth, where I had treatment. I had also seen a specialist called Mr Lemon, who had given me a cortisone injection. In 1986 I contacted the legendary Dr Carlo Biaggi in Scotland to ask him if he would have a look at my hip and use the cortisone treatment. Biaggi was a bit of a legend in speedway racing and he always seemed to be able to patch riders up so that they could compete in the important meetings. He agreed, and his efforts were effective. Biaggi inserted the extremely long needle, about six inches, deep into my hip joint and as soon as he started to empty the syringe's contents it was like he hit the bulls eye, as I experienced instant relief from the nagging pain that I had to continually endure.

I was well aware that this treatment would only give temporary relief, maybe up to three months, and continued treatment was not recommended. By this time, if I rode in a meeting it would take a couple of days for the aching to settle down, so if I rode three times a week it was a bugger! Anyone with this problem will tell you that while you are active and moving, the troublesome aching is something that you can tolerate, but sleeping is a problem. I had been taking painkillers to sleep for some time, but they had stopped working. I was also concerned with the health issues of continually taking fairly strong painkillers, so after a time I just stopped taking them altogether and decided that I had to put up with it.

As the bone reaction within my hip joint increased, my regular physiotherapy was essential to maintain movement and what flexibility I had, which was minimal and reducing. All this was starting to change my riding style. I reckoned I had a few more years left, but I knew it would be my undoing. Technology that could have helped me had not been developed yet as it was at least ten years off and what hip replacements there were were strictly for the over sixties with low activity. International speedway riding would not be considered low activity. Being the philosophical chap that I am, I reasoned I should just get on with it.

In 1986 I was offered full sponsorship for equipment by Jawa and, although they were slightly behind the GM in their development, as the Individual World Speedway Final was in Poland that year, the help from them would be a benefit in the East and I was confident that we could get them quick enough.

I qualified fairly comfortably through all the qualifying rounds – including a third place in the Commonwealth Final – to the Intercontinental Final that was staged at Bradford. As I went into my last ride I had scored only 4 points and looked out of it. My hopes of qualifying for my fifth Individual World Final were hanging by a thread. We had made some changes to the bike, but I decided to swap to my spare bike for this important race. Heat nineteen was the last-chance saloon and all four were desperate men. As I sat down digging deep for whatever I could find to make this happen, I knew I had most of the requirements and desire was not an issue. I had done it before, so ability was not an issue either.

But something that was creating a tension was the thought of not making it, and was once again proving incredibly painful to accept. I realised that my intense desire to qualify was a hindrance in this situation, so I made myself accept that this could be the end of my World Individual Final road for another year. I could live with it. Accepting that situation relieved the pressure I was putting myself under. I would give it my best shot; if I failed I would accept it.

I faced Mitch Shirra and Jan O. Pedersen, who had 6 points and Paul Thorp, who had the same number of points as me. Thorp had been a bit of a sensation that year as he rode for the National League team Stoke and was promoted into the line-up to replace Kelly Moran, as he had to pull out of the meeting following his near-fatal hotel accident. However, my personal game of psychological ping-pong paid off, as I won the race and qualified for the World Speedway Final to be staged in Poland. My team and I were elated!

It was ten years since I had qualified for my first World Final at the same venue. I was older and wiser and no longer grateful just to qualify like I had been in 1976 – this time I wanted to put in my best World Final performance. To that end I approached former World Champion Michael Lee to prepare some engines for the meeting. He had been doing some engines for some of the other lads with good results and he was an excellent tuner. I was hoping that he could bring some of that knowledge and experience to bear on my Jawa engines. When he won the World Final in 1980, he was mounted on a Jawa.

After only having one World Finalist in 1985, England now had four in the shape of myself, Kelvin Tatum, the new British Champion Neil Evitts and

Marvyn Cox. Denmark's Erik Gundersen arrived at Katowice aiming to equal Ivan Mauger's record of three successive World title victories. The Cradley rider was one of the favourites along with his fellow countrymen, Hans Nielsen and Tommy Knudsen.

My first race was against the Russian Viktor Kuznetsov, local favourite Ryszard Dolomisiewicz and Cox. I raced hard too for my second place behind the fast-riding Russian Kuznetsov and we were reasonably happy with my first ride. However, third in my second ride was disappointing. There was never any room for machine problems in these meetings, which is what happened in my third and pivotal ride. I had carburettor problems which resulted in me scoring no points. With 3 points from three rides it was about getting a better score than I had in the past.

In my next ride I was about to get a fantastic view of yet another controversial World Final race. Heat fifteen saw a clash between the eventual winner Hans Nielsen and fellow countryman and rival contender Tommy Knudsen. It had been well documented during this period that Nielsen was a Dane out on a limb, having had fallings-out with Danish team manager Ole Olsen. Moreover, significantly, Nielsen had been the bridesmaid in the last two World Finals behind Erik Gundersen.

In my opinion, at the time, I felt that Hans had been the best rider in the world for a couple of years, but the guts and determination of Erik Gundersen meant that he could not own the world title. I think Erik had a way of going and getting it whereas Hans, up to this point, had relied on his outstanding skills, but he was getting pipped at the post every time.

At Bradford the previous year, an important heat saw Hans Nielsen run a third after being given a hard race by Tommy Knudsen, which possibly cost him the title. For Hans Nielsen this all came to a head in heat fifteen of the 1986 World Final and this was when I think he took a leaf out of Erik Gundersen's book and decided if the World Championship wasn't coming to him, he was going to get it! Tommy Knudsen was in front and Nielsen was in second place with me in the grandstand seat of third. Hans had displayed good pace all night and was all over Tommy Knudsen, but Knudsen was riding a very tight and perfect inside line. As we entered turns three and four, Nielsen seemed to decide at that moment that this was one World title he was going to get.

I am sure his experiences the previous year were part of his concoction of motivation. He had the momentum to pass Knudsen but he just didn't have the room – so he made some in what was a masterful move. This happened on turn four. Nielsen was on the inside and he picked up some drive and powered alongside Knudsen. He pulled in front and he forced his way through into the lead. Tommy Knudsen was forced to give up his line and he lost control, drifted out and fell off.

It was possibly a difficult one for the referee to call as in most circumstances Hans Nielsen may well have been excluded. I believe the referee took a lot more into consideration than the incident on its own. I felt it was the right decision to award the race to Hans Nielsen, which allowed him to go on and win the World Crown. His move on Tommy Knudsen was one that bordered on foul riding, but Hans had a very subtle way of executing the move because he had the best close control of a speedway bike I have seen – only matched by the great Tony Rickardsson. Nielsen was able in this situation to be absolutely precise in how he placed his machine exactly where he needed to and create the gap to get through with the least disruption. Although, in this case, Knudsen did fall off, Nielsen made the move as cleanly as possible, which gave the referee the ammunition he needed not to exclude him.

It was another disappointing World Final for me, equalling my best to date with 8 points. It had previously been announced that the 1987 World Final would see a significant change by staging it over two days. Despite my disappointing performances so far, my quest was still on and I was not going to miss out on this historic event. I felt that I was worthy of a good World Final performance and I was already making plans for my next world title campaign.

ENDNOTE:

1. It was reported that Kenny Carter committed suicide on Wednesday 21 May 1986 afte killing his wife, Pam, with a shotgun. He then turned the weapon on himself.

ELEVEN

THE WIND OF CHANGE

Green light on, study the tape mechanism, tapes up, drop the clutch, go, go, go! This could have been the start of any race, but it wasn't. This was the final race of the 1987 season against Cradley, the second meeting in an historic end-of-season double-header. The first meeting was against Coventry in the second leg of the League Cup Final and, although we won 40-38, it wasn't enough to win the cup from a very good Bees side. However, for this final race of the season, personal pride was at stake. With the scores at 34-38, Belle Vue didn't want to end their season on a losing note – but it was also going to be the last race staged at Hyde Road – ever!

It was an emotional night, heightened by the fact that Cradley and Coventry had pushed us hard. I'm sure that the reason that the Heathens and the Bees were able to apply so much pressure was because it was the last speedway meeting at The Zoo and the atmosphere was emotional. There were protests on the terraces trying to keep this famous old stadium open and, overall, the Midlanders came and took full advantage.

For a race that had no bearing on any result and could give no financial gain, its only significance was its stand-alone status. Its importance crept up on me. It was while I sat on my bike that the race became one of the most desirable races to win – I just had to win because this place had meant so much to me. Like many, I was nothing short of disgusted that it was being sold off for a car auction, and suddenly the next 69.8 seconds would be the final tribute to the last sixty years of speedway at Belle Vue.

I loved what this place had allowed me to do. The Belle Vue speedway track wanted to race, and embraced the riders that could race. It brought the best out of Peter Craven, Peter Collins, Ivan Mauger, Erik Gundersen, Kenny Carter, Barry Briggs, Jack Parker, Bill Kitchen, Max Grosskreutz, Eric Langton, Frank Varey, Cyril Maidment, my inspiration Soren Sjosten, Hans Nielsen, Shawn Moran, Billy Sanders and many, many more who were always tough to beat because Belle Vue allowed riders to fully express their racing skills.

Just like many riders before us, both Peter Collins and myself got to know this track so well that we had many tricks that we could use to pass riders. Like many good race tracks it was easy to ride on but, ironically, it was very hard to win on because beating the specialists required a lot more than making a start. You had to ride fast, be on the right line for whatever the conditions were that night and at any specific time during a meeting, as the fastest way around would change from race to race. The majority of riders fell into the trap of riding Belle Vue about two yards off the inside line, which was the natural riding line that the track would draw you into. But any rider worth his salt could pass someone on this line either on the inside or outside.

During a meeting in the first two or three races, the fastest way would be around the inside, but as the meeting progressed the dirt moved out and the fastest line got wider and wider, so any dirt that was good early on in the meeting would get left on the inside. Peter and I, both being aware of this, would save this last bit of dirt for a situation when we needed to pass someone. Later in the meeting, when everyone was riding wide, you could get just one or two very fast lines around the very inside and use this last bit of dirt to produce a passing move. We would agree to save it for a needy moment as once you had gone over it once or twice it would be gone.

Few riders were aware of these hidden opportunities and, as the meeting got towards the end, the line got really wide as the dirt got nearer the fence. It was then about being brave and bold and taking the wide, deep line just off the fence. I used to really enjoy stalking a rider for a few laps and taking control of where he went as he tried to cover the line he thought I would take to pass him. I would plug away at the inside, making him have to cover that line, then on the last corner feint to take the inside again but as soon as he committed to cover the inside I would switch to the outside and have an easy but spectacular pass around the outside. When I came up against one of the Belle Vue specialists it was never easy because they also knew most of the lines and tricks and had them covered. But I had one slightly ruthless trick that I only used on occasions where nothing else had worked.

This move only worked on the pits bend, turns three and four, the pits exit gate was about two-thirds of the way around the fence line – I mention this as that was my target. I remember a specific occasion against John Louis, who was a Hyde Road specialist. He was in front of me and I was trying all the tricks, but John was riding the fastest line and was riding very fast and very wide. It was late in the meeting and there was no way to get around him, and to go inside him was not fast enough. We were on the last lap and there was only one thing left – forgive the pun, but I pulled out my ace!

If you took a lap as having a straight, turns one and two, a straight, then turns three and four; I started to execute my move as we exited turn two heading onto the second straight. I rode up against the fence, but about halfway down the straight I started to peel off. My plan was that, knowing John would be taking what appeared to be the fastest line at that stage, which was about two yards from the fence around turns three and four, instead of following him I made a straight line from the middle of the straight, cut across the inside line of the track going into the corner, and maintained a straight line towards the fence near the pits exit gate, two-thirds around turns three and four, but still not turning. As I was going straight and John was turning, I passed him and was about a yard up on him as we both headed for the pit gate area of the track.

The problem for me now was that I had not yet made a turn, while John was starting his exit of the corner. Meanwhile, I still had a ninety-degree turn to make – with the fence waiting to collect me should it go wrong! But the trick was in the knowledge and the surprise, the knowledge being that at that section of the track where I was heading – which was just a little wider than where John was going – there was a fresh, untouched four inches of shale that I used as my cushion and drive to turn off as I slotted myself in front of John. The element of surprise left him with no time to counter the move, using the old adage of upsetting the balance of the race. It was quite a ruthless move, but a bit risky and that was why I used it rarely; but done right it was very rewarding – I went over the line to take the chequered flag ahead of John. I have ridden many, many tracks around the World, and there are some that allow you to use your racing skills and are very rewarding to race on, but Belle Vue was the best of them all – a perfect speedway race track.

Rumours, gossip and speculation had been rife for months until it was revealed in early October that British Car Auctions (BCA) had put in a planning application for the redevelopment of the whole Belle Vue site – that included the stadium. An action committee was set-up to fight the demolition of Belle Vue, and if history was anything to go by then the prospects looked good. Hyde Road was the only track to remain operational during the Second World War. Not even Adolf Hitler could stop Belle Vue. But in the end it was the cold heart of modern-day business that forced Hyde Road to close. The loss of Hyde Road, warmly called 'The Zoo', was a huge blow to the sport. The loss of Wembley was a shock, but Hyde Road's demise broke speedway's heart.

According to reports, Stuart Bamforth had sold out to British Car Auctions for £10 million. There was little respect or dignity given to the establishment during its final weeks. Before the bulldozers moved in, on Tuesday 2 December 1987, an auctioneer sold off relics of Belle Vue Speedway's glorious past: the starting gate that had commenced so many famous races, the flags, floodlight pylon, signs, photographs and even a urinal! Sadly even some of the trophies that had sparkled in the small manager's office were put up for sale – tradition and history meant nothing that afternoon. As the hammer came down on the termination of each bid, its short, sharp, knock was the countdown for the final commencement of the final act – enter the bulldozers.

In 1986 I won the Peter Craven Memorial meeting for the third time. After the presentation, Stuart Bamforth gave me the trophy and said: 'Here, you can keep it now.' At the time I thought that it was a nice gesture because I had won it three times, but I think Bammy knew what was in the wind and realised the significance of the trophy and wanted to make sure that it went to a good home. I don't consider myself to be the owner of this magnificent trophy, but merely the guardian of it. Not only is it part of the history of Belle Vue Speedway, but also a big part of speedway's heritage. I am so pleased that it wasn't sold off in the auction for the highest price like a piece of family silverware. In speedway racing, the Peter Craven Memorial Trophy is an important trophy that is a permanent reminder of one of the sport's greatest riders.

The editor of *Speedway Star*, Richard Clark, has been a friend for a very long time and he wrote this piece called 'Remember Belle Vue' that is a fitting epitaph to that great venue:

The wind seems puzzled down Hyde Road way. On a March Saturday night it breathes slowly past the Manchester Apollo, snaking along a road that once crawled with traffic – pedestrian and motorised – heading for the speedway. Gone are the countless red and

149

black scarves, uniform of the devoted Aces followers. Gone, too, was the excited chatter about the night's 'big match' against Halifax, Coventry, Sheffield, Cradley, whoever. As the wind took its familiar right turn, it double-checks.

Gone also was that famous old speedway stadium. The moon that once glistened on the black shale covering one of the world's most renowned racing circuits now danced across the windscreens of cars for sale. History, it seemed, was also on sale. The wind briefly traced a path around the concrete forecourt. This was how Peter Craven used to slide into the pits turn; this was Jack Parker's favourite trick, how about this routine by Peter Collins? That rider out by the safety fence? That's Chris Morton.

We're just ghosts now. The stadium, the track, the pits, Peter Craven and all the riders who graced this super place over the years, ghosts. That's progress, they say. But I'm as puzzled as the wind. Where is the throaty roar of speedway bikes, the harsh scrape of metal shoe on shale, the screams of excitement sweeping the terraces and stands? Progress has exchanged them for the sound of an auctioneer's hammer and the folding of paper money, the rattle of coins and the ringing of tills.

The wind seemed puzzled down Hyde Road way. Like me, it remembered a more innocent time, before progress started to flatten everything in its way. I can recall a time of heroes, summer holidays that went on forever and a time when we raced until the petrol can ran out.

For that final season in 1987 the Aces had signed Paul Thorp from Stoke and he took to the wide-open spaces of Hyde Road very well. He brought the Aces fans to their feet when he defeated Hans Nielsen during a Test Match. Once again I was captain and we enjoyed a reasonable season by reaching the League Cup final against Coventry – who by now had the basis of a very strong team that would serve them well in 1988 as well.

That final season at Hyde Road began with us saying 'farewell' to Peter Collins. Peter had taken the decision to retire from racing at the relatively young age of thirty-two. Belle Vue staged a special farewell meeting that attracted a star-studded field of the top of riders of that time and Bruce Penhall came out of retirement to compete in some special match races against PC. The meeting was run on a traditional twenty-heat format, with the top six scorers entering a winner-takes-all final race. Shawn Moran was the overall victor and I took a third place that was a very satisfactory way of starting off my new campaign.

I was still chasing my dream of winning the World Championship, but at the Overseas Final at Bradford it looked as though my hopes of making the final in Amsterdam were over. As I entered my last race I had scored 7 points and needed only a point to secure my place in the Intercontinental Final. I faced the

Americans Sam Ermolenko and John Cook and the Australian Steve Regeling. We all needed points to ensure our places in the next round. I was in third place behind the two Americans when my engine blew and, despite his best efforts, Regeling ran into the back of me. I was excluded from the rerun and Steve was able to take his place in the race while I was out. I faced Kelvin Tatum in a run-off for the reserve spot. It was hardly the situation I wanted to be in, but I won the race and left Odsal Stadium with the knowledge that I would be travelling to the next round at Vojens as one of the meeting reserves.

As it turned out, that race win over Kelvin was very important. Kelly Moran finished third in that meeting, but during one of his trips back to America he crashed and broke his shoulder. This meant that I was next in line to take his place. It seemed highly unlikely that he would be able to ride as the Intercontinental Final was only a few weeks away, but the reports coming from California were that he would be riding.

It was his younger brother Shawn who called me to say that his brother had lost his fitness battle and he wouldn't be racing. It was ironic really; almost a year since his hotel accident, and now he was unable to take his place in the last round of the World Championship and I was replacing him.

I had qualified for the 1987 two-day World Final by scoring 7 points at Vojens. This was my sixth World Individual final and I had made a decision earlier in the year that although the Jawas suited me better from the start, they were not fast enough so I had changed to GM for their speed – which I found harder to get good starts on. So I did a lot of work building up to this World Final by improving my starting technique – and at club level it was working. At this stage I was taking stats at every meeting by recording my position as I entered the first bend and my stats were showing that I was making three out of five starts with me in a strong second place in the other two. All I had to do was transfer this to the World Final event.

I asked Peter Collins to help me in Amsterdam and I was hoping that his advice could provide that little bit extra. I felt good in the practice, but everything I had learned seemed to desert me in the final. I could offer many excuses, and the reality may have been down to my equipment not suiting the track conditions, or it could be that I did not adapt myself and my equipment to the conditions. It was a very difficult track to pass on and once again my starts were letting me down. By the end of the first day I was out of the hunt and my second day was just as disappointing. It was frustrating as I knew I was running out of time to fulfil my dream of becoming World Champion. Meanwhile, Hans Nielsen made a successful defence of his world title.

The British League Riders' Championship took on an extra significance in 1987 because it was going to be the last BLRC held at Hyde Road. Even now, over fifteen years since the stadium closed, there are many people who still recall vivid memories of those magic BLRC nights. During this time the BLRC was regarded as being just as hard as the World Final because it comprised the best riders from each club in Britain. They were very special nights. A big crowd had gathered and the action committee collected signatures to try and save Belle Vue from demolition. Labour Councillor Gerald Kaufmann added his support and it was planned that he would present the petition to the council at their next meeting.

I had decided that the GM still didn't suit me out of start and, in planning for the 1988 season, I rode a Godden for the first time in that meeting. Hans rode Goddens and they seemed to be able to get me out of the start better. I met Nielsen in my second race and made a brilliant gate and blocked his every move to inflict his only defeat of the meeting. Later, Hans said: 'I got a bit of a shock when Chris made the start on me – until I found he was on a Godden.' As I entered my third ride I was leading the scores, but I finished third behind Jan Andersson and Kelly Moran and with Hans winning his third outing he was back at the top of the score chart. I didn't drop another point, but neither did Nielsen. Overall I finished in second place behind him with Moran in third.

The brightly painted sign above the main stand at Hyde Road proudly proclaimed 'Home of the Aces.' Only the Aces were now homeless. We were, however, quite literally, going to the dogs. As the sale and demolition of the stadium commanded column inches on the back pages of the *Manchester Evening News* and the sports press, the only silver lining to counter these upsetting events was the reports that PC had joined forces with a local businessman, John Perrin, to move the Aces to the Greyhound Stadium at Kirkmanshulme Lane – the venue where speedway was first staged at Belle Vue in 1928.

It took a while to get all the relevant red tape and negotiations under way. But Peter was successful and also pulled off an impressive stroke by getting British Car Auctions to donate a cheque for £25,000. Most of the team remained loyal to the club so when the new promotion could actually get around to assembling a team, the riders were there.

Kenny McKinna moved to Glasgow, but we began our new era with myself as captain, Paul Thorp, Andy Smith, Peter Ravn and three newcomers in the shape of American Mike Faria, Roland Danno and Glenn Hornby. We began with away matches but, ironically, we were due to open our new season against Bradford on 1 April 1988. Perhaps we should have taken more notice of the date as the meeting was abandoned, although everyone was encouraged by the number of people attended.

We finally managed to kick off our new era with a league match against Wolves that we won 51-39. Some supporters had gone as far as predicting my demise at the new venue. But I saw it as a new challenge that would mean that the one thing that had plagued me for most of my career – my starting – would have to improve on a week-to-week basis at club level if I was going to maintain a 9-point average. I was going to have to work hard at this challenge because the new Belle Vue was a track that produced some good racing and was physically demanding, and was one of the hardest tracks to ride well. I was pleased with how I dealt with this change.

A new track meant that there was a new track record to be established, and Peter Ravn, Mike Faria, Erik Gundersen and Hans Nielsen all held it at different times until Gundersen set the record of 59.3 seconds that stood for the remainder of my career with Belle Vue.

The sixtieth anniversary of speedway racing in Britain was in 1988, so the BSPA (British Speedway Promoters Association) put together a special international tournament to commemorate the occasion that involved the world's four leading nations: England, Denmark, Sweden and the USA. This competition was run on a mini-league basis in a similar way to the *Daily Mirror* International tournament in 1973. Each nation would meet each other once and the top two teams would then qualify for a one-off final to be staged at King's Lynn.

England's first match was at Bradford against the USA. The Americans were not quite the force that they had been and we had gained the upper hand over our transatlantic cousins during the previous two years by winning the Test series. The meeting was not only a good one for England but also for me too. I raced to a paid maximum on a track that really suited my style and equipment. I particularly remember the last race when I enjoyed quite a dice with America's Lance King to complete my maximum. I came from last to first to complete my maximum and received a standing ovation from the crowd at Odsal.

It was a convincing 57-33 victory and gave our team a lot of confidence for the forthcoming international season. Previously there had been a lot of stuff in the press questioning my inclusion in the team, given the number of young riders around at that time who wanted a piece of the international action. I didn't have to defend my inclusion as my performance that day spoke for itself. It was refreshing to hear the England team managers, Colin Pratt and Eric Boocock, say that they would always consider me if my form warranted consideration. Booey said in the press: 'Chris Morton? He's like wine, he improves with age.

And he had nothing to prove to Colin and me. He'll always be considered for England if he's going well and this season he's flying, whether its wet, dry, slick or deep.'

England went on to win all three of their matches to qualify for the final against Denmark at King's Lynn. Although we fancied our chances of winning this trophy, the Danes – who were already dominating the sport – were at their peak and they defeated us at Saddlebow Road 52-38.

The World Team Cup reverted to its one-off format and was staged in America. This time I was included in the team and I travelled to Long Beach, California with Gary Havelock, Kelvin Tatum, Simon Wigg and Jeremy Doncaster. As I said before, Denmark were at their peak and they breezed into California and raced off with first place. Unfortunately, England was locked in a battle with Sweden for third place and Per Jonsson defeated Tatum in a run-off for the bronze medal. It was, statistically, England's worst World Team Cup Final performance since the England team was re-formed to ride in the World Team Championship in 1974. Although America was a disappointment, it was clear that England had some very talented young riders emerging, including Havelock and Martin Dugard, with other internationals such as Paul Thorp, Andy Smith and Richard Knight also knocking on the international door.

Since the first year I qualified for the World Long-Track Championship in 1980 I had ridden in it every year, qualifying for the final seven out of the ten times that I had entered. I had an ideal arrangement thanks to the enthusiasm of Martin Bean and his understanding wife, Sue. Martin was in the RAF and was stationed in Germany and was in charge of the Jump Jets. My bikes for the long-track were with Martin and he prepared them and took them to the meetings – all I had to do was turn up and ride – the easy bit! This arrangement also made it easy for me to do other international meetings as well. I used to ride about every other weekend in Germany at various long-track qualifiers or grass-track meetings. Martin's RAF background made him a good mechanic, he was very thorough in his work and he provided an excellent base from which to run my long-track campaign.

By the mid-1980s it was accepted practice that top international riders would compete in both the Speedway Individual World Championships and the long-track. Erik Gundersen had managed to win both titles during the same year – the first rider to achieve this since Ivan Mauger in 1972. Therefore, Erik had reset the standard and riders like Nielsen, Ermolenko, Shawn Moran (who had won in 1983), Schwartz, PC and Simon Wigg (who went on to win five long-track titles) were all eager to make their mark on the long-track scene.

I was finding it hard to compete against the very fast German-tuned special long-track engines. Then, in 1988, highly respected German tuner Hans Zierk offered me the use of one of his engines at the long-track final at Scheessel. Martin and I had a short discussion about taking his offer and decided, without hesitation, to use his engine. It was without doubt the fastest thing I had ever experienced on the long-track. Not only was it fast at the top end, but it was also a rocket from the start. One of the issues with long-track racing is getting filled in from the shale coming off the rear wheel of the rider in front of you. But when you hit the front on a 1,000-metre circuit, it was one of the most exhilarating feelings in the world as you peeled off flat out into the wide sweeping turns at over 100mph – it truly was sensational. Hans Zierk's engine made all the years of hard work trying to compete against the Germans worthwhile, as in 1988 I finished on the rostrum in third place in the World Long-Track final at Scheessel.

As the Danes had been such a force at international level they were rewarded with the staging of a World Final at Vojens. Vojens is a good race track, but just like Norden in 1983, it wasn't really a location that was suitable for the grandeur of the Individual World Final. Nonetheless, my first priority was to qualify for the big day.

I made consistent progress through the various qualifying rounds and found myself in Vetlanda, Sweden for the Intercontinental Final. Two points from three rides at the interval was a seriously 'bad scene' and I needed two race wins from my last two rides. In the pits with me were Ged and my brother Dave and, during the interval, there was a strange silence in our corner of the pits as we had made as many changes as we could. From my mechanics' perspective it didn't look good; and it didn't look good from my perspective either! This was a situation I had got out of before, but this occasion was as extreme as it could be. The maths made it possible, probability said not. Ladbrokes would have given you 1000 to 1, but I really wanted to be at the World Final in Vojens – the task was monumental.

I sat down in my pits corner and to onlookers it probably looked like I was wallowing in my disappointment with my head down staring at the floor. But the truth was I was planning out my last two rides, getting everything clear in my head, I was not going out of the World Championship. My head was fit to burst with frustration, desire and determination – I had squared it all up in my head during the interval.

In my fourth ride I got a win. Suddenly with 5 points it looked possible, but the real test was to come. Jan O. Pedersen was unbeaten and I would have to out-gate the rider who was the best gater on the night. As I stared at the starting mechanism I welled up with fortitude; in that split second I knew it had come together, I was going to do it. Against all the odds, I won the race to qualify for my seventh World Final –my third in a row.

I approached the World Individual final at Vojens with a strong desire to emerge as the champion. I had put a lot into my riding that year and I felt I was riding as well as I had for a few years. I had a very positive start with a race win in my first ride over John Davis, Sandor Tihanyi and John Jorgensen. In my second ride I was against the big boys, Hans Nielsen and Erik Gundersen, with the hard-riding Roman Matousek in there for good measure. However, I finished in last place and then followed that with another last place in my third ride – it was game over for me.

I was never one to go down without a fight, so in my final ride in heat twenty I fought hard and bravely for a good result. It was a race that was considered by some to be the best race of the afternoon. Sam Ermolenko and I did a display of determined close-contact racing, which was made doubly hard by the onset of driving rain. We battled for four whole laps, changing the lead several times, and it was the type of race we both revelled in, with Sam squeezing into the lead as we went over the line.

Although the World Final was a disappointment, I took some consolation from that race as it turned out that was my last World Final appearance. My last race was a metaphor of my whole World Championship quest. I genuinely gave it everything I had, the record shows I wasn't good enough to win the title, but it also shows that in qualifying for the seven World Finals I could beat the best at their best. But I never did myself justice on World Final night. I still carry that frustration, but take solace from the fact that I provided some raw entertainment for thousands of people and, on many occasions, some personal satisfaction and great times.

TWELVE

ON HER MAJESTY'S SPEEDWAY SERVICE

It was around September, getting towards the end of the 1989 season. It had been a year that had seen my average drop below 9 points for the British League Averages for the first time in fifteen years. I had, in the past twelve months, been involved in more crashes than I was used to. As a consequence I had more time out injured that year since I had broken my collarbone in 1974. I had other injuries in the past, some of which should have kept me out, but they didn't.

Due to my ongoing hip problem my riding style had changed, and I was finding it hard to get into the corners properly on the smaller tracks. I almost had to learn the trick of speedway all over again – something that had come so naturally to me since doing it as a kid, had deserted me. That action of dropping the bike into the corner in a smoothly actioned broad slide was getting harder and harder to do as the flexibility in my joint got less and less. I was also taking more chances than I had in the past. It may not have appeared that way to look at me racing, but in my earlier years I always had a level of risk I would go to. If I wasn't confident about a move I wouldn't do it; but in these later years I was pushing beyond my confidence levels to get the results, which meant more crashes.

Belle Vue was changing too. Peter Collins decided to step down from his duties and it was a very different Aces now. The Moran brothers, Shawn and Kelly, joined us after Sheffield had closed and sixteen-year-old Joe Screen became a sensation with an incredible debut year.

I made my final appearance for England at Belle Vue in the Second Test against the USA. It was a tight meeting, full of fast and furious racing but the Americans won by just 1 point, 54-53. I am proud of the fact that I top-scored with 14 points in what turned out to be my final appearance in an England race jacket.

The Aces team struggled to be a force at the top with Kelly Moran sidelined for most of the season with a broken finger and I had only scored double figures on eight occasions that year. It became clear to me that it was time to retire. I did not want to just keep riding until I was completely knackered. However, as this season had been so poor by my previous standards I made the decision to do one more season in 1990 and, knowing it was going to be my last year, I could give it my best shot and finish my career on a positive note. Having made that decision, I suddenly felt a sense of relief. That sense of release seemed to me to signify that the time was right to hang up my leathers.

As the 1990 season got closer I had great enthusiasm for what would be my last season as a professional speedway rider. It wasn't the best season I had ever had, but it was better than 1989 and one I was proud to retire on. My very last race at Belle Vue was a run-off for the bonus point against Bradford. I was nominated to race for the bonus point against Gary Havelock; and like the last race at the old Hyde Road track this had great significance to me and provided the motivation I needed to go out and win – which I did in true style. Havvy out gated me but I slipped through on the inside on the first corner, and raced to the finish to win my last ever race for the Belle Vue Aces. It had been eighteen glorious years.

Later, in the winter of 1990/91, I was just driving along the road when a realisation overwhelmed me that I would not be riding speedway anymore. I thought I had dealt with it in my own mind, and I had, but what struck me by surprise was this feeling of bereavement. This was it – I had ridden a speedway bike for a living since I was sixteen years old and now, at thirty-four, it was over. It took me some time to come to terms with that. I suppose what it really took to get that feeling out of my system was my five-month comeback with Sheffield in 1993, which confirmed that I had made the right decision. I thoroughly enjoyed my short spell with Sheffield – Dave raced for the Tigers for five years in the early 1980s – but still consider that I retired in 1990 as it was then I gave it up as a profession. I won my last meeting at Sheffield, winning the Northern Riders' Championship for the third time – and it's worth getting hold of the video of that meeting.

I entered the last race on 11 points and faced Sean Wilson – who was my nearest rival – and the wild Czech Republic rider, Roman Matousek. I made a reasonable start and took the lead, but it was all happening behind me. The red lights came on and the race was stopped. Wilson was excluded after a clash with Matousek. In the re-run I emerged in front again and was all set to clinch the title when my bike stopped on the last lap. Even in my comeback, I was still one not to go down without a fight and pushed the bike over the finish line for my crucial 1 point for third place. It proved to be enough, and I finished my final competitive speedway race as Northern Riders' Champion.

On 24 March 1991, Belle Vue staged a farewell meeting for me, which comprised of a team event that pitched the 'Hyde Road Aces' against the 'Kirky Lane Aces.' The result was immaterial, but Hyde Road won 55-52. Riders like Paul Tyrer, Michael Lee, Eric Broadbelt, Taffy Owen, Geoff Pusey, Ken Eyre and Keith White all turned out to race – I scored 7 points for the victors!

When I retired in 1990 I started my new career as a financial adviser and, in 1991, I found time to be the team manager for a new-look Berwick Bandits in the First Division, finishing fifth in the league. It was Berwick's first and only season in the top division and they had assembled a useful side that included an experienced heat-leader trio of Kelvin Tatum, Jimmy Nilsen and Richard Knight – all of whom had been World Finalists the previous year. This gave the team a spearhead that was an equal to any other in the league, but having such a strong top three meant that the rest of the team wasn't quite strong enough to win the league. But when we signed the Swede Mikael Blixt to replace David Blackburn, it gave the top three a bit more consistent support and we did win the Gold Cup. Unfortunately, having three top-class riders proved too much of a financial burden for the ambitious promoter, Terry Lindon, and the Bandits reverted to the Second Division for 1992. I didn't continue as team manager as I needed to concentrate on my new career in financial services.

As with any other day, the postman shoved some letters through the door and carried on his business. But this would not be like any other day. 'I think you had better read this,' Jackie said as she handed me an envelope with a letter in. We were at home, it was November 1991 and Jackie was opening the post. I was on my way down the stairs when she met me halfway up with this letter. My initial thought when I looked at the envelope was 'letter from the tax office!', as it had 'On Her Majesty's Service' on the front, although the envelope was a little flash for the revenue.

Jackie watched intently as I took out the letter and read its contents. I was gobsmacked; happily it wasn't a letter from the tax office, but instead a letter from the principal private secretary at Number 10 Downing Street. It informed me that I had been recommended to receive an MBE for my services to speedway. It went on to say that if I found it 'agreeable' then I should complete the form and send it by return post!

I had been retired for just over twelve months, and was just getting on with life after speedway, when this accolade came out of the blue. There had not been, up to this point, an English speedway rider who had received an MBE – for whatever reason my mate PC had been overlooked, although I am pleased to say that that has since been rectified. I really was incredibly surprised, but pleased that my efforts for the past eignteen years had not gone unnoticed.

In March 1992 I received my MBE from The Queen at Buckingham Palace. On that day, former England rugby union captain Will Carling was there to collect his MBE, and Jimmy Saville was being knighted. I was so incredibly proud and pleased that I had joined a small group of speedway people like Ivan Mauger, Johnnie Hoskins, Barry Briggs and Ronnie Moore to be honoured in this way. Sometimes words are not enough to describe that feeling of pride and happiness.

EPILOGUE

My youngest daughter, Charlotte, was going to be twenty-two in two months. She was talking on her mobile phone to her mother, Jackie, outside the accident and emergency at Leighton Hospital defending her father's impetuosity – or was it stupidity? It was clear from the way the conversation was going that Jackie considered it to be stupidity. When Charlotte's phone rang, knowing it was her mother following up the message explaining where we were, she went outside as she realised that she may need some privacy.

Ironically, considering where she was (outside under the veranda with the waiting room windows open), it was like an echo chamber; the whole waiting room of about twenty-five people – some injured, some offering a supportive hand – received Charlotte's side of the conversation loud and clear. 'But it's the only pleasure he gets these days,' Charlotte offered in my defence. Not quite true, but I was grateful to her for her support. I could just imagine what Jackie was saying: 'He's forty-six years old. He still thinks he's twenty-five. What is he going to do about work? I told him not to go on his own. I can't believe it, the stupid idiot!'

Two hours earlier, on this beautiful summer's day in August 2002, I was in Delamere Forest. It was a Saturday and I was laying on my side at the bottom

161

of what was called the 'Bomb Hole'. I knew I had broken my collarbone; I could feel it and hear it grating. In my dazed state I got myself together, and my first thought was 'She'll kill me' – Jackie that is. Her last comment, as I drove off in my car with my mountain bike, was: 'Should you be going in the forest on your own?' I usually went with my road-racing mate Sandy Dranfield or a gang of us, so if we had any problems you had back up. But my reply to Jackie was: 'I will be alright. I'm not going to do anything stupid!' Famous last words.

I had attempted what is called a drop-off. I had already done it successfully. I then tried it from another angle that made the drop higher – about six feet. I got it all wrong as I took off and landed on my head and shoulder first. Then, as I landed badly, crunch went the collarbone – matching the other side that I did while grass-track racing twenty-eight years earlier.

I staggered to my feet, picked up my bike with my good arm, leant it against a tree and quickly sat down as the pain kicked in. I started to feel nauseous, and I must have looked a sight, covered in crap and probably as white as a sheet. I planned to just rest a while then push the bike back to the car and drive the five miles home. My car, being an automatic, I could do that.

I wanted to keep it low key, not make a fuss, typical of me. A few people went past asking me if I was alright. I didn't mention the collarbone, and said: 'Yeah. I'll be okay in a few minutes,' and they walked on. Then a lady on a horse took one look at me, and said: 'Are you okay? You don't look it.' She wasn't letting me get away with a simple 'I'm okay'. She was very helpful and realised I had a broken collarbone, and made a sling from a spare shirt she had with her. She helped me back up to the car, and I knew she wouldn't let me drive, so I faked a call to Jackie to come and pick me up – who I knew was going to hit the roof. I could just hear her saying: 'I told you not to go on your own.'

Anyway as my helpful horse rider left me to supposedly wait for Jackie, I somehow got my bike on the car and drove the five miles home. I walked into the lounge – Jackie was out – and Charlotte was there on her own. When I announced: 'I have broken my collarbone, you will have to take me to hospital,' she thought I was joking. However, looking at the state of me she realised I was not joking. 'Mum will go mad,' she said.

Why is it that men have to endure? I get injured having a bit of fun and there is no sympathy, just 'It's your own fault'. I cleaned myself up, cut off the T-shirt and mistakenly left that lying on the bathroom floor for Jackie to find – who I could not get in contact with as she was out somewhere. Off we went to Leighton Hospital to get sorted.

I always considered I would have to have two careers: riding speedway was not going to earn me enough money to retire before I was forty, and riding beyond forty is possible, as shown by a few, but not realistic. In my case, due to a knackered hip, I hung up my boots at the comparatively early age of thirty-four. I sometimes wish I had pursued the desire to be a rock star. They rock until they drop! But talent would have been a restriction down that avenue. For me, speedway was a very satisfying and rewarding choice. A few more years would have been preferable, but under the circumstances I know I made the right choice.

Breaking out of the cocoon of my speedway world into the big wide world was quite a challenge; but a challenge was not something I was averse to and I successfully made the change from speedway rider to financial adviser – and hopefully author. People often ask me if I miss riding, and I answer without hesitation a bold YES! If I could have ridden speedway for another ten or fifteen years I would have done so, but it would have to have been at the top level. I suppose that is what I miss, competing against the best, the buzz you get from winning and competing.

Speedway provided me with some great times with some fantastic people. Don't get me wrong, I have a great life, I don't yearn for those times and I have it in perspective. I just miss it in that I know they were special times and am very appreciative of having a gift that I was able to express. That often gave me great satisfaction and I know, without being conceited, as time allows me to look at my riding in a detached way, I was entertaining.

Since I had my hip fixed in October 2001, I have had a new lease of life and get my kicks – and knocks – from mountain-bike riding. It is a way for me of keeping quite fit while still having a challenge. I just need to compete, whether it is against people or just setting a time for me to beat myself. It is a basic need.

I often say when I go out mountain biking: 'It's been a good day if you draw blood.' The broken collarbone was just a bit beyond that principle! But I don't think I will ever lose that desire to get stuck in and have that physical or mental challenge – I certainly don't intend to. I sometimes feel that failing in my quest to be World Individual Speedway Champion has left me with something still to prove to myself. Or maybe I'm still a kid at heart? I don't know and although my quest to be the best speedway rider in the world may not have been achieved, it was one hell of a journey that I would not have missed for the world.

And while reminiscing, my thoughts will always take me back to where it all started in my childhood times, when I can clearly remember those hot summer days when I could fill my gallon can up with petrol, take it down to the track with my bike to meet the rest of the lads, and ride until the can ran out.

ON A STORYTELLER'S NIGHT

This final section was inspired by an evening when we all got together and told stories about our eras in speedway. We talked long into the night as time passed by unnoticed during an evening of great memories, great stories and pizza. Some of them couldn't appear in the main body of the book, but they were so good that they couldn't be overlooked. Of course, this ballooned into something bigger and telephone lines were burned with renewed vigour to create our own version of outtakes. They appear here, in no particular order.

Hilary Morton, Mother

Early in Chris' career, when he was riding grass track, his father would do the driving because he was too young to drive. But on this particular weekend his Dad had to work so I had to do the driving. The bike would go on a trailer that we towed. We were going along and we missed the turning. 'You should have turned,' said Chris. I didn't go far past it because I had put the brakes on, so I had to reverse back. And I tried to back this damned thing (the trailer) up and I couldn't do it. It was going everywhere and in the end Chris said: 'Get out Mum. I'll back it up.' So we swapped over and he backed it up and I was hoping that a policeman didn't come past. Then I got back in and drove the rest of the way. I still can't do it now.

We were quite proud in 1976 when Chris qualified for the World Final. There were five or six coaches that went from Belle Vue to see that meeting. At the meeting, all across the top of the stadium there were Russian soldiers with machine guns keeping everyone in order. It was as if they were saying: 'You will stay there and watch this meeting.' It was a good track, but it was raining a bit at times and they had no covering, so when the people put their umbrellas up you couldn't see anything.

People were coming out of the country with more money than they went in with – I don't know how – and you weren't allowed to take zlotys out of the country. I bought everyone a meal with my money at the station because it was so cheap.

Richard Clark, Editor, *Speedway Star*

Historic partnerships: Lennon and McCartney, Jagger and Richards, Laurel and Hardy, Morecambe and Wise. All clear indications that two heads are better than one. But the one that lives in my memory is that of Chris Morton and Ged Blake. They never managed as many 5-1 victories as Mort and PC (to my knowledge they never managed one), but as a debating quorum around a pub fire, they were second to none.

It's a laugh-a-slurp with those two and many a speedway trip was enlivened by knowing I'd be able to catch up with them in some fun-forsaken place (Vetlanda springs to mind). Chris, of course, was the riding side of the partnership, Ged the oily rag. But that was never likely to satisfy Ged forever. The man lusts after just a brief whiff of what it smells like to be a top speedway rider, which is how he happened to be bending Mort's ear a lot more than usual one late-season night at Oxford.

Confession – I wasn't there. If I had been, the first thing thrust under the eventually prostrate Ged's nose would have been an autograph book, but I've insisted the two tell this story to newcomers so many times. And I have seen the video!

It was the last meeting of the season and, in those particular days, one regular ritual was for a mechanics' race as part of the farewell entertainment. Needless to say, Ged was well up for it. Equally needless to say, Mort wasn't.

'Mort, I know what to do.'

'Ged, you'll hurt yourself.'

'Mort, I won't, I know what to do.'

'Ged, you'll come off and end up in hospital.'

'Mort, I'll take it easy.'

'You're not using my brand-new bike.'

'Oh Mort, go on, give me a break.'

Finally, Ged's big break did come… and how! Much against his better judgement – and that's very unusual – Mort allowed Ged to clamber aboard said brand-spanking-new 500cc's-worth of snarling, snapping speedway machinery. On the video, you can see him offering last-minute advice, possibly along the lines of 'it's mostly left turns,' because that was the sort of detail that probably wouldn't have occurred to Ged.

Up to the tapes and then Ged was away, the direction in which Chris had possibly turned his head too. All was sedate until the end of either the first or second lap. That's when things began to go sadly wrong. Into the pits bend at a rampant 15 miles an hour or so, Ged suddenly discovered that his next twist of throttle actually took him past an opponent. This was no longer an end-of-season mechanics race. This was Ged Blake, in front of 20,000 screaming speedway fans at Hyde Road, starting to pick his opponents off one by one to ensure Belle Vue remained unbeaten at home. Coincidentally, this was also the moment Ged was no longer really in control of the bike in front of a more modest 2,000 or so at a bitterly cold Cowley watching a mechanics' race. It wasn't stardom beckoning as he charged into the home straight. It was the Cowley safety fence. Ged caught it a beaut. That snarling, snapping speedway thing spat him off. One of his knees took the full force of his landing upon Cowley shale. And our new-found hero lay there while others rushed to his rescue.

Not Mort. Oh no. On his arrival upon the carnage, Ged looked up at him remorsefully, saying: 'My leg really hurts, Mort.' The family-friendly version of Mort's reply was something along the lines of: '*******s to your leg, look what you've done to my bike!'

The wonderful postscript to all this is that Ged's a mad-keen 'boater', or narrowboat owner, and loves nothing more than negotiating the fascinating nooks and crannies of Britain's canal waterways. Soon after that abrupt end to his forty-second-plus speedway racing career, Ged set sail at a more sedate pace with that injured leg duly plastered from thigh to toe. And managed to fall into the canal!

Forget Batman and Robin or Del Boy and Rodney (Dave), few historic partnerships have made a bigger splash on me than Mort and Ged. On a slightly faster racing note, one of Mort's mighty moments has to be the Intercontinental Final at that fun-forsaken Vetlanda in August 1988. This was the last step to the World Final at Vojens that season, with eleven qualifying slots on offer. Twelve heats into the event, the interval stage, Mort had a not-so-mighty 2 points to his name with just two rides remaining. I can recall watching his pit from a safe distance. Ged and Chris' brother Dave busied themselves on machinery checks, while Mort sat collecting thoughts and any reserves of determination he had left. He promptly came out to win those two remaining races, net 8 points overall, and sail through to Vojens in seventh spot. Typically, the ever-modest Mort simply explained it away afterwards as: 'I knew my best gates were coming up, and knew I had to make the most of them.' My already huge admiration for him as a competitor went through the roof that afternoon. I also recall, during the days of the late, lamented Speedway Writers' and Photographers' Association (SWAPA), drawing Mort's name in a pre-British Final draw at a SWAPA lunch in 1983. Prior to tapes-up, I visited Mort in the pits and showed *him my ticket, telling him I'd share the winnings if he won the meeting. He pinned the ticket to his pit programme and, 12 points later, was crowned British Champion! It's the nearest I'll ever come to being British Champion, so perhaps Ged and I have more in common than we first thought! Mort and Ged, the REAL dynamic duo.*

Steve Cooney, Mechanic (1978–85)

I remember having really good times, but some of the best times that we had were when we were in the garage working. When we were working on the bikes and so on they were really good. We had a good crack.

I remember 'The Big Trip' in 1981. We had a meeting in England on Thursday and then we had to get over to Poland for the World Pairs Final. It was Manchester to Munich, Munich to Katowice, Poland; but we couldn't go through Czecho because we never had visas. We did the practice at Katowice, had one night in a bed there and I remember Mort having a shower. When he turned the shower on it came out like chocolate! It was horrible. And I said to Mort: 'I'm cleaner than the water, I'm staying as I am!' We had one night in the bed and the next day it was the meeting. The Americans won, Penhall and Schwartz and Bobby came back with us. We went to get fuel, but there were queues for petrol and we all just started filling up and this guy kicked off. Then one of the guys who took us to the station just pulled out some letter. God knows what it said, but everybody just shut up and walked away. We had a jerry can and filled it up.

We had to get from Poland back to the West because we had to race in a grass-track meeting on the Sunday. Chris drove to the border and I took over from there. We were there for ages, and we were tight on time. It was an early start on Sunday as well. Mort was in the back and Bobby was in the front. There was a speedway bike in the car with the rear seat out, but there was just enough room for a body length to lie down. Chris was trying to sleep in the back, it was absolutely hammering it down with rain and I was just nailing it. We were on three figures on the speedo and there were cobbles in places and all Chris could hear was: 'Bang! Bang! Bang!' We got so far into East Germany, then had to put the jerry can in and carried on. Later the gauge started blinking so we put the methanol in and carried on again. But when you run a car on methanol, because it's an alcohol fuel, when you put the throttle down it cuts out. So you drive it on the choke. You accelerate on the choke – using more fuel!

When we got through the border into East Germany we didn't get more than a mile and a half when we were stopped for driving on the wrong side of the road. We went round a corner and we found ourselves on a railway track, and I thought: 'Shit! We shouldn't be here,' but the road on the other side was wide enough, so I pulled over onto that side. But when we got to the bridge the arrow was pointing to the railway track. So we should have been on it after all! A police car pulled out and stopped us. He's ranting in German and we couldn't understand him, and Bobby Schwartz was trying to tell him that he's a World Champion and trying to give him his autograph! This copper's stood there with his hand on his gun. Eventually he set a fine of 25 Western DM (Deutschemarks) and Schwartzie asked him for a receipt! A big argument followed because obviously this copper was going to pocket it for himself. So there was a big row about that. Eventually he let us go and we got to the stage where we were really low on fuel, so we drained the fuel out of the bikes. We eventually made it to the border and we asked how far for gasoline and he said: '60km,' or something. But luckily we didn't have to go that far.

So we are off again at million miles an hour down the autobahn. I remember getting near the track, and Chris was in the back and Bobby was in the front with his feet up on the dashboard. I had got so far that I couldn't drive anymore because I had been driving at that speed for all that time and my eyes were on pins – I was shattered. So I said: 'I can't drive anymore. One of you guys will have to take over.' And Schwartz says: 'Yeah, yeah, I'll do it.' So I get out of the car and walk round and the air woke me up. I was sat there in the passenger seat and eventually that warm feeling came over me when you can feel yourself falling asleep. Well, after about two minutes I felt the car stopping and I wondered what was going on. Schwartzy said: 'Gee man, I can't drive anymore. I'm too tired!' I had about three minutes kip and then I had to jump back in again. And then we did another meeting on the way home in England!

'The Flying Phlegm' was a Mercedes van that was really narrow but really long. Of course, there were two up the front and the rest of us thugs in the back. On the boat you would get really packed in, and who ever was in the front opened the door and smacked this bloke's car. This guy got out and was all aggressive, but just as he got out, the door slid open and all five of us from the back got out and he just got straight back in his car!

At a European grass-track meeting in Germany we all stayed at the same hotel so we had a good time, played a bit of football and generally enjoyed ourselves – as you do. We were late, not for the meeting, but the last ones in. We were shouting abuse out to everyone we knew and Old Mort (Dave Morton) was shouting: 'Don't mention the War', and generally caused a bit of a fuss when we turned up. But when we got back there was an article in the Motor Cycle News, saying that we had been out all night – trying to imply that we were blathered – turned up late in the meeting and giving us a bit of a slagging. Then the last two paragraphs showed that we were first and second!

I can also remember a couple of occasions when I really stuck my neck out for Mort. It was at an indoor meeting – Old Mort (Dave Morton) was there – and I remember it was freezing cold and I had left a camera in the van over night and it was frozen solid the next morning. You couldn't press the shutter and the lens wouldn't turn. I remember Egon Muller came underneath Mort who just stood his ground and Muller went down. He came round and started kicking off at Mort, so I waded in and said: 'What are you

*talking about? Look at your throttle there, that goes both ways, you've got the choice.'
And Old Mort was behind us going: 'Hit him, Steve, hit him!' Another one that comes
to mind was at Eastbourne. There was a massive, big bloke. As usual I was warming
the bike up while Chris was on parade, and he came over and said: 'Stop that now!'
That's what he was like, dead arrogant and I just carried on. He was threatening me
out loud and I just said to him: 'You've got your job to do and I've got mine. When I've
finished....'*

*With Mort, as his mechanic, everything was discussed, but at Wimbledon one time he
came in from his first race and said that we needed to change the engine for his next race
– which was about two or three races away. So you can imagine what it was like, taking
the nuts and bolts off and everything in a short space of time – I had no fingerprints for
about two months after! I remember running out to the car and picking the engine up and
running back with it under my arm. I was warming the bike when he was getting his gear
on and we made it right at the death. That was Chris' decision – I had no say in it. But
generally everything was discussed.*

*Most of the time, if Chris missed the start his ability would get him through. It was
only on the odd occasions, those big occasions, when the pressure was on to do it. In his
final meeting Chris did a lap on his own and I remember talking to Clarkie at the time
and said: 'You know, I still get the impression he missed the gate!'*

Peter Collins MBE, 1976 World Champion, Belle Vue (1973–86) and England teammate

*Chris and I were born and bred in the same town. Our fathers were friends before we
were born and we lived and grew up within a quarter of a mile of each other. I was very
friendly with his brother Dave as well as he was the same age as me, whereas Chris was
two years younger. The partnership that Chris and I had going at Belle Vue was just
fantastic and people still talk today about the old heat thirteen when we used to have
the thirteen-heat format. If the score was close then Chris and I nearly always managed
to pull off a 5-1 at Hyde Road, and often on the away tracks too. We had a fantastic
understanding as far as team riding went. With both of us riding together at Belle Vue, it
was unbelievable.*

*Chris used to like riding around the outside and I used to like the outside and the
inside and enjoyed riding anywhere. But Chris favoured the outside more. He wasn't a
very good gater, and people used to say that I wasn't a good gater, but I could make some
starts if I had to. But at Belle Vue we never needed to make good gates. I used to like
to get ahead of Chris in heat thirteen, but I knew he was coming round the outside so
I just had to take care of the other two around the first turn and just glance across and
I knew he would be there. We had to change lines and direction, but we never used to*

discuss it – it just came naturally. We had a great understanding and in all those years as teammates we never ever fell out. Our predecessors at Belle Vue, Tommy Roper and Soren Sjosten, were the riders who would be in heat thirteen during the late 1960s and they used to argue over gate positions. In those days they weren't fixed gate positions and they would often be fighting in the pits after heat thirteen and there would be swarms of people in the pits watching them scrapping and trying to break it up. But Chris and I had a much, much better understanding.

I think the thing that put the top hat on it for us was when we won the World Pairs at Lonigo in 1984. The pleasure we got from that win was unbelievable – an absolute dream. The fact that our Dads had been mates, we grew up together, we lived less than a quarter of a mile apart and were born in the same hospital meant we truly were World Pairs Champions. It wasn't like me and somebody who came from Kent or something like that. Chris had won quite a few World Team Cup medals, but his World Pairs with me is probably one of the most prestigious things that he had won. It was one step away from winning the World Final. To win that after what we had both been through; the team riding we did at Lonigo was like a series of heat thirteens. Hans Nielsen and Erik Gundersen were paired together, Ivan and Mitch Shirra, Shawn Moran and Schwartz. We didn't dominate the meeting but we were the most consistent. Maybe there were riders who scored more points on the day, but we had something that the rest hadn't got and from the start we just helped each other. It was fantastic to do that after our history.

Kelly Moran, Belle Vue teammate (1989-90) and double World Team Champion

It was only my second long-track meeting ever in Muhldorf, Germany and I was sharing a bike with my brother Shawn. Shooey's bikes were not working very well so we shared this bike that was tuned by Hans Zierk – who used to be Wiggy's (Simon Wigg) guy. I was more worried about what I looked like going along the straights. What do I do? Do I stick my left leg out the back and lay down, or hold onto the chassis with my head down? Because it was only my second long-track meeting I didn't want to look like an 'idiot long-tracker'! Shooey would finish his race and the pits were in turn two, so he'd have to go round and come back. He'd pull onto the centre green, lean the bike over and then I'd come out and get on it. It was said that because the long-track bikes were 'highly tuned' you shouldn't do back-to-back races on them, but what the heck! Shawn said to me to look out for the 'rooster' behind me as they were filling the bike up with methanol. The 'rooster' is all the shale and stuff that sprays off the back wheel.

This bike was like a rocket ship – it just flew! I had made the semi-final, but I missed the gate. I saw the 'rooster' that Shooey told me about and then I went from last to third, passing Egon (Muller) and all these guys, and then I came up behind Chris. This bike was so fast, and I prepared to go round him, but I thought: 'Shit, he's the guy who saved my life in Poland.' So I backed off. I got third and transferred to the final, but the bike's magic box broke down in the final. After the meeting we were sat around having a meal and a drink and this and that when Chris said to me: 'Your bike was so fast. Why didn't you pass me?' And I said: 'I couldn't pass you because you saved my life in Poland.' Ged was there too and I remember Chris giving me a little wink of acknowledgment. I am indebted to Chris and his wife for what they did in that hotel room in Poland.

Steve E. Casey, former rider and friend

I have known Chris Morton practically all of my adult life, but initially as just an acquaintance, on a sort of a nodding basis. Our paths first crossed on a dark and cold October night in 1972 when he was better known as Dave Morton's little brother. I had travelled over to Crewe with my mates for my first visit to the super-fast Earl Street bowl to watch Crewe take on Ellesmere Port in an end-of-season challenge match.

As the second half was about to start we wandered into the pits and there, about to go out to race, was a tiny figure in what appeared to be the biggest crash helmet I'd ever seen. 'Who's that?' I asked my mate. 'That's Dave Morton's little brother, Chris.' This seemed as good a reason as any to watch the first of the junior races that signalled the start of the second half. Chris won the race in spectacular fashion, as he did his other two outings and it seemed to me then, as a worldly wise seventeen-year-old, that here was someone destined for a big future in speedway. How right I was. I also knew he would end up at my local track, Belle Vue, that was famous for developing young riders into stars. The following January saw the start of the Belle Vue Training School, run under the guidance of Dent Oliver. I, along with countless others, attended as we tried to make our own mark as budding speedway riders. As I expected, there was Chris and, in no time at all, had attracted the interest of Dent Oliver who, as the weeks went by, showed plenty of enthusiasm for his latest discovery.

It was around this time that contracted team members from other tracks appeared to try out new equipment and get fit for the rapidly approaching season. These more-experienced riders were often put into races with the less-experienced riders such as Chris and myself. It was in one of these races that Bradford's Syd Sheldrick and his brother Mick came into close contact with the fast-emerging talent that was Chris Morton. Back in the pits, the Sheldricks were anxious to point out to a bewildered Chris that there was a right and a wrong way to go about speedway and they didn't 'appreciate' some of Chris's passing methods. A shouting match ensued as more of the Sheldrick family got involved. Enter one very irate Dent Oliver, who explained in no uncertain terms that if the Sheldricks didn't button it they would be 'requested to vacate the stadium and would not be welcomed back'. Nobody answered Dent Oliver back; he was giving people the 'hairdryer treatment' before Alex Ferguson's voice had broken. Needless to say, Chris soon progressed and established himself as the star pupil of the class of 1973 and took his place on the long list of training school graduates.

By now a clearer picture of his background emerged of his links with the Partington Speedway Mafia. Partington is a suburb of Manchester that produced so many speedway stars who made their mark in British and world speedway. As a habitual Belle Vue attendee I saw Chris progress from a young (and wild) hopeful to superstar in next to no time, and his performances with Belle Vue and England in general, and Peter Collins in particular, are well documented. Apart from being nodding acquaintances at speedway, or the odd Hollies concert, we didn't become friends until we met at an indoor karting event being run by Carl Stonehewer's sponsors in 1988/89. Chris was interested in financial services and we soon ended up working together. Over the years we've had many lively debates and discussions about many topics and he hates losing arguments as badly as he hated losing races. I'm pleased to report, though, that I have won more than my share, which is more than can be said for our speedway clashes! As his career drew to a close, Chris threw his enthusiasm and effort into business and it was during this period that he had a year as team manager at Berwick, decided to open a new speedway track at Buxton, was awarded an MBE by the Queen (but I must admit I had my own interpretation of what it stood for) and also decided he would build his own house! All this was when we were trying to develop a financial services business with targets to hit and the myriad of problems that came with it.

Through all the traumas Mort, being Mort, was never flustered and in the same way I had seen him so many times at Belle Vue, he'd shrug his shoulders and take it in his stride. It wasn't long, though, before the need to race re-emerged. I was racing karts by this time and he showed an interest that quickly evaporated when he realised that he would have to pay to race. So a brief spell at Sheffield (always one of his favourite tracks) resulted. The season at Sheffield was rarely dull, but unspectacular and I'm pleased to say I 'helped him out' at many matches, along with Darren Boocock, doing the technical stuff. Ged wasn't prepared to drop down to the Second Division!

I was also with him at his final speedway meeting when he won the Northern Riders' Championship amid a near-riot at Sheffield. We were chatting on the way over to Owlerton when he said he fancied his chances of winning the meeting. This seemed a little optimistic as the previous Friday he'd put in a none-too-startling performance at Edinburgh. Sheffield was a different proposition though and the Chris Morton of old emerged, so his final appearance resulted in yet another title. That's Mort all over. Thanks for the memories mate; I certainly have plenty of them. Bob Radford once said of Mort: 'He's only a small man but he casts a giant shadow' (especially in that big crash helmet!).

Eric Boocock, Belle Vue and England team manager

Having Chris Morton and Peter Collins at Belle Vue was like the dream team. If we needed a 5-1 in the last race I always felt confident that we could get it with those two in the race – they were phenomenal.

They were friends on and off the track and there was a friendly rivalry there. If Peter had won a race, then Mort would have to go out and win one as well. I think that helped because they would bounce off each other. Mort had outstanding ability. He was born to ride a bike and he was a trier. I can't recall a specific race because with Chris there were so many wonderful races, and it was because he was so exciting that he was so popular. He couldn't get out of the start and if he did make a good start he didn't know how he had done it, but in those days it didn't matter. With Chris, if he was going through a rough patch, I had to approach him differently to PC. I would say something like: 'What's the matter with you tonight? You were crap there, that rider who's just beaten you should have got nowhere near you.' He would have a go back at me and then go out like a rocket and he was off again. But that wasn't very often because he didn't need much motivation. He was proud to ride for the Aces.

It was a different era then. They were great times and if he raced now he would still be good, but it's changed so much. These days you have to be able to make good starts, and Mort's problem was that he couldn't make good starts. But back then you didn't have to.

Shawn Moran, Belle Vue teammate (1989-90) and 1983 World Long-Track Champion

I raced with Chris at Belle Vue and Dave at Sheffield and they are both really cool guys. Dave was the gater while Chris was the racer. I had many good races around the old Belle Vue with Chris and he was always good to race against: he wouldn't squeeze you up against the fence or pinch you off – he was fair and you could trust him. When the tapes went up you would just be looking around for him because you knew he would be coming from somewhere. Maybe half a lap or a lap and he would be on my shoulder. He was a good ambassador for the sport and deserves his MBE. As a captain he always had the right things to say. It really sunk in and it would stay with you.

Ged Blake, mechanic (1979-90)

I had gone over to Germany alone with all the equipment while Chris raced at Belle Vue on the Saturday night. Then he was going to fly in ready to race the next day and I would have everything ready for him. But the van kept overheating. It was only the radiator but then it blew a head gasket so I was stopping every twenty minutes. So it took about ten years to get to Abensberg where the meeting was! I got in touch with Chris and asked him to bring over some parts for the van because we needed to fix it. At that time it was

normal after a meeting on a Saturday night that the top riders would all rush off to prepare for a meeting on the continent the next day. So a lot of the riders would be coming
in on the same flight.

The plane came in and sure enough all the riders were coming through arrivals from
the British Airways flight looking smart with their bags carrying their leathers and so on.
And then Mort appeared among this bunch of top international riders, except in direct
contrast he was carrying a radiator, hoses and gaskets! It was so funny, one of the funniest
things I had ever seen, Mort the parts man!

It was never just a job because there was a lot more to it than that. It was a special time
because with Mort what you see is what you get. But with some what you see is not all
you get. I never felt an atmosphere with Chris, ever, even when we had a cross word.

Mark Winterbottom, friend and current employer

My experience of meeting Chris Morton was so much different from everyone else's. I
never knew Chris as a speedway rider; for me speedway was something that was on
Saturday afternoon between the football and Giant Haystacks, Jackie Palo and co. I
should add with Chris's careful coaching I have learned to appreciate it much more.
However, some ten years ago I was a sales director for Zurich Insurance and into my office
walked Chris Morton MBE (the MBE certainly made me sit up straight in my chair!).
I had been introduced to Chris via a mutual friend and hoped I could convince him to
join my sales team in Manchester. I remember talking to Chris and listening intently as
he recalled his exploits and achievements in speedway. After all, how often do you get to
share coffee with the best in the world at anything – I was very excited.

To this day, I can recall how this very confident, polite man modestly told his stories
and answered my questions, questions I'm sure he must have been asked thousands of
times. Of course, if he had, he didn't show it – Chris would never make anybody feel
deliberately uncomfortable. Here was a man who had achieved so much in speedway, had
a family, built his own house. It was never ending. After many meetings I convinced him
we could work together and we embarked on a joint-career, progressing together in what I
can honestly say was one of the best times of my working life.

Recalling a story about Chris is easy because there are so many great times to recall.
The one that will stick in my mind was about five or six years ago. Chris had enjoyed
great success and had built up his own sales operation to twelve people. We had agreed to
take the branch away for a day's development/sport, and Chris had booked a mini-stock-
car racing circuit in Northampton. We had a great day, racing 60mph mini stockcars and
Chris was being the perfect host. The fastest six had made it to the final – Steve Casey
and myself were among them. Now up to this time I had known Chris as the ultimate
professional sales manager and, indeed, up to the last corner on the last lap of the last race,

that was what Chris was. All I remember was following Chris and Steve Casey into the last corner of the last lap and seeing Mort get on Steve's back bumper and flick him round, and then storming through and coming first. I can confess, under my helmet, a smile came to my face – I had finally seen Chris Morton the racer and it was a sight to behold. I speak for so many. We have had some great times. What Chris might lose in height he makes up for many times over in heart. Here's to many more great times ahead.

Ivan Mauger OBE, MBE, Six-times World Champion and Belle Vue teammate (1973)

As an opponent, I have always enjoyed racing against Chris as he was one of the few guys who, win or lose, was a completely honest racer. He could, and very often did, use every part of the track – so he was difficult to beat. If I was leading him I never knew where he was likely to try to pass and similarly, if he was leading me, it was very difficult to set up a passing manoeuvre on him.

He was always a 100 per cent honest racer who was respected by myself and all his rivals as someone you could enjoy a great race with and know you were going to have enough (sometimes just!) space to stay on your bike. As I said, there are not too many guys around like that and respect deserves respect. Even in the hardest competition I always gave him the same amount of space.

Chris' loyalty to Belle Vue also needs to be respected, as he will admit that he was usually in the shadows of Peter Collins and I am not alone in believing that he perhaps would have blossomed a little more on the international stage if he had switched to another club at the top of his career.

I would like now to relate a couple of instances that stand out in my mind with Chris. He and Peter Collins won the World Pairs Championship in Lonigo, Italy, in 1984 and I think that was a great reward for him. PC had already been Individual World Champion, but I thought that it was just great to see the two of them, who were great mates in the same district as kids, then went through their careers with Belle Vue, end up winning the World Pairs Championship together. At that time I was at the end of my international career and for a few years I was really only riding on Sundays around Europe for fun, for something to do as much as anything else. I was enjoying myself away from the pressures of trying to be World Champion. My partner that day was Mitch Shirra and he was probably riding almost at his peak, so we were as happy as you were ever going to get by finishing third in anything. But what made the day more memorable for me was that I was really happy for Mort and PC that they won it. I've had quite a bit to do with both of them for a long, long time; it was fantastic to see the two of them win the Championship together.

Another situation that I think Chris will remember quite clearly was before I was associated with Hans Nielsen. Chris and Hans had a run-off for the British League

Riders' Championship at Belle Vue in 1984. Well we all know that Hans was an excellent starter, so there was a better-than-even chance that Hans was going to get to the first turn before Mort in the run-off. I had raced Hans quite a bit around Europe in the year or two prior to this and his style was always suited to small tracks, as he rode for Wolverhampton and Oxford. So he had one of those small-track styles and tended to come to a bit of a halt in the middle of the turns and then make a big long straight. The problem was that he usually did the same thing on big tracks then. Because we were all Cheshire/Belle Vue guys, there were a lot of people in the pits who really wanted Mort to win the run-off and he asked if I could give him any advice for that. We had quite a chat and I drew on the floor of the pits with a screwdriver what I believed Hans would do three-quarters of the way around the first turn, and told Chris he would have about ten yards to get past Hans right at that point. If he wasn't able to do it, he could wave bye-bye to Hans down the back straight. He did exactly what we discussed and actually collected Hans' front wheel in the process, which was something he wasn't expecting and he slowed right down – possibly looking for a re-run. But Mort won the British League Riders' Championship in that run-off and once again I was very proud that I had something to do with it.

All in all he is a great bloke, a loyal team member to Belle Vue, he was exciting to watch and a 100 per cent racer who was respected by all his rivals. That is a very short statement, but one that very few riders ever earn.

Bobby Schwartz, Double World Pairs Champion and World Team Champion

I could never beat Chris around Belle Vue, never could. He used to have a special super-cool style and he rode around Belle Vue like nobody else. He was a great racer. I remember riding at Lonigo in the Pairs and the track was full of holes, but they just rode through it. Chris and Peter used to go every year and ride in that Gala meeting that they used to have there. But he was a nice guy and we used to have a joke together. He had a nice family and he was always proud of his team and his country, and I had a lot of respect for him.

Reg Wilson, British Lions teammate 1975-76

I was Chris's team manager at Sheffield when he made a comeback in 1993. I never saw him lose his cool. He would never come in and kick the tool box or throw his helmet down or anything like that, he was very laid back. To come back after two years out of the saddle like that is a measure of the talent that he had because it's not easy to do that after that amount of time out of action.

I remember the Lions tour we did in Australia and Chris was a young lad beginning to make his mark. He was the youngest in the team and we were a bit protective over him although we used to take the mickey out of him because he was a bit slack with his bike. But that was because he was young and still learning. I didn't like the Aussies in those days, although I get on better with them now, but back then they were always trying it on and referring to us as 'bloody Poms.' I hated them then, but when I went over with Reg Fearman he could handle all their strokes that they tried to pull.

Chris got into a good race with the Australian John Langfield and Chris had beaten him. When they returned to the pits we could see what was going to happen as Lango was not happy and was going to have a go at him. But we all looked out for Chris and protected him and saved him from getting beaten up.

The local derbies between Sheffield and Belle Vue were always very tense and competitive meetings, but I never had any problems racing against Chris. He was always a fast rider but you could race with him side by side and there were never any problems – it was the same with PC. It was good, clean competitive racing. I had one or two problems with the other Aces riders, but never Chris or PC. In those days there was always the North and South rivalry, so when ever we went south to race, I would always be in the northern part of the pits with those lads and Dave Morton, Dougie Wyer and those riders.

Dave Morton, brother and fellow rider

There was always a lot of rivalry between us when we were racing because we both thought that we were better than the other!

After I had broken my leg I couldn't bend my knee fully, maybe only a quarter of the distance. I went to see Dr Carlo Biaggi and he tried to bend it back while I was under anaesthetic, but he said he couldn't do it and didn't want to push it too much because he didn't want to bend the plate he had put in. Chris and I were dicing at Belle Vue when I was riding for Sheffield. We always used to have a good race because of the rivalry, and we clashed and I crashed heavily. I banged my leg hard into the safety fence, but I didn't break anything. I was just a little sore. Well, after a couple of days full movement had returned to my knee again! The accident actually cured my knee problem and to this day it's been fine ever since. After all the people that looked at it, it took a crash to fix it!

I did the Lions tour with Chris and that was a good tour, we had a great time. I remember having a fight with Bob Valentine. What happened was that Chris had just beaten John Langfield and Langfield came in and dragged Chris off the bike and started laying into him. I wasn't having any of that, so I dragged him off and then Valentine was having a go at me. We were having a scrap and all the bikes were lined up on their stands and we knocked them over and they went down like dominoes, one after the other – that was funny, and it turned into a full-scale punch up.

Peter Collins, John Davis, Dougie Wyer, Chris Pusey and Gordon Kennett were with us on that tour. We did a lot of water-skiing and one time Gordon was having a go. Jim Airey was driving the boat and Gordon hardly got going before he fell. So we turned round to pick him up. When we got there he was drowning because he couldn't swim! He was clawing at the water and the boat and he said he couldn't swim. I don't know why he didn't tell us – maybe it was because he was embarrassed. We used to play water polo in the pool and we used to split up into teams. I would throw the ball into the deep end so that Gordon would have to go and get it! But he never would.

I would have liked to have ridden for Belle Vue, but when I started at Crewe Len Silver asked me if I would like to ride some second halves at Hackney. I said yes, and then he started to put me into the team. I was also having second-half rides at Belle Vue too at the time, but when Maury Littlechild died that link with the Aces was broken and I went to Hackney. I would have liked to have ridden for Sheffield before I had my injury. I think I would have achieved more. We were always riding at places like Halifax, Belle Vue, Sheffield and Hull. All the northern lads would ride regularly with open meetings and guest bookings – it was a great time.

I remember that later in my career I was having a good season and Ivan Mauger was riding for Exeter then. He called me and asked if I would ride for the Falcons during their match at Belle Vue as a guest for Scott Autrey, and I said yes. Ivan was being clever because Scott had only ridden five matches, so he had an artificially high average and I could come in as a guest. I scored a maximum and Exeter won. Belle Vue were complaining about it and they said it wasn't right that they had me in place of Autrey – but that was Ivan, he was clever like that.

When we went to the World Final at Vojens I really thought Chris was going to have a good final because he had been riding well that year. Chris' problem was that he couldn't make consistently good starts; it's no good giving fast riders like Hans Nielsen a ten-yard advantage – especially round a track like Vojens. It was disappointing and he only scored 6 points, but Ged used to get more depressed than Chris! Ged was so enthusiastic and wore his heart on his sleeve. He was a bit over the top sometimes, but Chris just dealt with it and moved onto the next meeting.

George Morton, father

I remember I was walking from the garage with Bill Collins (Peter's father) when Chris was young and we could hear this bike going. Bill said to me: 'Can you hear that?' 'Yeah, he's giving it some stick isn't he?' 'You know who it is don't you?' And I replied: 'No.' 'It's your Chris.' That incident stuck in my mind because that really sounded like the real thing.

When we went to the World Final in 1976, we were met at the Polish border by a courier, like the Polish Gestapo, as Poland was a Communist country at that time. Derek (work colleague) and I worked for British Airways. We were interested in the aeroplanes because there were all sorts that we hadn't seen before. The courier thought that we were some kind of spies. He was dead scared and he said: 'Don't show any interest in any of the aeroplanes.'

Katowice was a dead dirty place, there was black smoke belching out of the chimneys because it was an industrial area. It probably isn't like that now, but back then it was and you could see them all working and there wasn't much safety. For example, there was one where there was a big blast furnace and all they had was just a wire netting and as you walked past you could feel the heat.

Before we went into the stadium we were all warned about the Russian soldiers and there was one who was being a nuisance. He was parading up and down and he was just being a nuisance, but no one would say anything because he was a Russian. If that had been in England he would have got clobbered! The currency regulations were very strict. You could only have 60 zlotys and that was what you were allowed, but it went a long way. You couldn't use any other currency.

On the way back we were stuck at the Polish border for hours and hours. We thought it was because a Polish rider hadn't won the World Final because speedway is a big thing in Poland. We were the last coach to get away, and we couldn't have any heat on in the coach because the radiator was knackered! Fancy having a coach go all the way over there with a broken radiator!

Gary Miller, Mechanic 1973-76

We had the same sense of fun, the same taste in music and the sense of humour – we got along really well. I had worked with a few other riders but Chris was the most profes-sional. I was working at the Smithfield Wholesale market at the time and I used to finish around 3 p.m., so I could then go and help Mort as his mechanic. But I had to start at 4 a.m. at Smithfield, so sometimes if we had been down south racing I would get back and go straight to work without any sleep. But they were magic times.

I suppose we were a bit of an odd couple, because Mort is not that tall and I am 6'2"! In the early days we went down to Plough Lane, Wimbledon, and we went to the van and Cyril Maidment came along and said: 'Oi, you kids, out now!' And Mort said: 'But I'm riding tonight.' 'Yeah, I've heard that before, go on, get out.' Because we were young and Mort never looked his age, Cyril thought that we were kids who had got into pits, but thankfully Wilkie (Alan Wilkinson) stepped in and came to our rescue – good ol' Wilkie!

At Birmingham I saw Mort lose his temper, which was a side of Mort I had never seen before. He had a tussle with Alan Grahame and put him down. At first I was pleased that he had done it, because Grahame had done the same to him earlier and I was glad that he got him back. But I realised that he had broken his leg. Mort came into the pits

179

and I said: 'Bit iffy that wasn't it?' At Birmingham you had to walk behind the main stand to get to the dressing room, and it wasn't very nice. One or two people were trying to hit Mort and saying some very nasty things. When we got to the dressing room people realised what was going on and the police escorted us out of the stadium. They stayed with us until we got to the A34 and then we continued the rest of our journey home. When we got to Knutsford, he said: 'I've learnt a very important lesson tonight. I'm never ever going to do that again.'

Another time was at King's Lynn. He had a crash and injured his elbow. He had a big gash that should have had stitches. But he went out for his next race and rode a blinder and won the race. I was waiting for him at the pit gate and as he came in I touched his elbow. He rode into the pits and collapsed in agony and was rolling around the floor.

'What's up Mort?'

'Some bastard has touched my elbow that I injured!'

I didn't tell him it was me. I did later and he just laughed, but he got me back though. Before the 1976 Intercontinental Final, it was a really hot day and we went to the Twickenham pool where we did a bit of sunbathing and then had a dip before the meeting. I got sunburnt, and when he came in after he had clinched his place in the World Final, he jumped off the bike and embraced me – God that was absolute agony! That was a great meeting and when he took Ivan Mauger round the outside that was out of this world. When he came back to the pits, we got the 'God Nod' from Ivan. We used to call it that because Ivan wouldn't really say anything to you, but if you did something on the track that was worthy he would give you a nod of acknowledgement so we called it the 'God Nod.' Ivan was brilliant, so smooth and fast.

I can remember Chris' stag night too. Dave was the number one for Hackney so Chris travelled with him and then after they had done the meeting they went out on the town. I went with Peter Collins because his mechanic couldn't make it and I ended up helping him as well as Chris and another Belle Vue rider, Russ Hodgson. On the way back I was driving and we stopped at the services. In those days the riders were wearing clogs, as they were all the rage among speedway riders. Mort was in the back and he said that he wanted a drink, and I replied: 'I'll get it for you Mort, what do you want?' He insisted that he wanted to come with me, but I said to him that he was pissed and should stay in the car. I left him scrabbling around in the car because he couldn't find one of his clogs. Then he emerged and I could hear clunk, clink, clunk, clink, when I looked round he was wearing a clog on one foot and a pint glass on the other! He didn't even know and I told him to go back to the car.

Mort used to give me his engagement ring to look after when he was racing. I used to slip it onto my little finger, but one night after a meeting at Wolves he said: 'Can I have my ring back?'

'Yes. Oh shit, Mort, I haven't got it. I must have lost it somewhere!'

I went to give it back to him and it had gone! Obviously I felt bad about it and I said to him that I would buy an exact replacement. But it turned out that he had already done that because he lost it while he was racing in Australia! We told Jackie and I wasn't very popular.

They were great times and I got along well with all the lads. It was brilliant, just going to the meetings, the atmosphere, the camaraderie and the racing – it was great. I had to give up because I was starting a family so I needed some stability, but I still followed Mort's career when I could. Now I take my son along and he said to me: 'Can I buy a badge, Dad?'

'Yeah, sure.'

He came back with a badge that had a silhouette of Mort on it. He said he picked it because it looked exciting. Mort was the most spectacular rider I ever saw, and when I introduced Mort to my son he was so excited to meet him.

Tony McDonald, Editor, *Backtrack Magazine*

It was 1979 when I first had the pleasure of meeting Chris Morton. He was testing the new Godden machine one chilly winter's morning at my local track, Hackney, just ten minutes' drive from the Speedway Mail *office where I worked. I had joined the* Mail *around six months earlier, more or less straight from school and when the owners asked me to line up a couple of big-name riders as regular, new columnists for our weekly paper, Mort was my first choice. Not because he had a string of major titles to his name, but because he had still to really make his mark on the international scene. I wanted him on board for what he represented at that time – a very spectacular, courageous and popular rider who was young, English and going places. Chris couldn't have been more co-operative with his column, often returning from gruelling weekend trips across Europe to meet our Monday morning deadline with tales of his adventures, on and off track. Thankfully he never lost his natural modesty, or his ability to see ironic humour in sometimes the most difficult situations. As any speedway hack of Mort's era will gladly confirm, he was always a delight to talk to and interview.*

As a teenage kid supporting the old Hawks in the mid-to-late 1970s, I couldn't help but admire and marvel at the daring deeds of this diminutive racer from Manchester. It was even a pleasure to see him beat our riders because he invariably did it the hard way – from the back. Chris' elder brother Dave was our number one in 1975 and 1976 and though the brothers were similar in size and stature, Dave was significantly faster from the gate, even if he lacked Chris' more spectacular endeavours. I would've loved to have seen them as Hackney's twin spearhead but I'm sure the Belle Vue management wouldn't have entertained the idea after Len Silver snatched Dave from under their noses, moving him up from Second Division Crewe (where Chris subsequently began his career in second halves) to The Wick!

Although Chris seriously contemplated a move from Hyde Road and out from under the shadow of his great mate Peter Collins at the end of 1979, he stayed with the Aces and, indeed, went on to achieve major success for club and country. There was talk at one stage that he could sign for Coventry but the slick Brandon circuit would never have provided Mort with the same kind of platform on which to display his talents as the wide-open spaces of Hyde Road. He was tailor-made for the famous old Manchester track and no fair-minded supporter will have begrudged Chris his victory there in the BLRC of 1984, when the annual league riders' final still had genuine prestige and was taken very seriously by competitors, promoters and fans alike. In the '70s and '80s, tracks were much more conducive to overtaking and none perfected the art better than Mort, who would give the very best a head start and beat them in style. It seemed effortless at times but, of course, his heroic, fearless passing manoeuvres were anything but. Thank God he never learned to gate as well as many of his rivals!

Neil Middleditch, Great Britain Team Manager (2001-)

My first memory of Chris was when he won the British Junior Championship at Canterbury, I finished third and it was really the first time I had seen him race. He was the hot favourite and he didn't disappoint. Chris went on to become one of the truly gifted riders and was always Mr 110 per cent. The crowd loved him for his never-give-up attitude and exciting style. You knew if Chris was in a race it was going to be a good one.

He was a lousy gater! I know he will agree, but anybody who raced him knew that until that race was over they would have a little terrier snapping at their back wheel. Our paths crossed many times over the years and some years later we had the rare distinction of racing in Kuwait, Abu Dhabi and Egypt. It was a demonstration tour and sixteen riders from GB went over to show them what speedway was about. I remember when we were racing in Cairo, Chris won the meeting and the crowd was huge, with riot police, the works. After Chris and the top three had collected their prizes the crowd then shouldered Chris through this sea of Arab faces – I think he was terrified that he would never get away but needless to say he did.

There has always been a bit of a north-south divide within speedway – all in good humour I hasten to add – but Chris crossed that barrier and has remained a friend for many years. Although we don't see each other very often these days it is normally when Poole are at Belle Vue. It's always good to see him. Speedway is a big family and riders, no matter how far apart or how many years pass, will always have that same bond of racing. Chris was one hell of a racer and it has been a pleasure to know him over the years.

Sam Ermolenko, 1993 World Champion

When I first enrolled into the British speedway scene back in 1983/84, my experience of speedway was only a few years old so my eyes were wide open, looking at other competitors' racing styles. To that date my only experience was the American scene and at the time Lance King, Kelly Moran and 'Cowboy' John Cook were racing Stateside and the difference between their styles and the locals was very noticeable, even to me, with so little knowledge of the speedway game. My only way of moving through the ranks back home was to watch and learn, and try to develop my own style.

Once I got into the swing of racing overseas my learning curve jumped into another gear. You had the gaters who would leave you at the start and go! Then you had the ones that would pull off a trap, then stay on the line for the four laps around the racetrack and not move an inch off it. Then there were the riders that would rely on the big cut back, following the guy in front of them and taking up the whole track. But then there was the Chris Morton type! If he made the start, he was usually across the finish line first; if he didn't – which was a lot like me – he would then work the track until he had you tempted to move off your line to try and stop him from overtaking. Then he would make his move or he would just go right around you, track permitting, but with that never-say-die racing style that definitely appealed to me as a racer!

In the 1988 World Final at Vojens, Denmark, in the race that we met, Chris and I had a battle on the track that really sums up exactly what I mean and admire about him. It didn't matter that it was wet and muddy because we live to race, look forward to the next challenge on the track and we don't give up until the flag waves as we cross the finish line! Plus, he always seemed to have a smile and a good word to say and was probably one of the nicest guys in the game – I'm sure if you know him, you will agree.

Eric Broadbelt, Belle Vue teammate 1973 and British Lions teammate 1974-75

My last season at Belle Vue was in 1973, which was when Chris Morton joined the Aces. He had a brilliant year in 1974 and was picked to go to Australia with the British Lions in 1974/75. He started off slowly in Australia, but by the time we finished in Perth he had really got to grips with riding the big tracks. One of the last meetings in Perth was an open meeting. Michanek was also there and Mort had been going really well. The television cameras were there prior to the meeting and the two riders were filmed practising together. I think Michanek was the current World Champion at the time, so it was a real honour for Mort to be filmed alongside him. Clearly, the organisers recognised the star quality of the young Mort.

Darren Boocock, mechanic at Sheffield in 1993

Chris's final season was the easiest he ever had because all he had to do was turn up, get changed and race. He won his last meeting and pushed the bike over the finish line to win the Northern Riders' Championship. One breakdown all through his comeback – wasn't bad was it?

Brian Burford, co-author

As a youngster, getting the opportunity to experience the big meetings like the World Finals, Test Matches and other international events was an encounter not to be missed. Like many others, Chris Morton was always involved and I can clearly remember waiting patiently for his autograph at a Test Match at Swindon all those years ago. Who would have thought that that wide-eyed speedway-mad kid, who used to plan his entry into the pits with all the stealthy cunning of a Special Forces soldier, would be helping him to write his book? Life has many mysterious ways.

It was during one of these 'big meetings,' the 1976 Intercontinental Final, when Ole Olsen ruthlessly took Chris out wide on the second bend, and Mort illustrated his displeasure by spraying the Dane with shale on the slow-down lap – much to the amusement of the fans. On the TV afterwards Olsen was having a bit of a moan about his elimination from the World Championship, his exclusion and how it was that the ref didn't give him enough time and all that. When it came to putting this down on paper, I remembered how Olsen used to hold up meetings protesting over someone's tyre, so I basically reported him as having a 'whinge and a whine.' Although Chris could see the funny side to it, he didn't really agree and wanted this remark of bellyaching removed – no problem, he's the boss. When we met up with a friend of mine, Phil Handel, Chris retold this story of my artistic licence, and as Phil also had experience of my ghosting/editing capability he found the tale highly entertaining. I promised to take it out – but I forgot! So, when I sent Chris the first half of the book for his perusal, it was still in there and he said: 'I've put a note here and it says "No, Brian you can't say that!" 'Oh, is it still in there?' 'Yes.' 'I'll take it out.' 'You're not going to put it in anywhere else are you?' 'No Chris,' – of course not! Chris Morton, diplomat, we salute you!

Chris Morton, author

It was September 1984; it had been a year of mixed fortunes for me, having left the Individual Championship charge at the British Final stage in frustrating circumstances. Erik Gunderson had gone on to win his first World Title, Denmark were World Team Champions, with me and my old pal Peter Collins stopping Denmark's dominance by taking the World Pairs Title in Italy. I was laying on a grass bank soaking up some afternoon sun while I waited five hours for a flight connection that would get me back home for a meeting in the UK, having had a couple of days racing in Germany and Denmark. As I relaxed in the sunshine I reflected on the games that sportsmen play trying to outdo their opponents, and the mental trickery that was sometimes practiced in many sports. I was then weighing this against the unrealistic idea of a professional sportsperson accepting getting beat in a sporting manner, and how you should be magnanimous in defeat. I thought that's all very well, but you can't beat winning, and sometimes a bit of trickery is the cherry on top. I did have five hours to kill, and I wrote this. This is an observation, it may be, or may not be my opinion. Who knows?

SPORTSMANSHIP 'PAH'
Sportsmanship does not exist
between true Sportsmen only Gamesmanship
Sportsmanship is the imaginary acceptance
in the eye of defeat that none Sportsmen have invented

But Gamesmanship is reality that true Sportsman quality that enables you
to heighten your chances
While reducing your opponent's
Usually by mental sabotage

There is nothing more rewarding than beating an opponent
with your skills of the sport
Coupled with
Your powers of Gamesmanship

The reality of Gamesmanship
Will always win over
Transparent Sportsmanship

CAREER RECORD

BRITISH LEAGUE CAREER AVERAGES

Maximums

Year and Club	Matches	Rides	Points	Bonus	Total	CMA	F	P
1973 Ellesmere Port★	22	91	128	15	143	6.28	–	–
1973 Belle Vue	16	55	67	11	78	5.67	–	–
1974 Belle Vue	26	95	152	20	172	7.24	–	1
1975 Belle Vue	44	180	380	37	417	9.26	2	6
1976 Belle Vue	42	178	406	18	424	9.52	3	6
1977 Belle Vue	39	179	386	15	401	8.96	6	4
1978 Belle Vue	44	183	445.5	17	462.5	10.10	7	6
1979 Belle Vue	34	147	318	15	333	9.06	1	2
1980 Belle Vue	36	178	435	14	449	10.09	5	5
1981 Belle Vue	42	199	466	19	485	9.74	11	3
1982 Belle Vue	47	196	476	23	499	10.18	8	5
1983 Belle Vue	48	205	508	20	528	10.30	10	7
1984 Belle Vue	49	206	502	29	531	10.31	11	8
1985 Belle Vue	39	169	393	20	413	9.77	5	3

1986 Belle Vue	39	173	380	24	404	9.34	3	3
1987 Belle Vue	49	212	440	33	473	8.92	3	1
1988 Belle Vue	44	211	429.5	46	475.5	9.01	–	2
1989 Belle Vue	34	150	235	18	253	6.74	1	2
1990 Belle Vue	31	134	216	19	235	7.01	1	1
1993 Sheffield★	31	15	235	28	263	6.66	–	–
Totals	756	3,299	6,998	441	7,439	9.01	77	65

CMA (Calculated Match Average) is the total points divided by the number of rides, multiplied by four. The above statistics cover all official matches only.

★Denotes Second Division

WORLD CHAMPIONSHIP RECORD:

1976: Katowice, Poland, 6 points, tenth
1980: Gothenburg, Sweden, 8 points, eighth
1981: Wembley, England, 6 points, eleventh
1983: Norden, West Germany, 7 points, tenth
1986: Katowice, Poland, 8 points, eighth
1987: Amsterdam, Holland, 9 points, thirteenth (held over two days)
1988: Vojens, Denmark, 6 points, tenth

BRITISH LEAGUE RIDERS' CHAMPIONSHIP:

1981: 13 points, second
1982: 6 points, eleventh
1983: 5 points, twelfth
1984: 13 points, first
1985: 12 points, third
1986: 11 points, fifth
1987: 13 points, second
1988: 12 points, fourth

OTHER MAJOR HONOURS:

Awarded MBE (Member of the Order of the British Empire): 1992; World Pairs Champion (with Peter Collins): 1984; World Team Champion: 1980; World Team Runner-up: 1981, 1983, 1984, 1987; World Team Championship third place: 1986; British Champion: 1983; Intercontinental Champion: 1980; World Long-Track Championship third place: 1988; British Junior Champion: 1974; Grand Prix Champion: 1978; Northern Riders' Champion: 1983, 1987, 1993; Peter Craven Memorial Champion: 1974, 1975, 1986; 350cc British Grass-Track Champion: 1974; British Grass-Track Pairs Champion (with Dave Morton): 1975.

ENGLAND APPEARANCES: 128

CLUB HONOURS:

League Champion: 1982
Runner-up: 1974, 1975, 1976, 1978, 1984, 1988
Knock-Out Cup winner: 1973, 1975
Runner-up: 1978, 1980, 1982, 1984
League Cup winner: 1983
Runner-up: 1984, 1987
Premiership winner:1983
Runner-up: 1984
Inter-League Knock-Out Cup winner: 1975

Holds the club record at Belle Vue for the most appearances at 703
All-time top point-scorer for Belle Vue
Gold Cup Champion: 1991 (as team manager of Berwick)

BIBLIOGRAPHY

Books:

Websters Speedway Mirror 1974, Paul Parish (ed.)

1979 Daily Mirror Speedway Yearbook, Peter Oakes (ed.) (Studio Publications)

1980 Daily Mirror Speedway Yearbook, Peter Oakes (ed.) (Studio Publications)

1981 Daily Mirror Speedway Yearbook, Peter Oakes (ed.) (Studio Publications)

1982 Daily Mirror Speedway Yearbook, Peter Oakes (ed.) (Studio Publications)

1983 Diamond Jubilee Speedway Handbook, (Qualmist Ltd)

1986 Speedway Yearbook, Peter Oakes & Philip Rising (eds) (Sportsdata)

1990 Speedway Yearbook, Peter Oakes (ed.) (Front Page Books)

The Complete History of the British League, Peter Oakes (ed.) (Front Page Books, 1991)

Loaders International Speedway Annual 1992, Tony Loader (ed.) (Privately Published)

Peter Collins' Speedway Annual No. 4, Richard Bott (ed.) (Stanley Paul, 1980)

World Speedway Final, Maurice Jones (MacDonald & Jane's Publishers, 1979)

Speedway Grand Slam, Richard Bott & Ian Thomas (Studio Publications, 1981)

The History of the Ellesmere Port Gunners, Neil Evans & Howard Jones (Speed-Away Promotions, 2001)

Confessions of a Speedway Promoter, John Berry (Retro Speedway Publications, 2004)

Periodicals:

Speedway Star, Speedway Mail, Motor Cycle Weekly, Motor Cycle News, Vintage Speedway magazine, *Backtrack* magazine, *The Ace* magazine.

INDEX

If you are interested in purchasing other books published by Stadia, or in case you have difficulty finding any Stadia books in your local bookshop, you can also place orders directly through the Tempus Publishing website

www.tempus-publishing.com